Paris, A Homage

Raana Haider

tara press

tara-india research press
Flat No.6, Khan Market, New Delhi - 110 003
Ph.: 24694610; Fax : 24618637
www.indiaresearchpress.com
contact@indiaresearchpress.com; bahrisons@vsnl.com

2007

ISBN-10 digit : 81-87943-73-4
ISBN-13 digit : 978-81-87943-73-0

Cataloguing in Publication Data
Raana Haider
Paris, A Homage
by Raana Haider

Includes bibliographical references & Index

1. Travel 2. Paris 3. History
I. Title II. Author

Recreated from the 2000 University Press Ltd., edition.

Printed in India at Focus Impressions, New Delhi – 110 003.

For two Francophiles
My late father Mirza Rashid Ahmad
And my daughter Ramine

Other titles in the *Travels with a Nomad* series.

Fragrance of the Past, A Middle Eastern Itinerary
Fragrance of the Past acquaints us with the extensive, sophisticated and influential culture of the 'cradle of civilisation', the Middle East. We journey to the heart of a people whose traces linger in their fabulous monuments. Meticulously researched and always accessible, these lively essays bring a region to life that has enriched all aspects of our human heritage.

India : Beyond the Taj and the Raj (forthcoming)
The author, on a journey through India, explores its diversity and researches the past and discusses the present of twenty-two cities and ancient sites in India. Raana inspires us with her writing on India's ashrams, rock-cut temples, splendid palaces, formidable forts, whitewashed churches and magnificent mosques.

Contents

Foreword

The author is a Bangladeshi Anglophone and a Francophile and Paris is a feeling and not a city. It is *un cri de coeur* (a call of the heart). This book is written in such a sentimental spirit. *Paris, A Homage* is a personal account and a chronicle of events and experiences. It translates into a subjective panorama of Paris.

I echo the sentiment expressed by Jean-Michel Wilmotte, noted French architect who has worked on the expansion of the Louvre, the restoration of le College de France and the expansion of les Champs-Elysées. "When you come to a country where the culture is different, you are like a sponge: you absorb things but always as a function of your emotions at the moment, for finally, the eye is selective."

The discussions of books on Paris are not book reviews. The discussions are rather presentations not exhaustive but selective. I have wanted to convey to readers of *Paris, A Homage*, the impressions, sentiments and information that I have gained from and shared with other writers. What we have is a chain of feelings and knowledge – a connection that engages the mind and expands the world for us.

The abundance of superlatives on Paris bears witness to the scores of its admirers through the ages – Parisians who have crossed national boundaries. What developed as a labour of love emerged as a mirror of similar sentiment on the part of countless others from far corners of the earth – Parisians not by birth but by choice.

Borrowing a phrase from Howard C. Rice Jr. in his preface to *Thomas Jefferson in Paris*: "This book is addressed to all Parisians: by birth, adoption or inclination." Paris celebrates the love of life and living and for that, Paris is the patrimony of all mankind.

Raana Haider
December 2006

Nostalgia Improves with the Passage of Time

"Paradoxically, the freedom of Paris is associated with a persistent belief that nothing ever changes. After an absence of twenty or thirty years, one still recognises it."

Marguerite Duras, French writer

... like good cheese, a comfortable armchair, a comfortable pair of shoes or a well-thumbed book. Returning to live in Paris after an interval of some forty years is an exhilarating experience, allowing one to partake in the sentiment of nostalgia in heavy dosages. I had a childhood residence in Paris during the years 1956 to 1958, when I accompanied my late father, Mirza Rashid Ahmad, a career diplomat then posted at the Embassy of Pakistan in Paris. I had visited on and off for brief periods during the interval of four decades. I returned to live in Paris in 1996, this time with my husband, Tufail K. Haider who had been appointed Ambassador of Bangladesh to France. We arrived in Paris in December 1996 from Cairo. I wore a new scarlet red coat when setting foot at Orly airport. I figured that if I had never worn clarion red before, now was the time and Paris was the place.

The odd forty years in a time-frame has spanned Paris of the 1950s – a decade or so following the end of the Second World War to the close of the 1990s and the start of a new millennium. This sweep of time has seen the rise and fall of nations and the reverse. It has seen the integration and disintegration of communities and its reverse.

Yet nowhere is the French aphorism, *plus ca change, plus c'est la même chose* (the more it changes, the more it is the same) truer than in Paris itself. As stated by Herve Champollion, noted French photographer in the introduction to his book, *Paris*, "for in spite of all the clichés, Paris is perennially itself, perennially unique unlike any other city in the world." For it is in Paris, the city of light, that one finds the rare and unique combination of extremes – reassuring tradition combined with revolutionary change. This visible coexisting paradox of classicism and modernity is closely interlocked and fluid in its flow from one to the other. Edouard Balladur, the former French Prime Minister once remarked, "French civilisation is a civilisation of uniformity while the Anglo-Saxon one is based on diversity."

France's twin serious preoccupations – history and culture ensure that Paris's unique blend of classical tradition and modernism creates an aura in the city's architectural homogeneity and an inviting ambience in its street life. This charming combination has often earned Paris the title – the most beautiful city in the world. The key has to be that "Paris possesses the exclusive weapon of total seduction and unconsciously infects us all with its eternal and irrepressible *joie de vivre*", notes *Places and History: Paris.* It is said that lovers of Paris cannot imagine the city more beautiful than in their memories. Many are proven wrong. For while the nostalgia remains, a kaleidoscope of new experiences, events and places renew one's energy, fervour and *finally* one's passion for the city.

Pierre Salinger, journalist, one-time Press Secretary to President John F. Kennedy and an ardent Francophile first came to Paris in 1925. His book, *Above Paris,* an aerial photographic odyssey of Paris was published in 1984. He wrote, "There must have been some kind of osmosis at work in a child; for Paris has long haunted me to return and then to live." That "osmosis" must be widespread for it has affected many others. The books about loving Paris continue.

Alex Carmel first came to Paris in 1949 after his first year at Columbia University. He also spent the summer in Switzerland and Italy before returning to France via the French Riviera and to Paris. "It was then that I discovered for the first time the pleasure of coming back to Paris; back to what had become the place in which I was most happy, despite all the fascination of Rome and Florence." Eventually, he came back for good. In his account of Paris he has written, 'A Corner in the Marais: Memoir of a Paris Neighbourhood' published in 1998.

Diane Johnson in *Le Divorce* (1998) delves into the clash of cultures – American and French. The plot revolves around one failed mixed marriage and one mixed love affair – both involving American sisters in Paris and their French partners. On the first morning out in Paris, the younger sister visiting her married sister observes what appears to be a very Parisian scene. "Those big-leafed trees and bookstalls along the Seine, and guys in berets on scooters, as in old Audrey Hepburn movies … boats came by, their loudspeakers announcing the names of this *pont* (bridge) or that. People waved at me from the decks, as if I was a Parisian. There were pink tablecloths on tables spread out in the street, where people drank coffee reading newspapers called *Figaro* and *Libération*, their dogs at their feet glaring at each other. *Libération*, I thought. Liberation! That was the first day." Subsequently, we have another emerging Francophile.

The quintessential Parisian entertainer, Maurice Chevalier in his autobiographical memories, *My Paris* published in 1972, which I found at Tea and Tattered Pages, a delightfully cosy second-hand English book-store in Paris reminisces, "Some streets, though, almost like those of villages within the great city, still seem to hang on to their human characteristics and their truths, as if they were determined never to have anything to do with the Paris that changes every day and that never ceases to become something else, while staying the same place of beauty." Robert Doisneau, the brilliant Parisian photographer, collaborated with Maurice Chevalier in *My Paris* and captured *la vie Parisienne* of the 1950s and 1960s in photographs of the period. The cover of *My Paris* notes that, "Here is that city as only her favoured sons know her – incongruous, humorous, whimsical, beautiful, poignant, inimitable. A daughter would also like to be so favoured!"

What is this 'Parisian' adjective that is so widely used? A description of 'Parisian' that I came across in 'A Guide to Paris' is the following: "Paris is the only capital in the world with a word derived from its name, with a sense of meaning which is both subtle and indefinable: Parisianism. It implies a way of thinking, of having a good time, of dressing, of laughing and of speaking, and of being well up on everything, which only exists in Paris. Parisianism automatically implies an air of superiority over all towns in France and over all other capitals of the world. It is not automatically accessible to those living in Paris or the privilege of those born in Paris. Outsiders – those who live in the provinces – and foreigners have always contributed to Parisianism, which is a form of snobbery." All Parisians do appear supremely confident and content.

Often asked whether Paris has changed in the last forty years, I reply, "*plus ça change, plus c'est la même chose.*" Certainly, Paris carries about it the same elegant tree-lined boulevards, vast expanses of vista, majestic monuments, flourishing fountains, spectacular buildings, colourful neighbourhoods, chic shops, corner cafés, well-stocked newspaper kiosks and a high density of dogs as I recall from earlier decades.

One of the most vivid childhood memories of Paris in the 1950s relates to the warm and musty smell emanating from the open grills on the pavements. This unique odour comes from the underground Parisian Metro system established in 1900. To this day, I am always swept back decades. I recall walking to the bus-stop in Trocadero in *le seizième* (the 16th *arrondissement* (district) to catch the school-bus. I have never come across this smell anywhere in the world. Neither the London, New York nor Tokyo underground systems have this peculiar and not unpleasant aroma. Thus it was with great amusement that I came across the following: "If I were to choose one single thing that would restore Paris to the senses, it would be that strangely sweet, unhealthy smell of the Metro, so very unlike the dank cold or the stuffy heat of subways in New York." So wrote May Sarton in *I Knew a Phoenix* in 1959.

Parisians will spare no effort to improve their capital city. After five years of research and testing on Metro commuters, French transport officials have launched 'Madeleine', a French perfume to combat that uniquely Parisian Metro aroma. 'Madeleine' is a composition of woody musk with hints of vanilla, citrus, jasmine, rose and lily. It is to be used extensively and intensively in the Metro subway system with cleaning products for the ceramic walls and asphalt floor. A childhood association has been swept away in the name of progress! However, long live French perfume.

In *The Secret Life of the Seine*, Mort Rosenblum, an American upon observing the tranquillity and beauty of a village alongside the Seine, remarked, "up the gravelled road was a regulation church with a pointing steeple. The cafés and shops had not changed for generations and likely never will. Ah, the poetry of *la France éternelle*..." So too is the poetry of eternal Paris.

This is probably far more due to design rather than as a result of default. Why speak of change in the past forty years? Divine Paris has from a physical perspective not changed much in the past 150 years. It remains an immense shed of marvels – the Arts prevail everywhere. A feast is spread for the eyes. Today's central Paris with its wide boulevards, open squares, large expanses of gardens, elegant buildings and grandiose monuments is largely the creation of Baron Haussmann during the second half of the nineteenth century under the direction of Napoleon III. "Gutting and levelling whole quarters, building others from scratch, laying out very broad streets to meet the new demands of urban traffic, within a few years he imposed upon medieval, baroque, romantic Paris a new modern, imperial vision of the capital," states *Places and History: Paris.* The Emperor also wanted a city design that in addition to outstanding aesthetic attributes would have a practical consideration – wide expanses would allow for rapid troop deployment.

Paris is structured like a snail, its twenty *arrondissements* spiralling outward from the Seine River. The river divides the city into the right bank (*la rive droite*) where the ambience is serious and the left bank (*la rive gauche*) which is bohemian. Thirty-six bridges span the Seine. The Pon Neuf (New Bridge) is actually the oldest, built in the sixteenth century and since restored but never changed. The 'heart, head and marrow' of Paris according to a twelfth century traveller, is the Ile de la Cite, the island in the middle of the Seine where the Gothic cathedral Notre-Dame de Paris stands. It was built, enlarged and embellished between the years 1163 and 1345. *The Hunchback of Notre-Dame* was the theme for a 1956 film based on the novel by Victor Hugo, starring Gina Lollobrigida as Esmerelda and Anthony Quinn as

Quasimodo. For a younger generation, the cathedral earned itself new fame – the Disney film, *The Hunchback of Notre-Dame.*

Victor Hugo in *The Hunchback of Notre-Dame* wrote in the 1830s, "The Church of Notre-Dame of Paris is doubtless still a majestic and sublime edifice. But, however beautiful it has remained in growing old, it is difficult to suppress a sigh, to restrain a feeling of indignation at the numberless degradations and mutilations which the hand of time and that of man have inflicted upon this venerable monument ... Upon the face of this ancient queen of French cathedrals, beside each wrinkle we constantly find a scar. *Tempus edax, homo edacior* (Time is destructive, man is more destructive) – which we would willingly render thus – Time is blind, but man is stupid." This declaration made in the early nineteenth century is even more valid at the close of the twentieth century.

L'Art de Vivre (The Art of Living), a journal of Maison de la France states, "Paris is a 'Capital Capital' which can be seen from any of the city's numerous high vintage points ... the subtle pattern of Paris spreads before you with its slate-grey roofs, green parks and major landmarks of the skyline." The 'Rooftops of Paris' is also a common reference. One is from the slender and soaring Eiffel Tower designed by Gustave Eiffel for the 1889 World Fair. A second site of what is possibly the jewel of the crown of monuments decorating Paris, is the regal and imposing l'Arc de Triomphe built by Napoleon Bonaparte to commemorate France's victories or the Sacre Coeur church in the artistic and bohemian *quartier* (quarter) of Montmartre or the high-tech Grande Arche de la Defense. The 'Rooftops of Paris' presents one with vast expanses of vista that delight the eye. Victor Hugo wrote, "I am not without hope that

Paris, as seen from the balloon, may yet present that richness of outline and opulence of detail – that diversity of aspect – that something grandiose in its simplicity – unexpected in its beauty – that characterises a checker-board." Surely Hugo in these few words has vividly captured all that is Paris – the Paris that so visually enamours one and all.

Dr. Edward Rigby in Paris, in his 'Letters from France in 1789' wrote, "We visited the church of Notre-Dame, a very beautiful Gothic building ... From the top of this church we had a complete bird's eye view of Paris, not so large as London, but the buildings being of stone, and white, the effect is more striking. We have now seen enough of Paris to be convinced that it is not that dirty, ill-built, inconvenient place, which our ill-tempered countrymen have described it. There are more magnificent buildings than in London; all the places worth seeing are likewise more accessible than in London; it costs less to be admitted and many may be seen without paying anything." A most generous comment coming from an Englishman.

This is the bird's eye view of Paris. The matchless notion extends to the micro-street-level as well. Parisians in their art of living *à la Parisienne* also create an unprecedented sense of detail – in the city's elegant buildings whose facades are a delight in proportion, balance and decoration with its black lace-like wrought-iron balconies, the graceful curve of an archway, the artistic flourish of the many fountains including the identification of illustrious individuals in whose names streets are named. In Paris, the twin sense of history and culture is all-pervasive. In today's age of fast food, fast buck, quick change and instant gratification, it is reassuring to feel a sense of continuity.

The Parisian aesthetic sense of continuity is, however, not by any means fossilised or fatigued. For frequently, behind the classical façade of the exterior of a building lies a high-tech, state-of-the-art interior with plastic, chrome, steel, geometric designs, luminescent colours and extreme modern lines; as in the many arcades and shops along les Champs-Elysées, the premier avenue of Paris. The Disney shop, Planet Hollywood restaurant, Virgin Megastore and FNAC, the audio entertainment shops and Sephora, the perfume and cosmetic consumer's dreamland, all on les Champs-Elysées are particular examples of the unique blend of the *ancien* and *nouveau* (old and the new). The new Louis Vuitton floor space dealing in exclusive baggage lines opened in the 1920s/1930s Art Nouveau style building of Arthur Andersen on les Champs-Elysées.

The reopening of the Dior super-boutique on avenue Montaigne in the heart of the Golden Triangle of French elegance and luxury in 1997 prompted Suzy Menkes to write in the *International Herald Tribune*, "Extraordinary transformation that the American-in-Paris architect, Peter Marino has wrought. It is a triumph of wit and workmanship ... subtle references to the heritage of the house ... far from being a homage to the past, Marino has also let the airy light of modern day into the pampered luxury that is the quintessence of French chic. For the French, Dior holds a position not so removed from the reverence accorded to an established church and eyebrows were naturally raised when Bernard Arnault, Dior's president compounded the ignominy of choosing a British designer, John Galiano, by picking an American architect. The bones (structure, façade) are classical eighteenth century architecture, but that is fleshed out with hyper-modern rails and fittings that stand away from the walls, as though an invisible pane of glass separated today's Dior from history ... 'In the store, the visual game is one of contrasts, so that modern is juxtaposed with fantasy. It is always about my reflection of old and new', says Marino." Once again we are talking Paris.

Paris is an accomplished mistress in blending the *avant-garde* and the past. It takes a certain *savoir-faire* (know-how) and *un grain de folie* (a touch of madness) to create an art museum out of a railway station. A cathedral-like nineteenth century grandiose structure housed the railway station, Gare d'Orsay from 1898 to 1939 when it was abandoned. In 1900 the painter, Louis Detaille exclaimed, "The station is magnificent, it looks like a *palais des beaux arts.*" (palace of fine arts). This observation materialised in 1986. The musee d'Orsay features paintings, photography, sculptures and decorative arts from the period 1850 to 1914. At its opening, the press called it "the most beautiful museum in Europe." It hosts the world's largest collection of Impressionist paintings, a testament to nineteenth century art. "The immense central nave, where the steam locomotives used to belch smoke, has been transformed into a labyrinth of clear light and suspended walls like theatre backdrops, which leave visitors free to wander, rather than imposing a particular path," is the description of the musee d'Orsay in *Places and History: Paris.*

In a similar fashion, Les Halles, one of the oldest districts of Paris which has been described by Emile Zola as "the belly of Paris" was for nine hundred years until 1969 the city's wholesale food market. Between 1850 and 1866, Les Halles underwent significant transformation. Emile Zola spoke of the 'new' Les Halles as a "Babylon of metal with a Hindu-like lightness, criss-crossed by suspended terraces, overhead corridors and flying bridges over the emptiness below." In the 1980s, the site became Forum des Halles, an urban complex of consumer culture – restaurants, movie halls, shops, banks, a swimming pool – all in glass and aluminium.

The ultimate coexistence of the *old* and the *new* is the startling presence of a grand glass pyramid and two smaller ones in the massive courtyard of the Louvre museum. They were designed by I.M. Pei, the eminent contemporary Chinese-American architect in 1989. The near juxtaposition of an ultra-modern glass and chrome structure among the classical columns, friezes and sculptures of eighteenth and nineteenth centuries' architecture was at first visually jarring and jolting. However, the inclusion I now find visually stunning and an architectural marvel. It can only be called *magnifique et splendide.* The pros and cons of this inclusion are heatedly argued upon by one and all. It has given the Louvre a new lease on life. Upon contemplation, which is new and which is old? The pyramid architecture predates the main buildings of the Louvre by some 3000 years! *Plus ça change, plus c'est la même chose.* Mort Rosenblum in *The Secret Life of the Seine* wrote in 1994, "This sense of history and attachment to the river, is why every new flourish is debated in public, for months or years. If it is something significant like a glass pyramid outside the Louvre, the president pours over each detail as the kings did. Once built, it takes Paris a decade to pass lasting judgement."

Paris has done that. In 1999, acknowledging the ten years of the existence of the I.M. Pei pyramid, the magazine *Paris Capitale* declared in an article celebrating its decennial: "The Pyramid of Louvre: From Condemnation to Glorification." After all, prior to its construction, the newspaper *Le Figaro* had declared in 1985, "*Double Non à la Pyramide*!"

Paris is a walker's paradise, i.e. an urban dweller's dream. It is possible to criss-cross the city. Criss it one day and cross it the next. Paris is only 13 kms across and 10.5 kms north-south. It is the only way to see, smell, hear and taste (at the inevitable and highly desirable cafe-stops) Paris. Richard Cobb in 'Streets of Paris' writes, "Paris should be walked, because much of it, the most secret, the most modest, the most bizarre, the tiniest, is only discoverable by the pedestrian who is prepared to push behind the boulevards and the long straight streets of the Second Empire."

Meandering through the Parisian streets one is struck by the sweep of history surrounding us. Not for the French are unimaginative numbered roads but a panorama of historical personalities greet one as one walks down. Stanley Karnow writes in *Paris in the Fifties*, "Unlike my native New York's monotonously numbered thoroughfares, Paris street names were a necrology of famous and forgotten French artists, authors, composers, scientists, politicians, diplomats, marshals, admirals, clergymen and a multitude of saints, male and female." Also included are their dates of birth and death and their profession.

For any Anglophile in the Mother of all Francophone countries, a visit to the Paris branch of W.H. Smith is compulsory. It has been described as "an institution to English travellers in Paris since 1903." It is situated on the rue de Rivoli, one of the masterpieces in urban design of the official architects of Napoleon I, Fontaine and Percier. These two individuals are the creators of much of the Empire-style architectural glory visible today in Paris.

In my possession, I have two books bought at W.H. Smith in 1958, with the stickers still on one of them, priced at 8sh. 6d. net. One of the books is *Little Women* by Louisa M. Alcott, any girl's classic novel and the now appropriately titled *When We Were Very Young* by A.A. Milne. A.A. Milne's other creation is Winnie the Pooh that serves the current generation of young consumers in Pooh paraphernalia (T-shirts, mugs, pencil-cases, school bags, stuffed toys, etc.) at the Disney shop on les Champs-Elysées. In those days, a child's treat consisted of a book or two from W. H. Smith and tea and cakes in *le salon de thé* on the first floor of the same shop. *Le salon de thé* is no longer there. It ceased to exist in 1989. Bestsellers and children's books are now to be found in the old rooms. A child of today, my daughter can still get a book or two at W. H. Smith (recent purchases included Agatha Christie's *Death on the Nile* and *Murder on the Orient Express*) and then enjoy an ice-cream at a current global favourite, Hagen Daaz. W.H. Smith has faithfully served three generations of book lovers.

For any subcontinental in the Mother of all Francophone countries, a visit to Saris is compulsory. There may very well be three generations of readers who are proud possessors of good investments – the French chiffon sari. Started soon after the end of the Second World War, it was located in an exclusive area close to the Madeleine, a classical Greek-styled church and walking distance from la Place de la Concorde, probably the finest and largest square in the world. Many a time, I had accompanied my mother on shopping trips to Saris France as it was then known. In 1994, it moved to the current location near the Paris Bourse (Stock Exchange) and the office of Agence France-Presse (AFP). The allure of French chiffon saris has not diminished and neither has its cost. Prices range from $200 to $600 per sari. It calls for further cherishing any French chiffon saris one may have been lucky enough to inherit from one's mother. I plan to introduce my daughter to Saris. She too, may one day become a third generation customer of an item that personifies 'a thing of beauty is a joy forever.'

As so well captured in *Places and History: Paris*, "Fundamentally we visit Paris on the pretext of the new in order to be reassured as to the fact that the old is unchanged, and it is on the subtle boundary between past and present that we find the eternity and uniqueness of this metropolis. In contrast with other capitals that resemble geological strata, Paris blends its past and future..." The harmonious blend of past and present has created a capital city of elegant equilibrium. All that has to be the *raison d'être* for France to be the world's top tourist destination. Some 67 million visitors per year!

Eloquence came easily to Henri IV. In order to enter Paris and save his throne, he was obliged to convert to Roman Catholicism, declaring famously, "Paris is well worth a mass." Someone else has felt it. William C. Brownell in 'French Traits' in 1889 wrote, "The sensation which France produces on the impressionable foreigner is first of all that of mental exhilaration. Paris, especially, is electric. Touch it at any point and you receive an awakening shock. Live in it and you lose all lethargy. Nothing stagnates. Everyone visibly and acutely feels himself alive. The universal vivacity is contagious ... Nowhere is there so much activity, nowhere so little chaos."

The French phrase, *Je ne sais quoi* (an indefinable quality), truly translates into that unidentifiable and elusive 'something' which either one has or does not have. Paris has it. And plenty of it.

Yesteryears

Old France, weighed down with history, prostrated by wars and revolution, forever vacillating between greatness and decline, but revived, century after century, by the genius of renewal."

Charles de Gaulle, *War Memoirs*

The Parisii, the Celtic tribe of hunters, farmers and boatmen settled on the island, Ile de la Cite in about 300 BC. Today's 'Paris' derives its name from its first inhabitants, the Parisiis. The first Parisian settlement was routed by the Romans who arrived in 50 BC and named their settlement Lutetia. "The gravel beach of that island was its first city wall, the Seine its first moat," wrote Victor Hugo in *The Hunchback of Notre-Dame.* The Romans expanded the increasingly urban habitation onto first *la rive gauche* on the Seine and then as the town continued to prosper, the population spilled over to *la rive droite.*

By the Middle Ages, the city of Paris was more or less settled along the following basis – the Ile de la Cité remained the heart and soul of the city and site of the Notre-Dame de Paris, the Gothic masterpiece cathedral started in the middle of the twelfth century by Bishop Maurice de Sully and continued to be built over some six hundred years; *la rive gauche* – the intellectual area, *Quartier Latin* (the Latin Quarter) which in time became the site of the Sorbonne University founded in 1231 by Robert de Sorbon; and *la rive droite* where commerce was located and Les Halles was established in the middle of the thirteenth century as the wholesale market for all of Paris. Les Halles was to be the supplier of food for Paris for some eight hundred years till it was dismantled and moved to Rungis on the outskirts of Paris, near Orly airport. Les Halles also used to be the place to indulge in piping-hot onion soup with melted cheese. Today, the *avant-garde* complex of Forum des Halles, a vast network of shops, cinema halls, theatres, cafes, restaurants, art galleries and a swimming pool stands in its place. Today's Louvre Museum was also built as a fort to defend the right flank of the Ile de la Cité in the thirteenth century on *la rive droite.*

In yet another account of 'their Paris' (everyone but everyone has their own Paris) – it has to be another credo along with *liberté*, *egalité*, *fraternité* which all foreigners espouse. Edmund White, American and Hubert Sorin, French in *Our Paris: Sketches from Memory* write, "The Ile St-Louis is the most perfect ensemble of seventeenth-century architecture one can imagine. For centuries, the monks of Notre-Dame grazed their cows here (it was even called the Ile des Vaches), but in the seventeenth century a group of speculators decided to develop the island all at once." One speculator, a Marie left posterity Pont Marie, the 'most poetic bridge', another a Regrattier gave his name to one of the north-south streets and a Poulletier left us another street in his name.

By the fifteenth century, Paris as Victor Hugo wrote, "was divided into three completely distinct and separate cities, each with its own shape, uniqueness, customs, traditions, privileges and history: *la Cité*, *la Université* and *la Ville*. Each of these three parts was a city, but a city too special to be complete and to be able to do without the other two. They therefore presented three individual faces. The *la Cité* was a city of churches, *la Ville* (town) of palaces, *la Université* of colleges; as if to say the island was the province of the bishop, the right bank of the merchants and the left bank of the rector." Thus, Paris had its Heart and Soul in the centre on the Ile de la Cite, its Mind on *la rive gauche* and its Body on *la rive droite*. In essence, the Paris of yesterday remains the Paris of today.

A little-known museum, the Archaeological Crypt of Notre-Dame de Paris in the Parvis de Notre-Dame (Square of Notre-Dame) is enlightening. Michel Fleury, now vice-president of the commission of old Paris and author of *Naissance de Paris* (Birth of Paris) published in 1997, documents the origins of the capital from a Neolithic village to a city in the Middle Ages. While excavating the Notre-Dame site from 1965-1970, Michel Flurry came across foundations of earlier constructions. Detailed maps show the evolution of the site through the ages. Remains are to be seen of what used to be a main street, rue Nerve (New Street) – seven metres wide and considered wide in its time – for transportation of blocks of stone from the nearby hills of Paris for the construction of the cathedral, Notre-Dame de Paris. Also to be seen are the piles of bricks used in a form of heating (hypocaust) where floors and chutes were used to heat walls some seventeen hundred years ago (1-3 AD).

In *The Hunchback of Notre-Dame*, Victor Hugo wrote, "every wall, every stone of this venerable monument is a page not only from the history of France, but also of science and art. Among all the old churches of Paris, this central mother-church is a kind of chimera: it has the head of this, the limbs of that, and the torso of another, something from everything. Each flux of time has brought its own alluvial deposit, every race has made its own contribution to the monument, each individual has added a stone." Victor Hugo argued that, "There are two aspects about a monument, one, its use and two, its beauty. Its use belongs to the owner, its beauty is the world's."

While the church took care of people's soul, it also took responsibility for people's body. And so the first Hotel de Dieu (Hotel of God), i.e. hospital was established in Paris, in the present square of the Notre-Dame de Paris. The early medical centres were run by religious orders, largely nuns. The tradition of human ailments being cared for by nuns continues today in the form of the well-known Catholic order of Sisters of Charity of which the late Mother Theresa was the most famous. The early hospital was in time destroyed. In the 1860s, the present Hotel de Dieu, the oldest and still running hospital was constructed in the Italian Renaissance architectural style. It stands to one's left as one faces the Notre-Dame de Paris.

Louis IX in the early thirteenth century built the Saint-Chapel cathedral on the Ile de la Cite. It has been variously called 'an architecture in glass', 'a symphony of stone and glass straining towards the sky', 'a bible of light', 'here is paradise regained'. One sees panels of mullet-coloured stained glass replacing walls of the structure. It is a sublime sight.

In the 1600s, the cultural phenomenon of the Italian Renaissance reached the banks of the Seine and the city of Paris which till then was a homogeneous city of an architectural and historical product of the medieval period was irrevocably altered. "That severe unity was blended with the dazzling luxury of the new style, and softened by the introduction of rounded Romanesque arches and Greek columns", notes *Places and History: Paris.*

Catherine Medici planned the Jardin de Tuileries, the extended gardens in front of the Louvre Museum which reach the spectacular Place de la Concorde. The first stone bridge across the Seine was built in the reign of Henry IV, the Pont Neuf. Earlier bridges had been constructed of wood. The practice was also to construct wooden houses on the two sides of the bridge. A fire on the bridge causing fatalities led to a new law being passed in the Middle Ages that banned housing on bridges. The oldest existing bridge of Paris is still called the Pont Neuf. The kings Francis I and Henry IV expanded the Louvre from a fortress into a palace and made it fit for a king and the city of Paris came to represent the ideal city of an urban civilisation in the seventeenth century.

Louis XIV, the Sun King (1643-1715) was a grandiose and monumental builder, constructing the Versailles Palace on the outskirts of Paris where he transferred his court from the Louvre Palace. Wide boulevards and expansive gardens were set up. Louis XIV is the source of the famous statement, "I am the State." The self-centredness of the monarchy came to an end in 1789 with the tearing down of the notorious Bastille prison and the guillotine of Louis XVI and Marie Antoinette in the Place de la Concorde in 1793. The French Revolution gave birth to the credo, "*Liberté, Egalité et Fraternité*" which became gospel words for the liberation of humanity all over the world. As Goethe said, "From this place and from this day, begins a new era in the history of the world."

La Place de la Concorde is described in the Michelin Guide to France, as "a perfect expression of the Louis XV style ... The square owes its monumental character to the colonnaded buildings defining it to the north, its octagonal plan, and to the massive pedestals intended for allegorical statues of French cities... The pink granite Luxor Obelisk, 3,300 years old, covered with hieroglyphics, was brought here from Egypt in 1836." Noting the uniqueness of la Place de la Concorde, *Places and History: Paris* states that, "There are perhaps few squares in the world with the magic atmosphere of enchantment present at every hour of the day in this square. Indeed at night, under the light of the street-lamps, its atmosphere becomes unreal, almost fable-like." It is all that and more. Ask anyone.

Notre-Dame de Paris cathedral was the venue for the self-coronation of Napoleon Bonaparte as Emperor and Josephine as Empress in 1804. A massive painting in the Louvre by Jacques-Louis David depicts brilliantly the scene. Napoleon vowed to make Paris the most beautiful city in the world – a task he set about with a vengeance. Had he not said, "if Paris is to be beautified there is more to demolish than to construct. Why not knock down the whole quarter of the Cite, that vast ruin fit to house only rats?"

Napoleon I is credited with some of the most imposing monuments Paris bestows on us today. For it was Napoleon Bonaparte who declared, "The French have vanity, levity, independence, and caprice, with an unconquerable passion for glory. They will as soon do without bread as without glory." He completed the construction of the Greco-architectural church at Madeleine. Four bridges across the Seine were constructed. Work began on the colossal l'Arc de Triomphe to commemorate his victory at the battle of Austerlitz. It was not only to honour the French army but also to "nourish French sculpture and sculptors for ten years." Victor Hugo called l'Arc de Triomphe "a mountain of glory on a glorious mountain of stone." Of the sculptures and high reliefs on the façade of l'Arc de Triomphe facing les Champs-Elysées, the masterpiece is Rude's 'La Marseillaise'. It depicts the departure of French volunteers to fight the Prussians in 1792. The flat surfaces are engraved with the names of 128 battles and 558 generals. L'Arc de Carousel in front of the Louvre was also commissioned to honour the Grande Armee of France. The wholesale food market at Les Halles was reorganised. The elegant arcades of the rue de Rivoli designed by Napoleon's official architects, Percier and Fontaine were opened. On the rue de Rivoli I remember from the 1950s, the bookshop, W.H. Smith and Sulka, the exclusive menswear shop which my father then frequented.

In his perpetual pursuit to further beautify Paris, Napoleon I in 1811 visited the hill of Chaillot, where stands today the Palais de Chaillot, Trocadero facing le Tour Eiffel. In the book *XVIe: Chaillot, Passy, Auteuil – Métamorphose des Trois Villages,* M. Copeland presents us with an insight into the architectural thinking of the day. Napoleon asked one of his favourite architects, "which is the most beautiful palace known?" Fontaine replied, "The most imposing but also one of the least convenient is the palace Farnese in Rome, the most gay are those of Genoa, the largest are those of Germany and the most comfortable are those of France." Napoleon observed that he had never seen a palace, or a castle that had pleased him. He criticised one by one all the residences he had lived in France and abroad and then explained his requirements. "I want to be living in a dignified manner, but I will not be like most rulers, imprisoned and ill-at-ease under the golden ceiling of my place of living; I need for myself in the same place, under the same roof two particular things. Above all, the lifestyle of the head of a rich family with all the conveniences of a private man who wants comfort and freedom: then, the reception rooms and the apparatus for representation should be that of a grand country, to which one would accord honour and respect." The man knew what he wanted.

Napoleon Bonaparte embellished les Invalides where he housed veteran soldiers and where his mortal remains were finally interred in 1840, although he had died on the island, St. Helena in 1821. "The re-entry of France was the last triumphal voyage of the Frenchman best loved by his people, most venerated by his soldiers and most feared by his enemies. In September 1840, a French ship carried the body of Napoleon to Le Havre, then slowly up the Seine as far as Paris. On September 15, in a snow storm, almost the entire city attended the funeral of the emperor, whose body moved in a slow procession along the great boulevards, passing under l'Arc de Triomphe and descending les Champs-Elysées to come to rest here in the Dome des Invalides and thus end at last Napoleon's long exile," notes *Places and History: Paris.*

The birth of modern architecture in Paris occurred between the years 1848 to 1914, according to *Architecture in the 19th Century*, a Beaux Arts special issue (1992). Charles Baudelaire observed this transformation: "For him, the chimney stacks were modern masts that competed in the city sky with the old church steeples." He lamented "that the old Paris is no more." It was also a manifestation of an urban transformation of towns and cities into larger metropolitan areas. Medieval Paris was being transformed into modern Paris. A skyline that once had been pierced only by church steeples and spires, was in the latter half of the nineteenth century increasingly accompanied by evidence of the changing urban landscape. Paris expanded rapidly; from 1851 to 1900, 1,240 houses and 3,588 in the adjacent suburbs were constructed states the Beaux Arts issue.

In a substantive work on the Paris of yesterday and today, *Paris, deux mille ans d'histoire* ('Paris, two thousand years of history') (1997), Jean Favier, a renowned French medieval scholar and former head of the National Archives observes that Paris already had some 240,000 inhabitants in the fourteenth century – a mega-population – for its time and was the largest western city in the Middle Ages. At the time of the Revolution in 1789, Paris had surpassed 600,000 people and by 1914 had a population of more than a quarter of a million. As a function of the expanding Parisian population, the administrative units, *arrondissements* also grew. While there had been twelve *arrondissements* in 1795, it grew to twenty by 1860.

Eighteenth century industrialisation created a new urban-based business, a skilled and professional class – a social class that was neither hereditary nor land-based. The French Revolution of 1789 had given the new *bourgeoisie* further rights. They contributed to the transformation of the Paris city centre by "wanting access to privileges that had formerly been denied to them: the luxury of public and private space and cultural activities (theatres, museums and libraries). The nineteenth century *bourgeois* monuments – banks, train stations, department stores – were to find their legitimate place within the city," (*Architecture in the 19th Century*). Similarly, in the private domain, luxurious new *hôtel particuliers* (town mansions) were built. A superb and sumptuous sample of such an abode is the Jacquemart-Andre home on boulevard Haussmann. Now a museum, it houses a private art collection worthy of any renowned museum.

There was also a growing realisation that since big and bigger cities were here to stay, then art and beauty had a great role to play. "The city is a work of art that exerts an influence on the mass of people every day, every hour," writes the Viennese architect and art historian, Camillo Sitte, in 'The Art of Building Cities' (*Architecture in the 19th Century*). He criticised the systematic nature of the urban transformations of his time, which were dictated by a technical concept rather than by an artistic design. Taking Paris as an example, Sitte conceded the grandeur and ambition of the city's design, emphasising its links with the Baroque tradition of 'showcasing' and 'positioning' the monuments. Of all the recent urban expansion and standardisation projects, the Paris solution deviates the least from the great Baroque issues ... We can therefore take the most spectacular cityscapes created in Paris as examples of artistic creations compatible with the practical requirements of our times."

It was in such a climate that Louis Napoleon Bonaparte became Napoleon III in 1852. For the radical urban transformation of Paris that he wished to achieve, he appointed the Baron Georges Haussmann as Prefect of the Seine in 1853. In receiving a decree from Napoleon III, Haussmann annexed the suburban communes to Paris, ruthlessly levelled and rebuilt whole areas; leaving Paris a massive construction site for some forty years (the period of a generation in the late nineteenth century). "Within a few years, he imposed upon medieval, Baroque, romantic Paris a new modern, imperial vision of the capita," (*Places and History: Paris*).

Haussmann's vision was to encompass "the total architectural economy of the great city, considering the entire city to be a single monument in which all individual elements were linked," noted Cesar Daly. Haussmann envisioned a monumental and rational plan for Paris, which would be constructed around a series of large axes, squares, boulevards and avenues. Jacques Ignace Hittorff, an eminent architect of the day eliminated the irregularities of the Place de l'Etoile by constructing identical *hôtel particuliers* at the end of each avenue intersecting the large square. (Observe this aesthetic symmetrical feature the next time you are at l'Étoile). A network of streets was created to facilitate the movements between the *arrondissements* and the traffic circles were admired by all and copied elsewhere in France and abroad. They became a model and a reference; there was a small island in the centre to protect pedestrians," (*Architecture in the 19th Century*), 'on which stood the graceful shape of a superb street lamp, similar to a beacon in the middle of a fleet of wild cars ... The most original and grandiose invention in modern urban design,' remarked the Viennese architect, Sitte.

Napoleon III's initial idea was for train stations to form the new gates to the 'new' capital. Implementation of this concept required a vast network of roads and support infrastructure. "Some 50 roads were created (for a total of 90 kilometres during the Second Empire) which formed new peripheral boulevards ... three new parks (including Parc Monceau) ... nineteen squares ... as well as aqueducts and a sewer system. The first railway station, Gare St. Lazare in the Quartier de l'Europe built in 1868 was the face of the modern Paris – a city both booming and blooming.

The neighbourhood attracted a generation of painters, the Impressionists, particularly, Manet, Monet and Marisot who lived in the area in the 1870s. More than one hundred years later in 1997, an exhibition of thirteen paintings by Manet, ten by Monet and works by other artists were on display at the musee d'Orsay in a tribute to 'Manet, Monet, La Gare St. Lazare'. The painters of the day captured the innovation of the new technology, the dynamism of the mood of the epoch and the ambience of the neighbourhood. As Alan Riding in an article, 'Paintings that Unlock a Paris Neighbourhood' in the *International Herald Tribune* wrote, "Indeed, with little effort, it is still possible to gaze at the oils and smell the smoke, hear the roar and feel the shudder as steam engines shunted in and out along the platforms of the Gare St. Lazare." It seems particularly appropriate that paintings of that period, commemorating the hustle and bustle of a new era, now be shown in what is an architectural masterpiece in iron and glass of the late nineteenth century–a railway station, the Gare d'Orsay which was transformed in the late twentieth century into the stunning musee d'Orsay. Once again, *plus ça change, plus c'est la méme chose.*

Haussmann created a new urban landscape, even within the old city, through devices that included quasi-standardised façades, rows of trees lining the major streets and urban furniture (lamp-posts, benches and fountains). Paris is the best example of this desire to recreate a city within a city," (*Architecture in the 19th Century*). Haussmann gave Paris the intrinsic features of symmetrical simplicity and elegance that today seem so quintessentially Parisian. It is that undeniable quality of French polish and studied classical properties, i.e. the country's trademark and justifiably the country's source of fierce pride and grandeur.

The *Geo* magazine tells us that, "Geography and History have joined together in making Paris a crossroad – financial, economic, touristic but also intellectual, scientific and artistic – all combining to earn Paris the capital title … The site is a huge amphitheatre … And so Paris became an international economic market where converged from all Europe, ecclesiastics, traders, lords, bankers and jurists."

A Polish historian and politician Bronislaw Geremek wrote in his review of Paris, *Two Thousand Years of History* by Jean Favier the French medievalist, "There are cities without identity which have a real history. There are others which have an identity at present but are deprived of a past. Paris, however, incarnates history. In the Parisian scenario, the past mingles with the present, the streets express the archaeology of the capital, the sites recall the grandest moments in the history of France – and also of Europe. I learnt the history of Paris well before I set foot on the banks of the Seine. Much later, while often visiting the city, I learnt, like countless other foreigners, to love it."

Charles Dickens was delighted with Paris. He enthused, "The crowds in the street, the lights in the shops and balconies, the elegance, the variety and beauty of their decorations, the number of the theatres, the brilliant cafés with their windows thrown up high and their vivacious groups at little tables on the pavement, the light and glitter of the houses turned as it were inside out ..."

The city of Paris, the city of light, so beloved by all, was in fact, designed in place in the nineteenth century. What we, today, so admire and marvel, is the abundance of the past in the present. And as Victor Hugo said, "Great edifices, like great mountains, are the work of ages ... Human intelligence is there to be traced only in its aggregate. Time is the architect – the nation is the builder."

"*Paris ne s'est pas fait en un jour.*" (Paris was not built in a day). Over centuries, architects have competed with one another to build or rebuild Paris.

Countdown to Year 2000

"The secret of this `eighth wonder' of the world is that it has kept its feet on the ground, in order to have its head in the clouds and see its reflection in the waters of the Seine."

GEO

1000, 999, 998 … 100 … 20 … 5, 4, 3, 2, 1, 0. These are not figures on a screen denoting the countdown to the next send-off of another spaceship to Mars. 1000 … 0 is the countdown to the next millennium – the start of the twenty-first century, the year 2000 at the Eiffel Tower, the jewel showpiece of Paris and the symbol of Paris.

The Mayor of Paris, Jean Tiberi lit the giant digital clock in April 1997 on the front façade of the Eiffel Tower that is clocking away daily the 1000 days to the year 2000. The digital clock says '*J – avant de l'an 2000*' (- days till the year 2000). The clock itself 40 feet high and mounted 330 feet above the ground is visible all 24 hours of the day. City of Paris authorities also inform us that it took 9000 hours to construct.

The sense of continuity – the connection of the old and the new in which Paris seems to have a particular expertise and flair is once again evident in this expressive illumination on the frontage of the most dominating monument on the Parisian skyline – the Iron Lady of Paris. According to Giovanna Magi in her book, *Places and History : Paris*, "Paris has always been able to renew its creative energy in infinite celebration of its own myth, and is always adept at finding ways of talking about herself, through music, theatre, painting, cinema, literature and architecture. Paris is a city of continual challenges and movement, bold in its imposition of the contagious youthfulness of the most excessive of *avant-garde* projects, whilst at the same time *une grande dame* ever capable of provocation and seduction."

The Eiffel Tower was built in 1889 by the French engineer, Gustave Eiffel on the occasion of the World Exposition held in Paris. Its creation was scandalous in its time and what is today the Iron Lady of Paris was then slammed as "a gigantic garish iron chimney piercing the Parisian sky … A hollow candlestick … What is this horror that the French have found to celebrate their much vaunted good taste? A ridiculously vertiginous tower, overshadowing Paris like some gigantic black factory chimney." So too does time heal architectural wounds.

Sylvie Genevoix, writing in *Paris: The Seine* remarks, "And if, one nightmare of the day they (the visitors) come to find her no longer there, they will leave bitterly disappointed, believing the unbelievable. Paris will no longer be Paris … Today it is the very symbol of Paris, necessary even to its everyday life. Built in homage to the industrial thrust forward of the 1900s, it is now the standard bearer of communications for the year 2000. As its summit, more than one hundred aerials or transmitters make it the nerve centre of Paris – meteorology, radio, television, the police, it serves them all … what would we be without it? … As sure as Paris will always be Paris, the Eiffel Tower will always be there." The rest of the world seems to agree with this French point of view. "The 301 metres-high Eiffel Tower, already the most visited monument in the world, had a record 6 million visitors in 1998. It nearest rivals are the Empire State Building (381 m) with 3.6 million visitors a year, and the Tokyo Tower (333 m) with more than 3 million visitors a year," states *Time* magazine. In this case, small is beautiful and more popular.

A collection of *Famous People in Anecdotes* by the Polish Wanda Rutkowska has this delightful entry on William Morris (1834-1896), a British poet, painter and socialist. Most people love Paris and William Morris was no exception. He loved the beautiful French city so much that he stayed in Paris for a very long time. The Eiffel Tower seemed to be his favourite place because he spent most of his time there. He not only had all his meals in one of the Eiffel Tower restaurants, but also did most of his writing there. One day a friend of his said to him, "I see that the Eiffel Tower is certainly your most favourite place in Paris." "My favourite place!" Morris cried. "How can you think so? I stay there most of the time because it's the only place in Paris where I don't see the terrible thing!" Well, we all have our individual forms of escapism.

The 1889 World Exposition held at the close of the nineteenth century celebrated the Industrial Revolution; the technological progress made and the scientific conquest achieved in the nineteenth century. Towards the end of the nineteenth century, according to *Places and History: Paris*, architecture also underwent radical changes: glass, iron and steel were the new construction materials, the most suitable ones to make buildings lighter, more dynamic and more modern. The engineer, in short, had taken the place of the architect. And indeed it was an engineer, Gustave Eiffel who designed – not on paper itself but on the surface of the sky itself – these extraordinary lines of metal, which soar above the Parisian skyline and seem to triumph over all the older monuments of the city."

The first proposal for a tower was made in 1884; construction was completed in an amazing 26 months and opened in time for the World Exposition in March 1889. The Michelin Guide to France notes that "despite its 7000 tonnes and a height of 1050 feet, its extraordinary weight rests on 4 enormous pylons with cement bases. It is a masterpiece of lightness. It is difficult to imagine that the tower actually weighs less than the volume of the air surrounding it and that the pressure that it exerts on the ground is that of a man sitting on a chair."

For the 1925 Exposition of Decorative Arts in Paris, Andre Citroen, the founder of the Citroen car company managed to obtain permission for the giant letters CITROEN to appear down the sides of the Eiffel Tower in gaudy neon. This was the first use of the novel neon lights for large-scale publicity purposes. Historically, the Eiffel Tower has served a number of needs.

'The Guide to Paris' provides an impressive array of facts. "To build the Eiffel Tower, 50 engineers and draftsmen drew up 5300 plans; 100 workers turned out 18,038 iron pieces and 121 others worked on the tower construction, 836,271 square feet of earth were cleared away for the foundations. The construction was finished in 1889; it lasted two years, two months and five days The Eiffel Tower is now repainted every seven years and 600,000 tons of paint are required to cover the 1,800,000 square feet of iron. The last time it was repainted, in 1995, the task required 1500 brushes, 5000 grinding discs, 1500 pairs of overalls and 2000 pairs of leather gloves." The Eiffel Tower has three floors at heights of 187 feet, 377 feet and 899 feet, each floor complete with restaurants and a panoramic vista. Visibility on a clear day can extend some 45 miles.

Built towards the close of the nineteenth century, the Eiffel Tower was also to appear as a symbol of the new millennium – the twentieth century, the Dawning of a New Age. In this context, it is appropriate that the same Eiffel

Tower built to herald the twentieth century today acts as an easel, the backdrop for the announcement – the countdown to he advent of the twenty-first century – yet another millennium, the Dawning of a New Age. So does Time inexorably tick away.

'This was the Year 2000 - The Paris of Utopias'

"A country where the impossible always happens and the inevitable never does."

Anon

An Eiffel Tower 'skirted' by an ornate palace halfway up the structure? The Arc de Triomphe with a hotel in a kaleidoscope of architectural designs perched on top of the Arc? Impossible? Ludicrous? Well, these were designs proposed by the cartoonist Albert Robida (1848-1926) to prepare Paris for the twenty-first century. Robida proposed in the late nineteenth century to modernise existing Parisian monuments for the Paris of the 2000s.

A Jules Vernesque futuristic odyssey through Paris was the theme of the exhibiton at the Paris Hotel de Ville (Town Hall) which ran from May to October 1998. Jean Tiberi, the Mayor of Paris in a statement on the opening of the exhibition remarked, "Between utopia and reality, there is often nothing but a margin which is the decision to undertake it or not to. Our predecessors had imagination. The exhibition '*C'était l'an 2000 – le Paris des Utopies*' ('This was the year 2000 – the Paris of Utopias') is the proof. In fact, the public is invited to a retrospective of Paris in the year 2000 by those who imagined it between 1860 and 1960 ... What is there of our utopia, our day-dreams, our dreams?

A series of spectacular and provocative photographs envisioning Paris in the twenty-first century reminds us of what might have been – if the fantasies of visionaries of the late nineteenth and early twentieth centuries had been implemented. For the Parisian capital is ambivalent. It loves the shock and controversy that is produced by *avant-garde* and audacious architecture. Yet Parisians deep down are extremely comfortable with their surroundings and dislike any major jolts in their scenic panorama. Time has proven successful two of Paris' unique landmarks – the Eiffel Tower and the glass pyramid at the Louvre. The two monuments (both in their times immensely controversial) constitute today veritable symbols of Paris. The Pompidou arts centre and the Mitterand national library have not been that well-received in the public eye.

Can one imagine skyscrapers surrounding and overlooking the Eiffel Tower? Well, so was a design envisioned in 1932. Horror of horrors. How about the Ile de la Cite island, complete with the Notre-Dame rebuilt one hundred metres above Paris like a Titanic afloat in the Seine? Surrealistic. This was the dream of the German architect, Ingrid Webendoerfer. Paul Maymont imagined a man-made lake in front of the Notre-Dame (where now stands the square) which would reflect the cathedral in its waters. The lake would be one hundred steps below the Notre-Dame at level with the Seine river. I like the idea. How about a new city district under the Seine? A 1962 project by Paul Maymont once again envisioned an urban setting complete with banks, shopping centres, theatres, and sport complexes, parking lots, offices and swimming pool well below the Seine. The metropolis of tomorrow was to cover fifteen kilometres. An intriguing idea.

A lighthouse for visitors from outer space? Such was the description of a 347 metres high (27 metres more than the Eiffel Tower) in la Defense area west of the city. The competitor would have chrome, laser lights flashing, facilities to guide supersonic planes; a cyber-lower designed in the 1960s by Nicolas Schoffer. Pure science fiction. Other turn-of-the-last-century visionaries included twenty-first century aero-abs flying with wings according to postcards printed by the Bon Marche department store on *la rive gauche* in 1990. It exists today in the form of helicopters.

The most incredulous? A photograph of la Place de la Concorde, les Champs-Elysées side showing a massive beach-front complete with waves, sun umbrellas and people in the water – utopia of the 1930s. I shall pass this one. Does there exist a more perfect urban landscape anywhere in the world than that vista which encompasss l'Arc de Triomphe, les Champs-Elysées, la Place de la Concorde and le Louvre – all that which makes up the Great Paris Axis? Mercifully, this projection of Paris into the twenty-first century never came off the drawing board.

'And God Created the French' by Louis-Bernard Robitaille

"The Almighty in His infinite wisdom did not see fit to create Frenchmen in the image of Englishmen."

Sir Winston Churchill, in a speech at Parliament, December 10, 1942

"If we are to believe the long-standing legend, France has been resented ever since its birth. All its European neighbours, to the north, to the east, even to the south, when they saw this new country in their midst, joined forces at once to pool their indignation and send emissaries before God to voice their complaints. To this single land, they said, God had granted everything: the Mediterranean Sea and the Atlantic Ocean, the fertile plain and the proud mountains, the sun of the south and the melancholy mists of the north, cooking with butter and cooking with oil, the inexhaustible subtleties of the most wondrous vineyards in the world and the conviviality of a land where beer flows freely. Was this his idea of divine justice? God gave ear to this torrent of arguments and in his heart of hearts admitted that on this occasion, yes, he had been overly prodigal. So to make up for those unfair benefits and bounties ... God created the French. And so the other Europeans went home, mollified, justice had been done."

Robitaille adds, "The anecdote may not be historically accurate."

On the other hand, "The European idea has stirred passions and polemics in France ever since romantic nineteenth century visionaries like Victor Hugo waxed eloquent about a future 'United States of Europe' – with

Paris as its capital, of course," writes *Time* magazine. Alain Duhamel in a 1999 bestseller, *Une Ambition Française* explores a united Europe with France *naturellement* as its driving force.

In the cheeky *Xenophobe's Guide to the French* (1997), Nick Yapp and Michel Syrett note that, "The French see brilliance in everything they do, and French statesmen from the Renaissance to de Gaulle and on to Chirac have likened France herself to a shining light. Their own role in relation to the rest of the world borders on the Messianic." Furthermore, in a map of La France, they have written 'Not French' in all its neighbours' territory; Britain, Belgium, Germany, Italy, Spain! How true.

Paris has always hosted writers – have been writers, would have been writers, will be writers and those chosen few writers whose writings sell. French-Canadian journalist, Louis-Bernard Robitaille happily falls into the latter category. With two books already published in Montreal and one novel published in Paris, *Le République de Monte Carlo* in 1990 – Robitaille achieved further success with the first English translation of his fourth book in 1997, *Et Dieu Créa les Français*. The author has been for over twenty years the Paris correspondent for the Montreal daily newspaper *La Presse* and the bi-weekly newsmagazine *L'Actualité*. Pierre Salinger in a review of *And God Created the French* writes, "A biting, loving and wonderfully knowledgeable insider's guide to Parisians. Few observers know France better than Robitaille."

Louis-Bernard Robitaille has been an intimate observer of Paris and of French society since the mid-sixties when he too, like countless others before him, sat at the Café de Flore on *la rive gauche*. "Dressed in a velvet suit and turtleneck, I sat myself down on the terrace of the Café de Flore, my left elbow lodged in one neighbour's ribs, my right hand with about six inches' leeway before it would capsize my other neighbour's glass. I thought I spotted Francoise Sagan – which seemed perfectly normal, and a happy omen of events to come. Having ordered a coffee, I flipped open the notebook I had placed in front of me, and took out a pen. No sooner had I done so when a terrifying waiter, strapping and moustachioed, boomed out in a voice that could not be ignored: "No writing on the terrace!"

No. Those bygone days are a thing of the past; a bit of history down memory lane. At the Parisian cafés where literary success was achieved (one has to discount all those who never made it); in the past, "owners of such establishments … would have been flattered by such cultural consecration. On the contrary. They were appalled by the ensuing invasion of penniless scribblers from hither and yon, who threatened to monopolise indefinitely – in exchange for the modest price of a small espresso – a precious table that could bring in at the very least the price of a large beer every half-hour". Alas no more wordsmiths in a Parisian café. Robitaille went on to write his first novel elsewhere in Paris in 1965-66 but "whose only copy I lost in the gents at Heathrow airport the day I returned to Montreal." Literary recognition finally came in 1982 with the publication of his first book.

One should not come to Paris, the City of Wonder to dream? Is he joking? Robitaille jolts the reader with the line, "But to come here to dream, no. Certainly one is taken aback, bewitched, overwhelmed at first by the beauty of Notre-Dame or the quays of the Seine. But wait six months or a year, and the astonishment will have fled. Well, almost. Now and then when you least expect it you'll be dazzled anew, on an autumn evening, say, as you cross over the

Seine. What endures is the respect and admiration you feel for the Beauty and Perfection you behold as you try to recall, just as it was, that first sense of wonder, the colours and the smells." Perhaps the writer's inspiration, the Muse, Paris succumbs to two proverbs - `Familiarity breeds contempt' (doubtful) and 'Absence makes the heart grow fonder' (undoubtedly). It was another Canadian, Sir Wilfred Laurier, Prime Minister who in an address in Paris, in 1897 said, "My eyes do not grow weary in gazing at this Paris, so full of marvels; Paris the City of Light, as Victor Hugo called it with such truth, beyond dispute the most beautiful of all cities."

One of the enlightening bits of information Robitaille provides us is on the subject of French nobility titles – such as the commonly aristocratic 'de'. The chapter is titled 'The *de* is not for burning'. Even though noble privilege was abolished in France in 1789, "an impressive number of people try each year to join ranks, officially and administratively, of the vague dead letter which is all that remains of the French aristocracy". In a matter of speaking I would add, since that vague *de* is yet sufficiently close to the hearts of many whereby "nobility now caters only to the variety of those who seek it. But the usurper doesn't risk much either, just a snigger here and there. There is no dearth of candidates, therefore, for an expanded name."

A French historian, Pierre Diudonnat has spent a quarter of a century listing the truly noble families and the bogus noble families. The 1994 edition of his *Encyclopédia de la Fausse Noblesse et de la Noblesse d'Apparence* (The Encyclopedia of False or Ostensible Nobility) in some 669 pages, defrocks some 4000 names of dubious noble affiliation. Another myth shattered. In order to understand the French strata, Diudonnat reminds us that "the *de* is not in itself an attribute of nobility. Many ancient noble families did not initially sport the particle, whereas it was found among some of the common folk. But it is true that, since for most people the two little letters were synonymous with aristocracy, nobles tended to affix them to the name of one of their fiefdoms. And families of the *grande bourgeoisie* followed suit to give themselves a semblance of nobility." For our information, Charles de Gaulle "was simply the issue of a very old *bourgeois* family, and we find as of 1720 a Jean-Baptiste de Gaulle who was prosecutor in the Parliament of Paris."

Further enlightenment on Parisian social makeup is provided for in Robitaille's discussion of '*la bonne societé*.' He defines it as, "a relatively unique French category, which groups, loosely speaking, the 'right crowd', the 'people who count' in the media and the state, the defenders of culture, intelligence, refinement and reassuring good taste. This cultural *bourgeoisie* will be hereinafter referred to by its French name, i.e. *la bonne societé*." And it is in the seventh *arrondissement* in which "the heart of real Parisian society beats, and nowhere else; so much power linked to so much discretion commands respect." The hallowed Golden Quadrilateral, a Forbidden City, includes the expanse covering the Rodin museum, any number of ministries, les Invalides, boulevard Montparnasse, rue Varennes, rue de Grenelle and preserved façades hiding members of the Parisian establishment. The social hierarchy extends to the extent that "The Parisian *bonne societié* may not lack for money, but neither does it consort with the moneyed ... Money exists, like bathtubs and toilets, but should not be shown off, nor publicly discussed. You may think about it all you want, just don't talk about it ... With a clear conscience one espouses what is worthy, cultivated, intelligent, enlightened, refined and reassuringly tasteful."

Yet, *quartiers* do evolve over the years – slowly. Barriers do become less defined. Robitaille remarks that ultimately, "A neighbourhood that yesterday was beneath contempt, today is declared chic by the arbiters of taste for the elite, and becomes acceptable. So goes the sociology of living space in Paris, and the price per square metre follows not far behind, at a moderate but constant speed."

We are in for a treat in his discussion of the Great Presidential Works (GPWs) – which they certainly are – since they receive direct patronage of the president (as they once upon a time did under Louis XIV or Napoleon I). The GPWs include the Grand Louvre, d'Orsay Museum, Arab Institute, French National Library, the City of Science and Music and the Defence Grand Arch. The author asked one manager of the work site for Cite des Sciences et de la Musique about the difference between an ordinary project and a GPW. "The response is classic in the French mode of expressiveness and expression. "Ah! He replied, with feigned dismay, as though I had asked him to cite, off-the-cuff, the various proofs for the existence of God." "Ah! You know, in such instances, there are no budgetary constraints." He gestured vaguely, and sighed, as though he was contemplating the Infinite or the Great Void. "There is, as it were, no budget at all."

Thomas Bentley in *Journal of a Visit to Paris* all the way back in 1776 noted that "The French have very magnificent ideas, and it is their delight to be laying magnificent plans. They begin work with a degree of vigour and expense that exhausts both their patience and their finances." The innate sensitivity of the French to such national needs was apparent even then.

So be it. Thus came about the Bastille Opera. President Mitterand and his Minister of Culture, Jack Lang put forth a plan for a poplar opera at the Place de la Bastille (the site of the popular uprising against the Bastille prison in 1789). Robitaille argues that, "the seats are as expensive as they were at the old opera, the Palais-Garnier, and they are just as hard to get hold of for the major productions. It cost twice as much as what had been estimated..." On the other hand, The Palais-Garnier, the mammoth classical opera house at the Place de l'Opera, "was one of the most beautiful opera houses in the world, with good acoustics, and it only needed a bit of modernisation: it had 2,200 seats (20 per cent of which had an obstructed view) compared to 2,700 today at the Bastille, not an enormous difference". Lt. Col. Nathaniel Newnham-Davis in *The Gourmet's Guide to Europe* of 1903 wrote, "An Englishman who loved his Paris beyond any other city of the world once said to me, as we stood chatting in the Place de l'Opera, 'If you find the central spot of this square, you may rap your stick upon it and say, "This is the centre of the world."

I know about the 'obstructed view'. In an umpteenth unsuccessful attempt to acquire 'proper' seats for a ballet at the Palais-Garnier, I reluctantly agreed to buy tickets at 60 francs – a ridiculously low sum. On the ticket was printed 'partial visibility'. Upon enquiring as to its meaning, I was informed that our vision of the performance of the 'Don Quixote' ballet would be partial, i.e. obstructed. Well, an obstructed view is better than no view – if one is ever to get into a masterpiece of nineteenth century architecture and see a prima ballerina perform. My husband unimpressed at my efforts, declined to see a 'partial' performance. I argued that at 60 francs, one could not lose. After all, we would see the interior, like a museum including what is acknowledged to be Charles Garnier's landmark staircase; at worst, see half a ballet and at best, with eyes closed hear a full concert. After all, when one comes to the opera, one wants to dream. My husband did not appreciate the bargain of my argument. He stayed. I went with our daughter and her friend.

In an excellent *exposé* on Paris – the heartbeat of France *vis-à-vis* the rest of the country – Robitaille finds that, "the saga of Parisian centralism harks back uninterrupted to the ninth century AD, and that all the great men and key events in French history have contributed to it … In France there are only two boxers in the ring; Paris in one corner, and in the other a huge anonymous mass referred to only in negative terms, as *la province*." An Englishman, Sir William Clayton in his 'Journals 1861-1914', wrote that "The heart of France beats in Paris, and the excessive centralisation of the French has centred the hopes and ambitions in their capital."

A brilliant manifestation of this fundamental Parisian thinking is the decision to relocate Ecole Nationale d' Administration (ENA), the National Management School to Strasbourg close to the German border. ENA, the bastion of Parisian establishment, produces the French political leadership and Parisian bureaucrats. The national powerhouse opened in 1994 at its new address – *en province*. Yet, "Out of 26 months at school they'll be spending seven in Strasbourg. That comes down to some boring return trips on the train and a few nights in a hotel. The ENA is now in Strasbourg without ever having left Paris." A magnificent compromise surely. *Plus ça change*, ….

Robitaille here paraphrases Prince Salina in the Sicilian author, Giuseppe Lampedusa's epic novel, *The Leopard* published in 1958 and later made into a film by Luchino Visconti. "We must change everything so that nothing will change" – a time-honoured teaching. *The Economist* in an October 1998 issue, discussed *The Leopard.* "To many readers, *The Leopard* is the greatest Italian novel this century perhaps the greatest ever and uniquely relevant to modern Italy." (And elsewhere). *The Economist* quotes Lampedusa's most famous line in the book, "If we want things to stay as they are, things will have to change." Change within continuity. Mobility within immobility. Are these the ingredients, the motto for the durability and attraction of a city, a people, a nation?

The author interviews a number of French celebrities. As the journalist observes, "It's an exercise that brings you face to face with the humbleness of your lot in life and the modesty of your profession." He interviewed Isabelle Adjani, the Algerian-German born French actress and President of the 1997 Cannes Film Festival. Remember thc masterpiece *Adele H* by Francois Truffaut where she portrayed at eighteen the daughter of Victor Hugo? The French have successfully overestimated the significance of a film festival. After all, Special Agent 007 Sean Connery on the steps of the Palais des Festivals declared at the Cannes Festival 1999 that, "There is a great charge there and the French do that rather well." Only the French could make a social bonanza complete with starlets and paparazzi and give it an intellectual aura – a meaning, substance, social conscience – and money-making to boot.

A much sought-after interview with the French music composer, Michel Legrand took place at Fouquet's on les Champs-Elysées at the suggestion of Legrand's secretary. It went like this. "There's only one solution. "You invite us to lunch on Wednesday. At Fouquet's. It's practical and it's not expensive. (In fact, it's the most famous show-biz eatery on les Champs-Elysées, and not the least expensive)" notes Robitaille. Legrand composed the music for the 1964 cult film *The Umbrellas of Cherbourg.*

A seasoned journalist, Robitaille is starry-eyed in his interview with Catherine Deneuve, a star since the 1960s. Can you blame him? He gushes, "Deneuve the Immaculate. Catherine Deneuve is a consummate modern incarnation of French perfection ... Perfection, of course, of her features, with their steadfast limpidity. It's perfection that is never laboured, that is imbued with intelligence and culture. Perfection, above all, of her musical voice, which with a slight effortless inflection shifts from coldness to amusement, from polite indifference to animation, from spontaneous laughter to boredom. She says, just like that, 'ah, you think so?' and you hear the angels sing."

A cover story on Catherine Deneuve in *Le Figaro* magazine is titled 'The Consecration of a Mythical Actress'. She is also named 'The New Idol of the Young'. A rap artist, a pure product of the 1990s, Stomy Bugsy in meeting Catherine Deneuve declares; "My greatest dream was to meet her. That has been done ... a bomb of charm ... Deneuve is a queen and I am nothing but her d'Artagnan, *Place Vendome*, released in 1998, takes place in the luxurious setting of Place de la Vendôme in Paris, a coolly elegant square hosting top international jewellers. Deneuve plays an alcoholic. The film is set in a high class jewellery business. She has received accolades at the Venice Film Festival for her role in *Place Vendôme*. Robitaille declares at the end of the interview, "She has become, to all intents and purposes, the one star of French cinema, even if she finds the idea "ridiculous. There are no stars in France." Notwithstanding her statement, the epitome of French beauty – the face of Catherine Deneuve graces the sculptured head adorning the Hôtels de Ville all over France.

Living in the '16th'

"Every French town has an avenue Victor Hugo."

Barbara Tuchman

Three medieval villages of Chaillot, Passy and Auteuil today constitute *le seizième.* Each village in its day had its own characteristics; Chaillot was aristocratic and conventional, Passy – residential and a centre for thermal treatment and Auteuil more rural. Until the revolution, the villages were host to convents, abbeys and country houses inhabited by affluent and fashionable Parisians. These villages were located en route to Versailles palace and in the course of the seventeenth and eighteenth centuries, these villages gradually acquired more architectural standing with mansions and hotels being built in the area and an ambience of pleasure and extravaganza started prevailing in an increasingly urban locality.

The ancient forest of Rouvray, the present-day Bois de Boulogne used to be the royal hunting-ground and it remained crown property till the nineteenth century. It was named le Bois de Boulogne in the fifteenth century. Napoleon III in 1857 inaugurated l'Hippodrome de Longchamp (race-course of Longchamp). And le Bois de Boulogne became a *promenade* – a public walking space. It transformed the forest. Henceforward, the Paris urban gentry went to le Bois de Boulogne for outings to see and be seen. How many of us who now go to le Bois de Boulogne for walks, drives, picnics, horse-riding, rowing or cycling know that from the thirteenth century till the close of the eighteenth century when it was demolished, there was a well-known royal abbey in le Bois de Boulogne established by Louis IX at the request of his sister Isabelle de France.

It was, however, Napoleon III in the second half of the nineteenth century who attached Chaillot, Passy and Auteuil to the city of Paris in 1860 and together they became the 16th district of Paris. The opening-up of imperial boulevards such as the present avenue Foch, avenue de la Grande-Armee which are two of the twelve majestic avenues taking off from l'Étoile (Star) and the avenue Henri-Martin, connecting the Trocadero with le Bois de Boulogne, added to the grandeur of *le seiziéme*. The extensive verdure of the area, its proximity to le Bois de Boulogne and the presence of numerous tree-lined avenues and boulevards lend itself to creating an impression of space, elegance and equilibrium.

The eye-catching Parisian tree-lined boulevards of Paris led T.J. Hogg in 1827 to observe in *Two Hundred and Nine Days on the Continent*, "Long straight lines of poplars delight the French; they suit the military turn of the nation." Notwithstanding the "military turn", one has to admit that the sense of symmetry, balance and proportion so amply evident in Paris – is what delights the eye. It is that delight which is a key feature in one's affair with Paris. Parisian boulevards, according to Rowland Strong, serve another purpose. In *Sensations of Paris*, Strong noted in 1912 that, "The ample proportions of the Boulevard are necessary to the Parisian for his gesticulations, and for the breadth of his ideas on moral, social, and political topics ... The Boulevard is the throat of Paris, and its palate as well."

A Parisian-born resident of *le seiziéme* for fifty years, Beatrice de Andia is a member of the Delegation a L'Action Artistique de la Ville de Paris (Delegation for the Artistic Action for the City of Paris) and the person responsible for putting together *Le XVIe: Chaillot, Passy, Auteuil – Métamorphose des Trois Villages.* It is a well-researched book with excellent pictures of old maps of the area; one map shows the 16th *arrondissement* in 1731 and another shows the 16th in 1992. Engravings, lithographs, sketches, and paintings of the changing *arrondissement* add to the charm of the book.

In an interesting comparative study of the various *arrondissements* of the city, she highlights the features of some of the districts with those of her beloved *le seiziéme.* In the 7th, the 'noble area', we find numerous *hôtels particuliers* with courtyards and gardens built in the eighteenth century that had belonged to the Abbaye de Saint-Germain. Since 1920, in those properties – now converted – a host of embassies and ministries are to be found. "Every morning, they invade the area and every evening, they leave." Béatrice de Andia notes that the shops of the area tend to be those of necessities. There are not many luxurious boutiques nor elegant shops to be found in the area. The residents appear isolated among the offices. "The area is more conservative and not open to progress; they are more old France and less cosmopolitan than the 16th."

In the 8th, we find opulent residential areas combined with the highly commercial les Champs-Elysées. Les Champs-Elysées has an influx of the office-workers in the mornings and recreation-seekers in the evenings; frequenting the theatres, cinemas, cafés, restaurants, nightclubs and fast-food outlets and many just taking-in-the-air. In comparison, the streets of the 16th are silent. The 17th is dotted with sumptuous Haussmannian buildings. "The network of streets are narrow, monuments are fewer and it has neither the air, nor the architectural quality, nor the historical heritage of its neighbour." On the other side of the river, the 15th lacks the homogeneity and the touch of grandeur of the 16th. "The laid-back atmosphere in the 15th pretends to neither the stature nor elegance of the 16th." The 5th and 6th form the heart of the ancient capital. It is where any number of churches, fountains, palaces, old and picturesque streets are to be found among boutiques, cafés and restaurants. This is the Latin Quarter where one finds the young and the intellectuals. In this happy bohemia, one is far from the dignity and calmness dear to our 16th." Acceptable alternatives appear to be the 5th or 6th *arrondissements.*

Not everyone would agree with Beatrice de Andia's assessment of other *arrondissements* and defer to her partiality for *le seiziéme.* However, one has to concede her fifty years residence and her obvious love for the 16th. On my part, I am unabashedly prejudiced. I lived in le *seiziéme* in the 1950s – on rue Spontini. I lived in *le seiziéme* in the 1990s – on avenue Victor Hugo. Where else could one live?

Le seiziéme of today owes its ambience and character to Napoleon III and a team of experts. The team leader and father of the nineteenth century Parisian urbanism was Baron Georges Haussmann. He is to be credited with the present-day architecture that is 'just-so Parisian'. Other technocrats who were also men of vision included the minister of finance and interior, the engineer in charge of water and sanitation and the director of the promenades of Paris, Jean-Charles Adolphe Alphand. A statue of him graces avenue Foch, the wholly residential and most elegant avenue by any standard. One can vividly imagine horse-drawn carriages with top-hatted men and parasol-holding women in them, en route to the races at Longchamp. Nowadays, the only four-legged animals one is likely to see on avenue Foch are a motley of dogs.

The current broad avenues emanating from Place l'Étoile existed in the nineteenth century. Present-day avenue de la Grande-Armee used to be la route Imperiale. The avenue Foch was the avenue de l'Imperatrice and before that avenue du Bois. At the far end of the avenue Foch was placed a statue of Maréchal de Lattre at Place Dauphine. This fulfilled Haussmann's *grande perspective* monument to monument', i.e. l'Arc de Triomphe at one end and Marechal de Lattre at the other end. The station at Place Dauphine received a number of foreign dignitaries following the end of World War I. They used to get off the train at Place Dauphine, travel up avenue Foch, down les Champs-Elysées and enter the presidential Elysées Palais. Today, the Université de Dauphine, renowned for its faculty of economics is also to be found here. In our immediate neighbourhood, the Trocadero avenue became avenue President Wilson and the avenue de l'Empereur became avenue Georges-Mandel and avenue Henri-Martin. The avenue de Saint-Cloud became our widened avenue Victor Hugo. The avenue Roi de Rome (King of Rome) became avenue Kleber and avenue Josephine became avenue Marceau.

At the Pont Neuilly, en route to la Défense, the Seine is 28 metres above sea level and also in the 16th, the place l'Etoile where stands l'Arc de Triomphe has an elevation of 58 metres. Archaeologists often observe that all sites well-placed invite early construction. So it was with the hill of Chaillot – the Trocadero of today. On the occasion of the forthcoming Universal Exposition in 1878, it was decided in 1876 to build a monumental construction on the hill. The other hill at l'Etoile became transformed with the construction of l'Arc de Triomphe – a symbol of grandeur. From this star-location, radiate the unique twelve avenues, often named after French generals and battles; avenue Foch, avenue Kleber, avenue de Friedland, avenue de la Grande-Armee, avenue d'Iena and French liberary giants, such as avenue Victor Hugo. The towering father of all French generals, General Charles de Gaulle – the architect of post-war modern France has been honoured with Place l'Etoile being renamed Place Charles de Gaulle. However, the old name is still *en vogue*. Bill Bryson in *Neither Here Nor There* made an accurate observation. "I know Baron Haussmann made Paris a grand place to look at, but the man had no concept of traffic flow. At the Arc de Triomphe alone twelve roads come together." Undoubtedly it is a hair-raising round-about.

The rich architectural heritage found in *le seiziéme* today hosts embassies, headquarters of foundations and corporations and museums. In *The Crazy Years: Paris in the Twenties*, William Wiser (1983) refers to an *insouciant* style which was sustained by inherited wealth." The turn-of-the-twentieth century saw a construction boom with big money – often from an American female source – combined with male French aristocracy. The merger of wealth and blue-blood have left us a legacy of architectural wonders littered all over the 16th. An opulent lifestyle involved grand balls, artistic, musical and literary salons where fierce rivalry competed for the painter, composer and writer of the day. Those endowed materially felt a need to encourage and endow the arts.

One such architectural jewel is the *hôtel particulier* built for the banker, Jules Ephrussi of Russian origin and his wife Fanny Von Pfeiffer of Austrian origin at 2 Place des Etats-Unis in 1886. It was bought by King Fouad I of Egypt. After the overthrow of his son, King Farouk in 1952 from the throne of Egypt, it became and remains the residence of the Ambassador of Egypt. The Hotel de Breteuil at 12 avenue Foch was built for the third Marquis de Breteuil. His financial standing combined with that of his American second wife allowed them to enlarge and embellish their residence and garden. The property along with a large amount of furnishings was bought by the Irish government and is today the Embassy of the Republic of Ireland.

The Heidelbach at 19 avenue d'Iena was the property of an American banker and President of the American Chamber of Commerce in Paris and his American wife. It was built early in the twentieth century. It is now an extension of the museum of oriental arts, musee Guimet. The imposing Polignac at 43 avenue Georges-Mandel we passed frequently during our walks. This magnificent mansion with a terrace and a garden some twenty feet above ground-level was built by Winarette Singer-Polignac. She was the daughter of the American sewing-machine industrial family. Her second marriage at 28 was to the Prince de Polignac who was 58. A young-widowed Princesse de Polignac in the 1920s went on to become "a substantial and legitimate cornerstone of French society," says William Wiser in *The Crazy Years: Paris in the Twenties.* Before her death in 1943, she bequeathed the building to the Foundation Singer-Polignac which still bears its name.

The 16th has the dimension of a large city with 7.5 kms. facing the Seine, 4.5 kms facing the centre of town (the 15th), and 3 kms bordering the forest of le Bois de Boulogne. The 1990 census counted 170,000 inhabitants in the 16th that places it as the fifth most populated Parisian *arrondissement* (after the 15th, 18th, 20th and 13th). The 16th's population equals that of the major French towns, Reims, Toulon and Grenoble. The population is more aged than it was thirty years ago. This is evident in the number of coiffed, elegantly-suited and bejewelled ladies walking their precious pets in the 16th.

Le seizième has more than seventy embassies in its area; about half of the totality. Our embassy is at rue Erlanger, Auteuil. Our residence is at avenue Victor Hugo. The Organisation of Economic Community Development (OECD) is close to avenue Henri-Martin and boulevard Suchet. The International Conference Centre is housed in a palatial building on avenue Kleber. The Quai d'Orsay (French Ministry of Foreign Affairs) hosts many of its social events in its magnificent salons. The 1920s rotunda-styled Economics and Social Council is to be found at Place de'Iena.

Some of the major museums of Paris are located in *le seizième.* The Musee Marmottan boasts the most impressive collection of the Impressionist painter, Claude Monet. In the basement are innumerable 'Water Lilies' and the renowned 'Impression: Rising Sun'. The novelist, Balzac's house is on rue Raynouard; one of the rare examples of the rural Passy that used to be. At 50 avenue Victor Hugo is the Dapper Museum honouring African art. The house where George Clemenceau, the French hero of World War I lived almost all his life is at 8 rue Franklin. The Palais Galliera, a stunningly beautiful eighteenth century palace belonged to the Duc and Duchesse de Gallira. She was from an affluent ancient Genoese Italian family. His money originated in banking and railways. She generously donated the palace to the city of Paris following her death in 1894. Today the Palais Galliera hosts extraordinarily rich exhibits on textile and fashion. One exhibition that I saw was on fashion and gardens. Another exhibition covered Parisian fashion at the turn-of-the-century–*la Belle Epoque.*

The Museum of Modern Art is at the Palais de Tokyo close to Trocadero, facing the Eiffel Tower. The Museum of Cinema is found in one of the wings of the Palais de Chaillot, Trocadero. The Museum of Mankind focusing on anthropology and the Museum of the Sea are located in the other wing of the Palais de Chaillot. The Mona Bismarck Foundation at 34 avenue de New York facing the Seine is another elegant and classical nineteenth century architecture. It belonged to Mona Bismarck, an American and le Comte Edouard Bismarck. She was one of the pillars of Parisian society early in the twentieth century – much celebrated for her beauty, elegance, lifestyle and generosity. The foundation is today engaged in primarily promoting Franco-American friendship in the form of hosting cultural events, seminars and exhibitions. Such was the wealth and such was the tradition of civic generosity in those days.

A scan of *Le Figaro* newspaper, a major source of real estate information in Paris shows the value that is put on nineteenth century Haussmannian architecture – "*ancien immeuble en Pierre de taille, Haussmannien, de haut standing*" (old building of dressed-stone, Haussmannian, of high quality). A building of Haussmannian architecture is a reference of quality in which the façade presents a delight in proportion, balance and decoration. Christian Geury writing on `Real Estate: The Return of the Promoters of Neo-Haussmannian' in *Le Figaro* notes that the intrinsic value of Haussmannian architecture remains steady and increasingly in demand for office space. For one is looking at large volumes of space, spacious entrance halls, marble fireplaces, parquet flooring and all on a 'noble floor'. Ideally, the second floor for first-time owners, since the ground floor had often shops and the first floor could have commercial usage, being reserved by shopkeepers as living quarters or storage space. Such an apartment we found on avenue Victor Hugo in *le seizième*. On a 'noble floor' (the second), the building was constructed in 1910 by the architect, Paul Raman as it tells us in markings engraved on the wall. It is an Haussmannian building.

It is at a minimum, a twenty-minute walk to les Champs-Elysées. I doubt if anyone has ever managed it. The window shopping along the way extends delightfully the walking-time. Drool at the mouth in front of the *boulangerie* (bakery). Be tempted by that essence of French casual chic clothes at Carolls and Francois Pinet for shoes. Imagination has no stops at Point a la Ligne. It has to be the mother of all candle shops. Their windows of *l'art de table* are superb pictures of art. And approaching l'Etoile, your pace will further slow down while you marvel at the sleek chic window-dressing and sleek *chic* contents at Yves St-Laurent, Celine, Lolita Lempicka …

I have to agree with James Grant who in *Paris and its People* wrote in 1843 that, "The window of a Parisian shop … is a sight worth going a day's journey to witness; it is quite a study – a perfect picture. It affords an exhibition of artistic skill of which the people of no other country can have any conception." Furthermore, Walter Bagehot in 1868 wrote in *The Economist*, 'One Difference Between England and France', "The French are better consumers than we are. They will buy nothing which is not what they want, will buy no more than they want, and will take care that what they buy is fitted and finished in the precise manner which suits them best. The consequence, is, that France, as a country has a kind of finish which England lacks."

In *Le XVIe*, Beatrice de Andia writes with immense and justifiable pride, "Those (the shops) of avenue Victor Hugo, those of the rue de Passy and those of rue d'Auteuil, count among the most beautiful of the capital and rival those of Fifth Avenue in New York, of London and of Rome," *Ah oui.*

Speaking Français

"To be introduced to the people of high quality, it is absolutely necessary to be master of the language, for it is not to be imagined that they will take pains to understand anybody, or to correct a stranger's blunders."

Thomas Gray, in a letter to Thomas Ashton from Paris, April 21, 1739

I beg to differ.

At a lunch hosted by the Association of Professional Women of France honouring Dr. Boutros Boutros-Ghali, former Secretary-General of the United Nations and present Secretary-General of the Association of Francophone countries, I was speaking to *une grande dame*, the President of International Women Jurists. The distinguished lady and I were mildly arguing as to who would invite the other home first.

It transpired that we lived in the same district, *le seiziéme.* I said that we were then living in the same *banlieue* (suburb). I had meant to say *voisinage* (neighbourhood) or *quartier. La grande dame* was highly amused at my choice of the word *banlieue* and said, "how very charming it was to use the word *banlieue.* She continued to commend me as a foreigner on the use of *banlieue* to convey the spirit of friendliness and congeniality; but … and I knew there was a Big But coming … She elaborated – the 16th *arrondissement* spells *bourgeois* living, a certain snob appeal – and the word for neighbourhood in this context is *quartier* and not *banlieue* which carries with it a strong connotation of suburban living in the outer reaches of Paris; somewhere Out There and not exactly It. The French phrase, *en province* (as Parisians dismissively describe the rest of France) captures the notion as stated in a journal *Living in France*. For us residents of the highly prestigious *le seiziéme* in central Paris, it was undesirable to be living in a *banlieue* rather than a *quartier*.

After all it was Rivarol who dismissively said, "What is not clear is not French" in his *Discours sur l'Universalité de la Langue*. Had not Samuel Taylor Coleridge said, "French is the most perspicuous and pointed language in the world?" On the other hand, there is the beauty and expressiveness of the language. That is what must have compelled E.R. Bulwer-Lytton in *Lucile* to declare, "Whenever I hear French spoken as I approve, I find myself quietly falling in love."

A most attractive *lingua franca*, French still has a grammar and verb construction that is daunting to put it mildly. The complexities have been well-presented by Stanley Karnow in *Paris in the Fifties*. He "agonised over grammar, especially tenses – the past, the present, the future, the conditional, the subjunctive, the past imperfect, the more-than-perfect and the tortuous imperfect of the subjunctive. Equally puzzling were verbs – regular, irregular, active, passive, indicative, reflexive." *Absolument*.

Paris has twenty *arrondissements*, each headed by a Mayor. The *arrondissements* then work out from the centre further out in a snail-like form. As the mark of an insider, a native, one always refers to the 2nd or the 8th, as "I live in the 16th," and does not reveal one's *nouveau* and *gauche* status by remarking, "I live in the 16th *arrondissement*."

A perceptive comment by a Frenchman is found in *French Toast: A Humorous Tour of What Living in France is Really Like!* by Harriet Welty Rochefort. Harriet, an American asks her husband, Philippe, "I've often noticed that Parisians make fun, not only of foreign accents, but even of French accents which are not Parisian. How do you Parisians situate yourselves in relation to other French people?" Philippe queries, "What other French people?" End of story.

The social hierarchy prevailing in France cannot be taken lightly. One must know one's place. An astute observation by George Mikes in *Little Cabbages*, confirms that placing. "To be a tourist is the lowest form of human existence. The population of Paris is divided into four groups: (1) The Parisians and other French, such as provincials and suburban dwellers; (2) resident aliens; (3) tourists." Mikes soothes one by adding another category; that of a visitor. "A visitor is less than a resident alien but certainly much more than a tourist." Now, I am a resident alien in Paris. However, on future trips to Paris, now demoted; I would so like to be included in the category of visitor rather than tourist.

A hilarious source of *la vie Parisienne*, Bluff Your Way in Paris notes that, "Lifestyle in Paris is often largely a matter of where you live and what you do for a living. If you live in the *banlieue*, wear leather jackets, drive a motorbike and are on the dole, then you are a *loubard* (good-for-nothing). If, on the other hand, you live in the *Seiziéme*, wear designer clothes, drive an Alfa Romeo, and are not on the dole, you are BCBG ... This is an extremely important social classification, standing for *bon chic, bon genre*, a concept with no direct equivalent in English, but which connotes wealth, style and a certain social *savoir-faire* ... The *Seiziéme* is more than just an *arrondissement*; it's a complete package of *haute-bourgeois*, expensive lifestyle ... they live the life of gross, selfish, morally and politically unacceptable capitalism, the lucky bastards. They are BCBG in a big way."

The importance of a good address cannot be

underestimated – therein lies what distinguishes the patricians from the plebeians and woe betide she who inadvertently misplaces the place. The subtleties of a language were amply illustrated in this amusing and highly educational incident. *Il faut chercher le mot juste.* (One must find the correct word). Never again shall I make this mistake. Nevertheless, a host of others remain to be committed.

Frantic gesticulation is expressively *Française.* You may have a good French accent but without the appropriate accompanying facial, hand and body motions and guttural noises one remains *un amateur.* George Mikes writing in *Little Cabbages* has vividly captured the body language necessary to identify a proper French speaker from someone who dabbles in it. Mikes writes of his son who attends a bilingual school in Lausanne, "When he speaks English, he speaks quietly, monotonously, without raising his voice or lifting an eyelid; but when he speaks French, he starts his gymnastics, using his hands, feet, eyes, face, toes, kidneys and appendix, like everybody else."

I know that I am doubly handicapped. Not only do I not have fluency in French and perhaps, more importantly, I lack the ability to raise my shoulders while dropping the two sides of my mouth (in order to express - 'I don't know'). I need to work on body gymnastics as well as French grammar and vocabulary.

Mark Twain once declared, "In Paris, they simply stared when I spoke to them in French; I never did succeed in making those idiots understand their own language." My experience in speaking French has never come close to that of Mark Twain. On the other hand, maybe they were too kind.

'Down by the Seine with Me'

"How would you like to be, down by the Seine with me
Oh what I'd give for a moment or two
Under the bridges of Paris with you
Darling. I'd hold you tight, far from the eyes of night
Under the bridges of Paris with you
I'd make your dreams come true."

Sung by Dean Martin

At a dinner in the Montmartre district of Paris, the topic of conversation turned to the symbol of Paris. In our party of six, two said the Eiffel Tower, one noted the Notre-Dame, I pointed out the Arc de Triomphe and two declared the Seine river. They reasoned that the Seine is the main artery, the lifeline of the city. The city owes its existence to the Seine, for through the years all commerce passed up and down the river. And would Paris be our Paris without the Seine, on whose embankments stand the city's architectural jewels? The Seine made Paris. The Seine is Paris.

I am an easy convert.

"Along the length of the river Sequana," wrote Strabon, "There are the Parisii (Par in Celtic meaning boat) who live on an island (Ile de la Cité) and have for their town Lucotecia." Lucotecia became Lutece (Celtic for dwelling on the waters) and over time the settlement became Paris – named after its first settlers, the Parisii tribe. And it was King Clovis, a Frank who gave the country its name and made Paris its capital. "Under Clovis, Parisians knew their city was the focal point of human enlightenment," writes Mort Rosenblum in *The Secret Life of the Seine*. For Parisians of today, make that – was, is and forever shall be!

In a loving and critical study of the river, Rosenblum writes, "Paris was the City of Light long before there were switches to flip. The *rayonnement*, that radiance which the French have always beamed to the less enlightened, emanates from the pinks, and oranges and sparkling flashes of the sun sinking into the Seine. When Baudelaire wrote that all around was nothing but *'ordre et beauté; luxe, calme et volupté,'* he was looking at the river off the Ile Saint-Louis ... There is not a river like it in the world, for beauty and passion along its banks ... As the French went from monarchy to republic empire to monarchy to empire to republic, the Seine remained their centrepiece ... People who live and work on the Seine reject the geographers' term *fleuve*, the French word for a river that feeds into the sea. Instead, the Seine is *la riviére*, which is supposed to apply only to gentle inland waterways. Sequana was a lady, Seine people insist, and so is their river." The river is feminine to the French as is their city Paris. Given the frequent confusion foreigners face with the masculine and feminine articles in French, it is a safe bet to opt for the feminine in addressing objects of beauty and reverence.

Who was Sequana? The Seine wells up from the hills of Burgundy, near the city of Dijon. The source was named by the Gauls after the river goddess, Sequana. Sequana evolved into Seine. It flows 482 miles long. The Seine is, however, not to be seen through only rose-tinted spectacles. Reality is grim. The nuclear plant at Nogent, "produces 50 million kilowatt hours a day, enough to electrify a small house for three thousand years. Under normal conditions, fifty gallons a second spill back into the Seine ... The Seine is a cocktail of lead, chromium, copper, and way too much zinc and iron. The cadmium level is 95 times normal. Mercury is 134 times what it should be. There is ammonium and arsenic. Farms and nitrates and phosphates from fertilisers, along with lindane and high doses of PCBs. Then there are compounds that elude testing ... "The water is disgusting," said Jean Allardi, among the few scientists on the case. With a smile of tender concern, he added, "But it's a wonderful river." Famous last words.

And Rosenblum lets us into a secret – that which I think each one of us discovers in Paris. One's senses become rarified to see the collective whole; the wood and not the trees – and what an impressionable wood it is. He discloses, "In time, I picked up some secret. Like France itself, the trick is not to look too closely at the river. You step back, let myth and romance blur reality into an impressionistic flight, and suddenly there is something exciting that exists nowhere else. When the sun starts to drop, or rise again ... we saw gold playing on the water ... a few odd lights mirrored gold on its surface, it is of a beauty words cannot approach."

Through the ages, the rising financial prowess of the city was largely due to commercial river-traffic and the transport of merchandise. "For 2000 years, the Seine was the alimentary canal to a nation that took its nourishment seriously," states Rosenblum. After all, it was a Frenchman Raymond Blanc who declared, "To eat well in France is a universal right – the realistic expectation of the majority, not the privilege of the few." According to George Bordonove, a writer, "The most beautiful avenue of Paris is a waterway. She has made her way through history and knows all its secrets ... Would it be an exaggeration to say that the Seine is a history book ?"

Francois Beaudouin, 'the high priest of the Seine', writing in *Geo*, in an issue devoted to 'Paris: Seen from the Seine – from Lutece to the year 2000', remarks that, "The principal charm of Paris downstream is that it offers us, along the most beautiful waterway that exists, a chronological panorama of urban monuments of all the styles which an imaginative Europe has known from the Middle Ages to the present." He describes the Seine "as a corridor of nature which runs in the heart of the capital." In les Invalides where lie the remains of Napoleon I, there is an inscription which reads, "I wish that my ashes rest along with the Seine among the people of France I loved so much." For Napoleon III, the Seine was, "that great highway leading from Paris to Rouen and Le Havre."

Along the vital artery of the city exists two thousand years of history. In 1990, UNESCO declared the banks of the Seine from Pont de Sully to Pont d'Iena as World Heritage sites. *Le Figaro* in a special feature on the occasion when the French celebrate their heritage in September of each year wrote, "The Seine offers the city its curves and sweep. She brings to the capital her femininity, fluidity and versatility. The Seine strikes off its masterpieces like the hands of a clock: the Notre-Dame, the Church of Saint-Chapelle, the Louvre, the Mint, the Concorde, the Invalides, the Eiffel Tower..."

An American living in Paris, David Applefield titles an article, 'Seine-sational Paris and its romantic bridges'. He declares, "I count between five and ten magnificent ponts which possess that special magic for transforming a mundane moment into a personal epiphany... For New York or London may excite your mind or body, but Paris on the Seine is a purely emotional experience. They provide modern-day refuge for what the American poet, Robert

Frost called, "a momentary stay against confusion." Among his highly recommended bridges are: Pont de l'Archeveche, where you can get a spectacular view of the spires and cornices of the Notre-Dame; Pont Saint-Louis which takes you to the jewel of an island full of nineteenth century town mansions and little lanes; Pont de la Concorde which takes you across the Seine from the massive Place de la Concorde to the steps of the Assemblee Nationale; Pont de l'Alma which has now become a must-see sight since it is in the area above the tunnel which claimed the lives of Princess Diana and others; and the priceless approach to the Bridge of all Bridges, the Pont Alexandre III with its winged horses, cherubs, nymphs and gold-leaf swords.

Of the thirty-eight bridges spanning the Seine, the Pont Neuf, despite its name, is not only the oldest bridge in the city- it is 420 years old, it is also one of the emblems of Paris, only more subtle. Connecting the right and left banks of the city, with its historic centre, the Ile de la Cité, the masonry structure is formed by two successive bridges, one that has five arches and the other seven. The first stone was laid in 1578 and was just about completed by 1607. The series of half-moon tunnels on the river gives the Pont Neuf much charm. It was honoured in 1985 by the artist, Christo who wrapped the bridge for nearly two weeks in pleated yellow-golden fabric to make a Parisian statement. Some ten years later, in 1994, Kenzo, the first Japanese *haute couture* designer to establish himself in Paris decked the Pont Neuf in flowers. How many bridges, old or new can claim such honour?

Which visitor to Paris has not boarded *les bateaux mouches* (cruise boats) on the Seine? From Rosenblum, we learn that, "The term *bateau-mouche* originated last century in Lyon, where little boats carried passengers on the Rhône and the

Saône. They were built in a sector called Mouche, and the name stuck because the first engines whined like river flies, *mouches*. Some of those "little boats" are now mini-Titanics, massive floating restaurants. It was on a cruising boat under the bridges of Paris that Cary Grant romanced Audrey Hepburn in the film *Charade*.

La rive droite, la rive gauche. The right bank, the left bank, "To the right money, to the left, spirit. Matter here, spirit there. Such contrariness which is very French and also old and inexplicable, comes to Paris, of a history of which the geography of the Seine has written, creating the two embankments as two irreconcilable worlds," so observes Bertrand Poirot Delpech, an historian, novelist and member of the Académie Francaise. Whereas money speaks loud on *la rive droite* with its banks, stock exchange, professional offices of doctors and dentists, estate agents and travel agents – *la rive gauche* is an area "where money has become invisible". It houses the arts, law and matters pertaining to the intellect including the Sorbonne University. The Seine has been and remains a mental barrier between the two embankments.

Some two hundred plus *bouquinistes* display their literary and print collections for sale along the Seine. The Seine has always been a source of literary inspiration. Writers, novelists and poets who have described its charm have included: Victor Hugo, Alexandre Dumas, Gustave Flaubert, George Sand, Anatole France, Balzac, Baudelaire, Oscar Wilde and Voltaire who died at house number 27 on the Quai de Voltaire facing the Seine. "Paris, besides being a beautiful city in the quarter that strangers most look to, … delights the eye of a man of letters by the multitude of its book-stalls … I thought, if I were a bachelor, not an Englishman, and had no love for old friends and fields, and had no decided religious opinions, I could live very well, for the rest of my life, in a lodging above one of the booksellers' shops in the Quai de Voltaire, where I should look over the water to the Tuileries (gardens of the Louvre), and have the Elysian fields (les Champs-Elysées) in my eye for my evening walk," wistfully wished Leigh Hunt in his *Autobiography*. Current commentators on the Seine include: *Les Inconnus de la Seine* (The Unknowns of the Seine) by Simon Lacordaire, *The Seine* by Anthony Glyn and foremost *Paris/ Seine* by Francois Beaudouin. Note the interchangeable names.

Artistic inspiration has not been short-changed. The monuments are strung like pearls along the river and form everlasting symbols of Paris. At any angle along the Seine, one comes across a scene of the Seine worthy of a postcard, (pardon the cliché). The sheer harmonious beauty of Nature and Human Endeavour takes one's breath away. Who has not stared in wonder at the majestic Notre-Dame seemingly afloat on the Seine, or the elegantly constructed Louvre framed along the Seine or the golden leaves of autumn shimmering along the *quais* bordering the Seine? As so accurately stated by Rosenblum in *The Secrets of the Seine*. "No one had thrown this place together one piece at a time. For two thousand years, people who loved it had shaped it with style and grandeur. Always they worked around a central theme, a languorous, life-giving, treacherous, life-taking river. I had enjoyed Paris up until then. Finally, I realised what all the fuss was about."

The "fuss" has affected countless others before us and will certainly dazzle many after us. William Hazlitt in his *Notes of a Journey through France and Italy* in 1826 recorded that, "Paris, where you can get a sight of it, is really fine. The view from the bridges is even more imposing and picturesque than ours... The clearness of the air, the glittering sunshine, and the cool shadows add to the enchantment of the scene. On a bright day it dazzles the eye like a steel mirror … Paris is a splendid vision, a fabric dug out of the earth, and hanging over it."

Although my parents had lived in Paris in the mid-1950s, my father's interest in French authors never diminished. I came across recently a book of his that he had bought in London in 1976, twenty years later. The book is *Lost Profile* by Francoise Sagan, *la rive gauche* socially *avant-garde* beatnik writer who received international acclaim in the 1950s for her novels, *Bonjour Tristesse*, *A Certain Smile*, *Those Without Shadows* (which is inscribed to my father from my mother in Paris in 1957). Sagan is very much part of the Parisian literary scene today. In a quintessentially Parisian novel *Lost Profile,* Sagan writes, "Paris was dazzling on this first evening of spring. The golds and blues of its façades were as elusive as the light that bathed them. Its bridges seemed suspended in mid-air, its monuments floating, its pedestrians winged. In my euphoria I went into a florists' shop…"

In Tehran, we saw an impressionable photographic exhibition of more than three hundred photographs of the city of Paris taken by an Iranian photographer, Y. Yaran. The black and white photographs of the City of Light and River of Light were lovingly captured in an exhibition titled, 'Paris: Seven Rounds'. One of the seven themes was – Paris, the Seine. His photographic eye was captivated by the *quais* of the Seine; the play of sky, sun, rain and light on the river, the reflections of the trees, buildings and Parisian monuments on the river, the stone stairs leading down to the *quais*, the people sitting/strolling beside the Seine … A year's stay in Paris was all it took for Yaran, a foreigner to capture forever the splendid beauty of the Seine.

For Yaran, it must have been as it was for a Frenchman Francois Bibal, a 'poet of the camera' who wrote in his book of photographs of the Seine, *Paris: The Seine*, "All these photographs started with a gnawing anxiety and ended up in that one brief miraculous moment, that fleeting instant when the light is at last in harmony with the running water and the stone. Unlike the lights in a photographer's studio or the colours of an artist's palette, the light from the sky cannot be controlled. It is there to be taken or be lost forever. Each time the light came to help me … giving me more than a simple record … magnifying the hidden qualities of the Seine, showing me an intense complicity, showing me that the photograph would be just right." The French photographer, Henri Cartier-Bresson spoke of "the decisive moment in photography, the single instant of timing that renders a captured image into a work of art." Beauty is in the eye of the beholder. That 'eye' may belong to a foreigner or a native yet beauty exists for those who take time to see it.

More than two hundred years ago, a twenty-four-year-old Nicolae Karamzine wrote to his Moscow newspaper from Paris, "Never have I approached a city with such excitement, Such curiosity, such impatience." In 1790, just after the French Revolution, he found, "Narrow streets, dirty and muddy, with foul-looking houses and people in torn rags." Then he saw the river, "The décor transformed totally when we reached the banks of the Seine. There were magnificent edifices, houses of six stories, rich boutiques. What a multitude of people! What a tumult! One carriage races after the other. Every second someone yells, 'Make way! Make way!' And the throng ebbs and flows like an ocean. This indescribable noise, this marvellous variety of objects, this vivacity of the people all threw me into a spin.

It seemed as if, like a grain of sand, I had fallen into an abyss and was sucked into a whirlpool." That was and remains Paris.

If the Seine has a biographer, the position has been filled by Claude Monet, the Impressionist painter. His home at Giverny is Impressionist country. David Applefield in an article, 'On the Monet Trail' writes, "The Seine meanders spectacularly below chalk cliffs, through lush meadows and is divided into secret wooded islands." Monet when asked about his art studio, pointed to the river and countryside outside and declared, "That is my studio … The subject is secondary to me. What I want to reproduce is what exists between the subject and me." At the final count, is it not "what exists between the subject and me" – that elusive "*je ne sais quoi*", that magic spell, that visual experience that transcends into the unforgettable? – and creates an impression?

Four visits to Giverny have not ebbed my appetite for the vivid palette of colours and scenery that Nature has bestowed on the area – a veritable colour laboratory. Monet built the story-book house and created the famed pond, the Japanese bridge across it and the brilliant garden which have all been captured forever by him in innumerable paintings. See them at the Marmottan musee, musee d'Orsay and musee de l'Orangerie in Paris. There is not a canvas of Monet to be seen at Giverny. But do savour the impressive collection of Japanese wood-block prints dotting the walls of his home.

Claude Monet continues to reign as one of the art world's most bankable stars. Tickets to an exhibition of his paintings at the Royal Academy of Arts in London from January to April 1999 were sold out even before the show had opened. The Academy was selling 500 tickets per hour and there was still a demand for more. In an unprecedented move, the exhibition was open non-stop for the last 36 hours in a bid to meet the overwhelming demand. Many of the paintings exhibited in London have moved to a special exhibition at l'Orangerie prior to its closing for a two-year period while it undergoes extensive renovation. Highlights of the exhibition are the series of 'Water-Lilies' Monet painted towards the end of his life, by which time his vision was impaired due to cataracts.

In 'On the River', a short story by Guy de Maupassant, he writes of meeting a neighbour – "an old boating-man, crazy on the subject of boats, and was always either in, or on, or by the water..." Maupassant asked him about his nautical experiences and, "Immediately his face lighted up, and he became eloquent, almost poetical, for his heart was full of an all-absorbing, inevitable, devouring passion – a love for the river." Maupassant once observing Monet's efforts to capture the Seine on canvas remarked, "I have seen him seize a glittering shower of light and fix it in a flood of yellow fires. And the full effect is an unseizable, dazzling brilliance." It was Monet's friend, Cezanne who said of him – "Monet is only an eye, but, my God, what an eye."

If the Seine and Paris are synonymous, then the comment on Rosenblum's book, *The Secret Life of the Seine* by Marcel Marceau, the French father of mime is appropriate. Marceau observes, "In Mort Rosenblum's pilgrimage my heart was filled with yes at every word. This is more than a trip through Paris, but rather the sound of the whole world through the silent language of the Seine."

Les Champs-Elysées: Yesterday and Today

'Paris appears to be a vast temple of pleasure; the whole population turning out at even-tide pour s'amuser, and such a sight as the Champs-Elysées near us exhibits by lamplight can be seen nowhere else ... The very business of Parisian existence appears to be pleasure, whereas the truest pleasure of London seems to be business; never was there such a contrast. But really I take it there is a great amount of merely childish innocent amusement in Paris gaiety: London may have sterner duties and guiltier pleasure."

Martin F. Tupper, 'Paterfamilias Diary of Everybody's Tour,' 1856

The most famous and unique avenue in the world has a long past. Like its host city, les Champs-Elysées was not built in a day but evolved over the ages. One has only to pause at any point along the two-and-a-half kilometres length and one is struck by the sheer splendour of the setting. This single thoroughfare has contributed immensely to the beauty and romance that is Paris. There is simply nothing comparable in the world. At one end towering majestically over les Champs-Elysées stands on an incline l'Arc de Triomphe. One commentator, Frederic Peguillon remarked, "Over and above the magnificence of the work, which radiates through the site from all angles; economic, architectural, historic, economic, geographic, artistic, touristic, social, it is the construction of it that captivates one." An emblem of Paris, it has to be counted as one of the international paragons of architecture. Twice as large as any of the triumphal arches of antiquity, l'Arc de Triomphe dominates the perspective of les Champs-Elysées by its impressive dimensions. It has a height of 49 metres above the ground, a width of 45 metres, a thickness of 22 metres and a massive foundation of 8 metres below the ground. At the other end, soaring into the Parisian sky towers the Obelisk of Luxor at la Place de la Concorde, the city square par excellence. In between lies a Parisian showcase.

Les Champs-Elysées used to be till the seventeenth century, open fields dotted with dairy farms and cottages. As the Louvre was expanded by successive rulers, a portion of the fields became planted as a promenade by Marie de Medici in 1616. It was named the Cours de la Reine (Queen's Way). The famed landscape architect, Andre Le Notre planted double rows of chestnut trees along the promenade in 1670 and gave it its current name. During Napoleon III's reign in the second half of the nineteenth century, the road was levelled to make it more accessible for the parade of stylish carriages which now made their way up and down the thoroughfare. The cut-off point between commerce and leisure was and remains le Rond Point. Les Champs-Elysées from le Rond Point to l'Arc de Triomphe is the consumer's paradise. The area between le Rond Point and la Place de la Concorde are gardens for contemplation and recreation.

The urban renewal of les Champs-Elysées has been continuous. Gutting and revitalising the thoroughfare is a constant feature. In 1786, it was levelled. In the nineteenth century, it was paved with wood. Paving in granite followed in 1938 only. The most recent improvements occurred in 1994. A promenade was created by banning parking on les Champs-Elysées. Plantation of a second-row of trees and widening the pavements were other urban works. This expansion lent a fresh lease on the glorious avenue. Les Champs-Elysées continues to reign supreme in the heart of Paris into the third millennium.

Catherine Trautmann, the French Minister of Culture

spoke of the scenario of festivities that heralded in the year 2000. It was titled *Les Portes de l'an 2000* (The Doors of the Year 2000). The twelve avenues radiating off l'Étoile and l'Arc de Triomphe represented twelve doors that resounded like twelve gongs at midnight. Throughout, les Champs-Elysées received special creativity. At the other end, les Jardins des Tuileries hosted a gigantic clock ticking away the time to the year 2000.

A grand avenue by day, it is transformed into a fairyland of lights at night. It is the venue of a permanent spectacle – some 300,000 spectators and participants by weekday which can reach some half a million by the weekend. If one is in front of la Maison de Danemark (the House of Denmark) towards l'Arc de Triomphe, one can see a sea of colourful and happy humanity before you right down les Champs-Elysées – a cosmopolitan throng.

There is one side of les Champs-Elysées *au claire* (in the light) and the other side is a *l'ombre* (in the dark). Coming down from l'Arc de Triomphe, on the left is the sunny side of les Champs-Elysées where are to be found the majority of shops, boutiques, cafés and restaurants and along with it – the sitting and strolling crowds. People are drawn to the sunny-side and amenities follow. Across the avenue, on the shaded-side, there are fewer consumer outlets and more banks and offices. The mood is sober and human congestion is less.

In the 1957 edition of my late father's copy of *Those Without Shadows,* a novel by Francoise Sagan, Alain Maligrasse, one of the main characters is on les Champs-Elysées. Sagan writes, "The pale, damp dawn breaking over the Champs-Elysées, the early morning perfume of Paris recalled the country and made him stop a moment and breathe deeply before lighting a cigarette. He smiled, murmured 'Delightful evening', then walked briskly homewards with the step of a young man."

The broad avenue is a main artery of the city and features prominently in literary life.

One establishment that has celebrated a hundred years of existence, is the renowned meeting-place of the rich and famous–Fouquet's–a cornerstone restaurant of les Champs-Elysées. Louis Vuitton first opened its luxury leather luggage and bag outlet on les Champs-Elysées in 1914 at the present Sephora perfume emporium site. It is part of the French luxury-goods conglomerate, LVMH Louis Vuitton Moet Hennessy. Another long-standing establishment is the refined Guerlain perfume shop that opened on les Champs-Elysées in 1913 and still retains its original marble, mirror and crystal chandelier and opulent grandeur. It was designed by Charles Méwés, the architect of the Hotel Ritz as an old haven of refinement. Just before the First World War Pougeot, Renault, Mercedes and Rolls Royce set up prestigious showrooms and so they remain along the avenue. The now up-market super-market Prisunic opened at its present site in 1932.

Le Deauville is one of the oldest cafés still in opeation on les Champs-Elysées. The likes of Napoleon Bonaparte and Maximilien de Robespierre both shared a fondness for the elegant restaurant, Ledoyen at le Rond Point. The likes of us have also been counted amongst those who have walked through their majestic doors thanks to a Japanese invitation. Opened in 1928, the cabaret le Lido remains a star attraction for international travellers more than half a century later. A visit is merited. Laduree, a remake of the prestigious Belle Époque tea-room and restaurant on rue Royale near la Place de la Concorde, opened on les Champs-

Elysées in 1997. We indulged ourselves here for a memorable meal. Their *mille feuilles* pastries and chocolates are renowned and justifiably so. The presentation at the counter is alone a feast for the eyes – never mind the treat of the taste. After all was it not Walter Bagehot who wrote, "The most exquisite diners of all nations say that the French are the most exquisite diners," in 'One Difference Between France and England', in *The Economist.*

La gastronomie française has neither received such accolades nor sensual description in recent years as that provided by an Englishman Peter Mayle in the bestseller *A Year in Provence.* Mayle was also the recipient of the 1989 Travel Writer of the Year British Book Awards. Mayle and his wife are having their New Year's lunch at a village restaurant. The menu? "*Foie gras*, lobster *mousse*, beef *en croûte*, salads dressed in virgin oil, hand-picked cheeses, desserts of a miraculous lightness, *digestifs.* It was a gastronomic aria which he (the restaurant proprietor) performed at each table, kissing the tips of his fingers so often that he must have blistered his lips ... The final *bon appétit* died away ..." In a delightful observation, Jean Anouilh in Cecile writes that, "Everything ends this way in France – everything. Weddings, christenings, duels, burials, swindlings, diplomatic affairs – everything is a pretext for a good dinner.

In the follow-up to the run-away success of his first book, Mayle in *Toujours Provence* analyses his love of the French palate. In a discussion with a French *gastronome* (Regis) on *la cuisine française* versus la *cuisine anglaise* (?), Regis explains, "It starts, he said, at babyhood. The English baby is fed on bland, mush, the kind of pabulum one would give to an undiscriminating chicken, *sans caractére, sans goût.* The French infant, however, even before he has teeth, is treated as a human being with taste buds. As evidence, Regis described the menu offered by Gallia, one of the leading baby food manufacturers. It included brains, fillet of sole, *poulet au riz*, tuna, lamb, liver, veal, *gruyére*, soups, fruits, vegetables, puddings of quince and bilberry, *crème caramel* and *fromage blanc*. All of that and more, said Regis, before the child is eighteen months old. You see? The palate is being educated .. And so it is inevitable that the French adult has a better appreciation of food, and higher expectations, than the English adult … I would have liked to argue with him, but I don't have the ammunition." Of course not, since "In France, cooking is a serious art form and a national sport," notes Julia Child, the renowned American cooking expert.

There is more! Towards the end of the meal, by which time the reader is salivating in the mouth and yearning for the same heavenly repast; Mayle continues as the dessert trolley is presented before them. "It would have caused deep distress to anyone with a weight problem: bowls of fresh cream and *fromage blanc*, truffled chocolate cake covered in more chocolate pastries, *vacherins*, rum-soaked *babas*, tarts, sorbets, *fraises des bais*, fruits bathed in syrup – it was all too much for Regis to take in while sitting down, and so he got up and prowled around to make sure that nothing was hiding behind the fresh raspberries." Even a literary meal with Mayle leaves one desperately famished.

At the close of the Second World War, in 1945, Madame Carven opened a *haute couture* boutique catering to *les petites femmes françaises* (the small-built French women). The Carven boutique no longer exists. A childhood association, my mother loved to wear the perfume 'Ma Griffe' by Carven. I searched high and low for it in Paris this time, but to no avail. Another childhood association too no longer exists. Special occasions like birthdays and a good report-card merited a family dinner at la Pérgola, a French restaurant near the present-day café George V on les Champs-Elysées.

For many Parisians, Paris has never ceased being a feast and at that moveable; in that the ardour and thrill of the city continuously renews and revitalises itself. That rebirth has manifested itself through the years. The evolution and renaissance of les Champs-Elysées has been well-researched and extensively documented with some historical and superb photographs in les Champs-Elysées: *Trois Siécles d'histoire* ('The Champs-Elysées: Three Centuries of History') by Roland Pozzo di Borgo. As president of the Comitee de Champs-Elysées for the past fifteen years, he has coordinated a group of historians and journalists in the production of this highly detailed and exquisitely presented book of 400 pages. In an A to Z of les Champs-Elysées, Roland Pozzo di Borgo, presents a historical perspective of the celebrated avenue. We are taken through 'A' for Arc de Triomphe, 'B' for bars, 'C' for cafés, 'G' for Galleries, 'L' for Lido, 'M' for Metro, 'S' for Sculpture...

Pozzo di Borgo treats us to a historical odyssey. As magnificent town-houses started being converted into commercial outlets, people decried the transformation, predicting the beginning of the end of les Champs-Elysées. By the 1930s when cinema halls started opening on les Champs-Elysées, it was again the end of an era. Today, one in five Parisians on les Champs-Elysées are there to see a film. We too must have been among those numbers, for we indulged ourselves thoroughly to this accessible treat. Seeing a film on a big screen while munching popcorn or savouring a chocolate is most enjoyable. Then ready-to-wear clothing boutiques and fast-food outlets sealed the fate of les Champs-Elysées in the 1970s. The masses had invaded and destroyed the sophisticated and luxurious reputation of les Champs-

Elysées. Then renaissance came once again in the 1990s. Luxury brands, trendy stores and fancy eateries have put the lustre back on the image of France's premiér avenue as it moves uptown. The Paris of legend takes up again the French motto - 'beauty by design'.

The French flavour and the Parisian ambience of the most visited thoroughfare in Paris is however, facing competition from largely American corporations. Gap, the clothing chain store opens a mega-store on les Champs-Elysées. Virgin Megastore is invaded by multitudes daily and hordes on weekends. It is along with FNAC, a perfect paradise for all those passionate about their audio needs. Classical, funky, hip-hop, jazz, opera, rap, rock and roll, salsa, tango, techno, waltz, world music ... it is all there. Any Planet Hollywood attracts the young. All Disney-stores attract the youngest. And McDonald's attracts us all. However, even McDonald's in Paris has adopted a Parisian look. They too have outdoor eating space complete with umbrellas on les Champs-Elysées just like all other neighbouring cafés. The building of our local McDonald's on avenue Victor Hugo has a bistro décor on the outside with glass doors that open on to the pavement.

Major events in France's history always took place on les Champs-Elysées. There were fireworks on les Champs-Elysées to celebrate the marriage of Marie-Antoinette with the future Louis XVI. They both met a grisly fate at the other end of the broad avenue – in la Place de la Concorde. The funeral of Victor Hugo passed down the same path. There was Napoleon Bonaparte en route to be buried at les Invalides – a son of France returning from death in exile. There were marches of celebration following France's liberation from Germany in two World Wars. The annual defence parade on Bastille day, July 14, marches impressively down the national avenue. The national cycling event, le Tour de France ends on les Champs-Elysées.

And who can forget la Coupe Mondiale 98 (the World Cup) that brought France its greatest national glory at the close of the millennium. It started and ended on les Champs-Elysées. The fervour expressed at such joyous occasions is infectious, as we witnessed as France progressed towards victory during la Coupe Mondiale. We too were euphoric and we too shared France's pride and celebrated along with a million others on les Champs-Elysées. Les Champs-Elysées has been and remains the venue for national triumph and glory. It remains the rallying point for France's citizens and a magnetic attraction for the rest of the world.

Homage to Perfume

"The French trades people display a very pretty taste in the arrangement and decorations of their shops & c. This is particularly observable in the shops of the milliners, the confectioners and other dealers in fashions and delicacies. The principal streets have a gay look from this circumstance and a stranger is tempted at every turn, to purchase, from the pretty and inviting manner in which the merchandise is spread to view."

Washington Irving, 'Notes and Journal of Travel in Europe', July 17, 1804

Armani, Balenciaga, Chanel, Dior, Givenchy, Hanae Mori, Issey Miyake, Nina Ricci, Ted Lapidus, Yves St. Laurent ... No, the above names are not alphabetical entries from an anthology of *haute couture* fashion houses in France. Although, they would be featured in any Who's Who of the French Fashion Forum. Armani ... Yves St. Laurent are names arranged alphabetically on the shelf headings of Sephora, an immense location dedicated to the universe of perfume with high-tech touches like a sensory auditorium and an Internet connection, reports 'Where: Paris' an up-to-date guide on the best of *la vie Parisienne.* Parisians are simply natural-born decorators.

Sephora opened in 1996 on les Champs-Elysées, the most celebrated avenue in Paris, close to another exclusive perfume house, Guerlain. While the Guerlain outlet retains every cardinal aspect of classicism–subtle elegance and understated refinement, Sephora is the antithesis in its interior. The use of black laminated surfaces, plenty of glass and chrome creates a cool, ultra-modern minimalist interior.

Sephora is an ultimate sensory and visual experience

and highly successful at that, judging from the crowds; men and women, young and old, French and foreigners. From the word go – from the entrance to the deep far-end of the wide expanse tunnel-like interior, it is a sensory delight of seeing, feeling and smelling perfume, and failing iron will-power to resist temptation, succumbing to some purchase. The perfume pleasure-dome is highly successful in breaking down any reservations one may have entered with, judging from the queues at the payment counters. Human frailty is thy name.

From the doorstep, all along the right wall are the best-sellers among women's and men's perfumes, *eau de toilettes* and after-shave lotions. About a quarter-way into the vast interior, are shelves and shelves of bottles – all beckoning. It starts alphabetically with the perfume house, for example, Chanel. Under the Chanel heading are all the sensory delights ever created by Chanel: Chanel No. 5, Chanel No. 19, etc. and Allure, the latest on the market. The shelf stocking the perennially favourite French classic perfume, Chanel No. 5 notes that it was created in 1921 and its composition is rose, jasmine and yang and the price of the particular-sized bottle. It also details the style for Chanel No. 5 that describes it as eternally-feminine! Allure was created in 1996 and it is made up of cedar, jasmine, vanilla and mandarine. Allure's style is: indefinable but irresistible!

Close to Chanel is Dior and there you find Miss Dior, Diorissimo, etc. and its latest creation, Dolce Vita created in 1995. Its composition includes apricot, vanilla and lily. Dolce Vita's style is: a sensual perfume which gives happiness and the joy of living. And so it goes on through the alphabet. Such is the uniqueness of every style that it is universally irresistible! It touches the core of every woman – every time! A brilliant marketing ploy. As if it is not enough to see and read about perfume at Sephora, and that too, as far as the eye can see; you can indulge yourself in handling the bottle and smelling the contents. Each and every perfume has a tester bottle. All along the shelves are jars with strips of paper on which is printed Spray Here and Name – . One is to spray the perfume of the strip and then note the name of the perfume. Such is the enticement to the senses, and it is such a pleasure; that one is tempted to go from shelf to shelf methodically spraying oneself (but after a while – spraying the strips of paper is advisable) and writing on each strip the particular name of the sprayed-on perfume. For after an orgy of spraying, one's senses are totally dulled and one's memory fails too. It is a veritable venue for some serious research on the power of perfume.

There is no gender disparity in sensory delights. The men's range is equally diverse and it occupies almost the entire left side of the hall and operates on the same alphabetical principle and self-indulgence. There are very large numbers of men in the crowds testing the products and succumbing as well to temptation. Marketing whiz-kids also know that women are major buyers of men's toiletries. For the connoisseur and well-heeled person, pricey coffee-table books on the history of perfume, aromatherapy, perfume through the ages, perfume and fashion … are also available.

By now walking in a cloud of sprays of scents, one can then further indulge oneself in sampling each and every kind of makeup: lipstick, blush, eyeliner, mascara, foundation … by international cosmetic houses–L'Orèal, Revlon, Clarins, Helena Rubenstein, Christian Dior … and creams and lotions to lighten or darken, to clear or hide, to flatten or puff-up, to loosen or tighten the skin. It is all there. Seek and ye shall find. A large digital screen flashes the price of a particular perfume, of a particular size that is available at leading duty-free airports in various cities and its price at Sephora. Just made for the bargain hunter.

Having free rein and accessibility at the fantasyland of hedonistic pleasures, one leaves Sephora in a sweet-smelling cocoon of perfume and a good deal of French francs lighter but feeling quite self-satisfied. I saw a young man spray his paperback book and coolly and casually walk out into the warm sunshine of les Champs-Elysées. I plan to return with a worthy tome – maybe, *War and Peace* or *A Suitable Boy* – a book which will do justice to Sephora.

In *Paris in August*, Adrian George suggested to friends that they see some exhibitions and museums. When they met a few days later, they were weighed down with shopping bags. What happened? "Well, we went to the musée Brasserie Lipp (restaurant), and then we went to the musée Christian Lacroix (designer's shop), and then the musées Saint Laurent, Chanel, Hérmes and Charvet (all designer shops), where I bought him this tie. We then went to that exhibition at Guerlain, do you like this scent? And then to the show at the Didier Lamarthe Museum, isn't this a divine handbag? Then because we had walked to so many exhibitions and museums, I just had to buy some shoes at the Sephane Kélian museum and I had to have my hair sorted out at Alexandre de Paris, and then by chance I came across Jean Laporte in the rue des Capucines, and fell in love with these scented gloves, and then just a few handmade chocolates from Debeuve et Gallais, they are museum pieces don't you think?" Absolutely. Parisian shops are mini-museums in themselves. Window-shopping in Paris is divine and shopping in Paris is absolutely divine.

"If work is people's primary reason for coming to

France, shopping must come a close second. It is quite possible to make a full-time career out of it here, where everything from fashion to groceries is presented so seductively. Napoleon may have dismissed the English as a nation of shopkeepers, but the term is more appropriate to his own countrymen," notes 'Living in France'. William Brownell in 'French Traits' in 1889, remarked, "Life is almost never in France taken *en amateur*, as it is so largely with us at the present epoch. It is taken, rather, *en connoisseur*."

Sephora, a stunning showpiece of a major French export product, perfume has been created with true Gallic glamour, flair and *savoir-faire*.

Travelling through Time

"It has a unique talent for anticipating, assessing and meeting travellers' needs – whatever the era, no matter how detailed."

Louis Vuitton

The history of Louis Vuitton is a chronicle of European history of the nineteenth century–a century that saw the rapid rise of extensive travel by train. Atlantic sea-corssings and colonisation; an age of discovery and travel far afield. Arriving in Paris at the age of fourteen in 1835, Louis Vuitton, the son of generations of carpenters. In time, the name became synonymous with the art of luxury travel. This was a man who created a need of the moment. The hand-made, sturdy, practical, monogrammed luxurious leather travel items are a byword in up-market travel.

Louis Vuitton invented the wardrobe-trunk in the 1860s. The Empress Eugenie of France became the first celebrity to prefer Louis Vuitton creations – a practice that has continued through the ages. Customers in the late nineteenth century included Sultan Abdul-Hamid II of the Ottoman Empire; Ismail Pasha, Khedive of Egypt, Tsarevitch Nicholas II of Russia and King Alphonse XVI of Spain.

In 1893, Louis Vuitton crossed the Atlantic in seven days. Ocean-liners vied with each other regarding speed and prestige of their respective companies–Cunard, P&O, Générale Transatlantique. The golden age of luxury liners was a major catalyst for the development of trunks since sea-travel was the principal form of long-distance travel. This was an era pre-dating charter flights and the Concorde. That period came to an end in 1914. In 1927, Charles

Lindbergh first air-crossed the Atlantic. Louis Vuitton's grandson, Gaston Vuitton, an admirer and then a friend of Lindbergh met him in Paris. By the time Lindbergh returned to America, he was accompanied by a set of Louis Vuitton cases. A special request by Pierre Savorgnan de Brazza for his exploratory expedition to Congo in the early 1900s, resulted in the design of a unique bed-trunk. This was the precursor of the ubiquitous sleeping-bag used by intrepid travellers of today.

Other Louis Vuitton original designs include the flat trunk created in 1854. Earlier, trunks had rounded covers. The innovative feature facilitated stacking the trunks under bunks in trains. The early space-saver. A zinc-trunk was designed for use in tropical countries in 1868. Ship cabin-trunks were introduced in 1896. The 1900s saw the arrival of the first steamer-bag (intended to contain dirty laundry). This item was the pioneer of today's hold-all – the one item in sturdy nylon or canvas that every traveller carries. The quick advances in transportation in the early twentieth century prompted the design of driver-bags and the aero-trunk. Specialised travel containers were introduced in 1925 –a toilet-case and the first shoe-trunk, a custom-order for a singer. The Maharaja of Baroda in India commissioned a tea-case in 1926. The first folding-secretary trunk was designed for the orchestra conductor Leopold Stokowski in 1926. The travelling whisky-set made its debut in 1955. A line of city bags in precious leathers was launched in 1995. In 1998, for La Coupe Mondiale, Louis Vuitton created a select series of Louis Vuitton footballs!

Always alert to the pulse of the market, Louis Vuitton opened its London shop on Oxford Street in 1885. Louis Vuitton was selling their products in New York and Philadelphia in the 1920s. Soon, Mary Pickford, Marlene

Dietrich, Cary Grant, the Rockefellers and the Vanderbilts were regular patrons of Louis Vuitton. In the 1950s, the Duke and Duchess of Windsor, the former King Farouk of Egypt, Audrey Hepburn, Yul Brynner, Kirk Douglas, Lauren Bacall and even Jerry Lewis were favoured *cliénteles* of the exclusive travel merchandise.

We visited the Louis Vuitton premises at Asniéres near the Seine at Neuilly in a visit organised by Bienvenue en France. The factory and museum present a fascinating journey through the past and into the present. We were told that a unique lock combination was offered to every customer. A second or third generation possessor of a Louis Vuitton trunk (it is an item worth inheriting – given its value on the market), can bring in the handmade product and receive the original and unique locking combination.

An Italian customer, we were told, wanted Louis Vuitton to create for her a single trunk that would contain her precious chinaware. They suggested a single unit was undesirable and did not take the order. She took her request elsewhere. She returned a year later, consenting to Louis Vuitton's suggestion of multiple containers. A byword in elegance, quality, durability and service, Louis Vuitton continues to cater to individual idiosyncrasies.

Sorbonne and its Soul

"The French are the only people, except the Greeks, who have been at once philosophers, poets, orators, historians, painters, architects, sculptors and musicians ... And, in common life, they have, in great measure, perfected that art, the most useful and agreeable of any, l'Art de Vivre, the art of society and conservation."

David Hume, 'Essays Moral and Political', 1741

The University of Paris Sorbonne was founded in the late twelfth century by Robert de Sorbon, as a theological college for sixteen poor scholars. By the early part of this century, it had become the principal centre for higher education in France – and today is the most illustrious of all the country's universities.

On the occasion of the eight hundredth anniversary of the establishment of Sorbonne, Emmanuel le Roy Ladurie, historian, professor at the College de France and a member of the highly prestigious Institut de France gave an interview to *Le Figaro* newspaper in May 1998. Ladurie was asked, "If a student in hibernation at Sorbonne for eight centuries woke up today, what would strike him the most?" Ladurie replied, "Above all, the enormous number of students. In the Middle Ages, students were numbered at hundreds or some thousands – there were only some two hundred in the faculty of medicine at Montpelier, for example – whilst today the Universites de l'Ile de France (Universitiés of Paris) have hundreds of thousands of students. Moreover, there were no women at Sorbonne ... nor among the professors ... Madame Palatini, a sister-in-law of Louis XIV was to my knowledge, the first woman to submit a thesis ... She came with a large court in attendance, which caused quite a stir at the time. Medieval teachers were almost all priests, Franciscans, Dominicans. And in teaching at the University, one spoke only Latin. Another surprise for the Hibernator, would be the absence of the practice in medieval colleges of living and eating within the premises, and all paid for by the fees. These colleges ceased to exist in France after the French Revolution, whereas they survived in England, particularly at Oxford and Cambridge."

Situated on *la rive gauche* in the 5th and 6th *arrondissements* of Paris, Sorbonne forms the heart of the intellectual life of the city and thus the haunt of artists, writers and musicians and would-be artists, writers and musicians. The greater area outlying Sorbonne is popularly known as the Quartier Latin dating from the time Latin was the medium of instruction – a period extending from the Middle Ages to the French Revolution. Romans had, however, settled in the area as far back as 50 BC. Today, some of the writers who can afford to live here tend to be well-established or well-to-do expatriates, many pretending to be Ernest Hemingway.

According to *Bluff Your Way in Paris* written by Jim Hankinson, a hilarious and tongue-in-cheek book on Paris and Parisians, Sorbonne was "once the centre of the student revolt of May 1968 still referred to neutrally by the French as *Les Evénements* (the events). Only Paris could have staged a revolution of University students and lecturers that all but brought down the Republic. Students fought a pitched battle in the Latin Quarter. Paving stones were hurled. Tear gas fired. The barricades went up. Half a million students and workers marched across Paris and occupied the Odéon theatre, the Opéra, the Opéra Comique and the Beaux Arts, presumably in Paris's age-old belief that he who controls the arts, controls Paris. Where the insurgents of other nations would make for the Post Office, the Telephone Exchange, the Broadcasting Centre and the printing presses, Parisians go for cinemas and dance halls."

And why not? For is it not "the honest opinion of every French man and woman that France has always led the world in matters cultural – architecture, painting, music, cinema, literature, sculpture, mime, theatre, ballet and how to die at dawn in a duel", observes *Xenophobe's Guide to the French*, an immensely enjoyable light-hearted study of the French by Nick Yapp and Michel Syrett. The French remember *Les Evénements* of May 1968 thirty years later with extensive coverage in the print media on television. The rabble-rousing students of then are today's greying middle-aged men and women with largely nostalgia on their minds.

The ambience in the Quartier Latin is one of youth, dreams, ideals and the eternal hope of youth – to refashion the world. Tomorrow shall be a better day. Such ideals require ample food for thought that is available in the plethora of cafes and bistros dotting the Quartier Latin. Creative thinking demands nourishment and an espresso café smoothly whets the intellectual appetite. If possible, such feeding of the mind should be partaken at the Café des Deux-Magots which opened in 1885 or Café de Flore where Jean-Paul Sartre and Simone de Beauvoir may have graced your table.

It was at Café des Deux-Magots that Pablo Picasso met Dora Maar, his muse and companion in 1935. Their relationship lasted some ten years. Dora Maar died alone in Paris in 1997 leaving a large collection of prints, paintings and etchings by Picasso. They fetched millions of dollars at an auction in Paris in late 1998 that made headlines around the world. That is the price of history. Both cafés were meeting spots for many writers and artists before the First World War. Its literary and artistic tradition is today sprinkled with tourists savouring its intellectual past and the ambience of present-day intellectual chic. *Un café* also costs twice as much as elsewhere – once again the price of history.

For visitors, all the cafés and bistros look more-or-less alike. For Parisians, it is *au contraire.* As Louis-Bernard Robitaille has observed in *And God Created the French*, "...It is not only that the indigenous Parisian is set in his ways and has his favourite bistro, but that, for reasons that are beyond your grasp, he or she will never go into other cafés. What you dimly sense to be a certain kind of bistro, the Parisian-born will immediately identify as a place with a bad reputation – unpleasant, or snobbish, or tacky, or old." One keeps to one's own café.

Grey matter is also cultivated by books, and the area abounds in publishing houses and book shops; selling old and new books–a wide range of material for thought in arts, religion, philosophy, languages and social and natural sciences. The intellectual heritage of the Latin Quarter also dates back to 1499 when the first printing press in France was set up at Sorbonne by Louis XI. Cardinal Richelieu, 1585-1642, the First Minister of Louis XIII is buried at the Sorbonne Church. As Rector of Sorbonne University, he reconstructed many of the crumbling university buildings. Academia has always faced a financial crisis and it took the King's First Minister to allocate funds and attention to the hallowed seat of learning.

Cardinal Richelieu established in 1635, L'Académie Française, the vigilant guardian of the French language. Its

40 'Immortals' are dedicated to upholding the purity and quality of the French language. Their word is the golden word and the last word to be enshrined in the dictionary of all French dictionaries – the Dictionary of the French Language. The ninth edition of the dictionary has appeared, with over ten thousand new words in addition to the thirty-five thousand of the earlier edition. L'Académie Francaise is the most prestigious – *la Grande Dame* of the five Academies of the Institute of France.

There has been a decline in the usage of French globally as well as in Francophone countries. The Anglo-American culture and English language are gaining a foothold the world over. English is also the global language of communication, business, science, technology and the information highway. English is to the twentieth and twenty-first centuries as French was to the eighteenth and nineteenth centuries. There are quarters critical of such a development and who criticise the conservative L'Académie Française for resisting any major changes to the language. A writer Serge Brincourt notes, "language cannot hum in a sealed jar" but requires constant change. Another writer, Claire Gebeyli blames the falling use of the French language on "the lack of motivation in the French-speaking community. Language is passed through education and culture." Without investment in these two sectors, particularly in Francophone countries, it will be increasingly difficult to counteract the prevailing dominance of the English language, particularly among younger generations. For as Gebeyli declares, "To be Francophone does not merely imply speaking French but belonging to a cultural reality which extends far beyond the historical, political and ideological boundaries of France."

One of the declared objectives of the recently-formed

Association of Francophone Countries headed by the Egyptian Boutros-Boutros Ghali, an ardent Francophile is to promote globally the French language. The first summit was held in Vietnam, a former French colony in 1997. In Vietnam, the French influence continued till the 1950s when it was over-ridden by the American impact following the war.

The other four Academies founded in the 17th and 18th centuries are assigned to cover arts and music – L'Académie des Beaux-Arts; L'Académie des Inscritions et Belles Lettres for literary history; L'Académie de Sciences tackles astronomy, mathematics, medicine and natural science and L'Académie des Sciences et Politiques covers philosophy, ethics, law, geography and history.

The bastion of intellectual life in France – Sorbonne continues its bid for intellectual stimulation amongst its Parisian population by having introduced in 1980 the Inter-Ages Programme. This academic programme is accessible to all regardless of age or level of education and does not provide a diploma. What it does offer is a diverse spectrum of courses on *n'importe quoi* (no matter what). The phenomenal success of the programme is attested by its attendance that has risen from 1700 persons registered in 1981-1982 to 8000 students in 1996.

The 1997-98 programme offers some 36 courses on topics as varied as :

The Pharaonic Presence in Sinai and Sudan

The Urban Environment: City Living in the 16th-20th Centuries

The Revolution in Communications and the Reorganisation of Exchanges

The Metaphysics of Liberty

The Media : Yesterday and Today

India and the West: A History of Spiritual Exchanges

Handel : The Cosmopolitan and Prolific Musician

Chinese Painting: Its Form and Spirit

The Grand Debate on the Year 2000

What appears to be a most interesting course, the Grand Debate on the Year 2000, in a series of 12 lectures include the following topics :

Globalisation: The confrontation between the old and the new worlds

The demographic, economic, social disequilibrium and international migration

The new global commerce: cooperation or economic war

The crisis of knowledge of the giant Japan

The economic explosion in East Asia

The old 'new order' of Clinton of the United States of America – a model of resistance in decline?

The Sorbonne continues to nourish the intellect of its Parisian inhabitants as it has throughout the ages. Such vibrant and varied courses are offered at a minimal fee and open to current students, long-time-past students, wish-I-were-a student-again students, and all those of us who yearn for those golden days at University. The out-reach programme of Sorbonne University should appeal to many mature and aspiring students wanting to relive those When We Were Young Days and be once again among The Young Ones.

Mementoes of Montmartre

"There is but one Paris and however hard living may be here ... the French air clears up the brain and does good – a world of good."

Vincent van Gogh, in a letter to an English artist considering moving to Paris, Summer 1886.

Mont des Martyrs (Mountain of Martyrs) is said to be the origin of the name by which we know that hill in Paris on which stands the white church – Sacré Coeur. The martyr Saint-Denis, the first bishop sent to Lutetcia by Pope Clement was beheaded at this site. Henceforward its name. The haunt of artists and bohemians; ateliers, cafés, restaurants and cabarets only since the nineteenth century, was earlier a village and the site of an abbey for ladies established by Louis VI and Queen Adelaide of Savoy in 1134. A financially well-off abbey, *les Dames de Montmartre* was in use till the revolution and had at its head a succession of forty-six abbesses. The last seventy-one-year-old abbess was beheaded in 1794 after appearing before a tribunal. So came to an end the six hundred-year-old religious connection with Montmartre. Not a stone remains today of the once-influential abbey.

Montmartre was in the Middle Ages a hill in the countryside with some thirty *moulins* (windmills) amongst fields and vineyards. Interestingly enough by the seventeenth century, fifty-four per cent of the residents of Montmartre were Parisians escaping the stress of living in the big city! The character of the hill took a turn in the late eighteenth century when the abbey started renting-out parcels of land. The till now rural and religious ambience of Montmartre changed. Soon, distinctly secular and urban features characterised the hill – by 1780, some twenty-five cabarets and numerous wine-shops were to be found in the locality. An old dictum states, "There is more of Montmartre in Paris than there is Paris in Montmartre."

Among the steep and narrow cobble-stoned streets, picturesque little houses were tucked away with enough presence of flowers and trees to encourage the first early nineteenth century generation of painters in Montmartre. By the late nineteenth century, every major French and European artist recognised today had been or would be in Monmartre. Bonnard, Cezanne, Degas, Gauguin, Manet, Monet, Modigliani, Picasso, Pissarro, Renoir, Sisley, Toulouse-Lautrec, van Gogh ... The greatest of European painters have all at one time or another experienced the magic of Montmartre. Montmartre was at its zenith at the turn of the twentieth century. Artists, comedians, dancers, singers performed in the numerous cafés, cabarets, restaurants and music-halls. The three famous entertainment establishments of the day came into being – le Moulin Rouge, le Moulin de la Galette and le Chat Noir. Roland Dorgéles, a French painter of the late nineteenth century in a tribute to those happy days spent in Montmartre wrote, "Often in the summer evenings, sprawled in the grass, we looked at the stars which twinkled at night and we made wishes. We said `Love'. We said 'Glory'. No one thought of 'Money'.

Amelie Chazelles has compiled a memorable book, *Montmartre: Vu par les peintres* ('Montmartre: Seen by the Painters'). She has documented an artistic chronicle on Montmartre. The first painting of Montmartre that she records is painted by an artist of the German school dated around 1500. It shows the Virgin Mary in front of the abbey Saint-Gemain de Prés and in the background the hill with the abbey of Montmartre and its fortified walls can be seen. The hill looks desolate in comparison to the vivacity of the city below. There is a 1937 oil painting by Elisee Maclet of '*La Place Pigalle a Montmartre*'. The square is serene and fresh and quite contrary to the Pigalle of today. Many know Place Pigalle. Few know that the beneficiary was Jean-Baptiste Pigalle, a talented and distinguished sculptor of the eighteenth century. '*Vue sur Paris*' by Alfred Renaudin painted in 1899 is a view of Paris. It has been drawn from a grassed portion of the hill that appears to be the site of the present-day and ever-popular grand stairway in front of le Sacré-Coeur. The stairway is always packed with visitors, musicians and trinket-sellers. In the background, one can see the just-built Effel Tower. The painting can be seen at the musee du Vieux-Montmartre, Paris. Jean-Hippolyte Marchand in 1912 painted in oil "*Le Funiculaire de Montmartre*'. The funicular cable-train was first constructed in 1887 and was in operation till 1931. After considerable repairs, it was newly inaugurated in 1935 and functions to this day. The attachment of the people of Montmartre is evident – since the Latin word for umbilical cord is funiculus.

A 1987 oil on canvas, '*La Butte Montmartre de l'intéricure de musée d'Orsay*' by Andre Renoux is a view everyone can recapture today. It is the hill of Montmartre seen from the interior of musée d'Orsay – through the glass front façade of a clock facing the Seine. One can see through the interior of the clock; trees bordering the Seine, a line of Haussmannian buildings and in the distance rising above the city, le Sacré-Coeur. The painting hangs at the Galerie André Roussard, Paris. Renoux is an artist intent on capturing the memory of Paris – a changing Paris. He gives credence to a remark by Bernard Dimey who said that "in a century, perhaps, the grand children of our sons will relate among themselves, in the midst of the racket of construction-cranes in their mushroom towns; they will repeat with disbelief, as we speak ourselves of Nineveh and Babylon. It seems that Paris was once the most beautiful city in the world."

'*Les Moulins de Montmartre*' painted around 1820 and to be seen at musee Carnavalet in the Marais quartier of Paris shows the hill covered with windmills; a rural scenery with few housing and people walking. A similar scene by Paul-Alain Villeneuve painted in 1834, '*Vue de Montmartre*' depicts mixed houses, i.e. small one-storeyed brick houses and stone-built more imposing two-storeyed houses. This painting can also be seen at musee Carnavalet. A 1910 painting, '*Le Maquis de Montmartre*' by Alphonse Quizer depicts a windmill surrounded by small plots of land and in the distance, the new landmark-of-the-day, the Eiffel Tower. One has to go to the Petit-Palais in Geneva to see this work of art. Louis-Jacques-Mande-Daguerre drew '*Paris, vu de Montmartre*' around 1830. From the windmills of Montmartre, he painted the city-scape of Paris. Daguerre wrote, "The night seen from Montmartre, Paris takes on a magic air, it rests in the hollow of a basin like an enormous jewel that breaks into pieces." See it at musee Carnavalet.

'*La Construction du Sacré-Coeur*' painted by Maxmilien Lucé in 1900 hangs at the musee du Petit-Palais in Geneva. It shows the scaffolding for le Sacré-Coeur being built on the hill. Two French businessmen, Rohault de Fleury and Alexandre Legentil vowed to construct a church dedicated to the Sacréd Heart of Christ, if France emerged victorious in the Franco-Prussian War of 1870. France did and work started on the basilica in 1875 and was consecrated in 1919 following the victorious outcome of another war – the First World War. Initially, estimated at seven million French francs, the eventual costing stood at 45 million French francs. Bernard Buffet in 1956 captured '*Le Sacré-Coeur de Montmartre*' in his definitive style of geometric lines in cool greys and blues. In a tribute to le Sacré-Coeur, *Le Petit Journal* in 1891 noted that, "less grand than Saint-Peters of Rome, smaller in size than the Cathedral of Cologne or the Dome of Milan, but built in a location superior to the rest, with the most beautiful city laid at its feet this basilica will be one of the wonders of the grand city and in no time it will become the most radiant of pilgrimages in the world." The comment is valid. The year-long crowd assembled at the summit of the hill is testimony to the attraction of the site of le Sacré-Coeur. I am not sure how many people actually enter the basilica. However, the teeming numbers feel a visit to Paris would be incomplete without a pilgrimage to the top of the hill.

"I paint madly, so that when I no longer have my sight, I shall have them at my finger-tips." So remarked Suzanne Valadon, one of the cornerstones of Montmartre; artist, muse and friend to many of the area's artistic residents. She painted in 1916, '*Le Sacré-Coeur vu du jardin du Rue Corot*' (The Sacré-Coeur seen from the garden of Rue Corot) where she had her atelier. The painting can be seen at the Pompidou Centre.

Regarding Maurice Utrillo, Amélie Chazelles notes that, "... in paintings of Montmartre, one cannot see Montmartre without thinking of Utrillo." He is buried in the cemetery of Montmartre. In '*Place de Tertre*' which he painted in 1930, one sees only a snow-covered square, bare trees and a few people strolling in the empty square. It is a far cry from the present touristic art-market-place. The desolate scenery at Place de Tertre contrasts vividly with the hustle and bustle of commercialism pervasive today.

Yet, some memory of the magic of Montmartre remains. For we too, sat at one of the cafés just off Place de Tertre with two *cafés au lait* and people-watched, took in the feeling and stored the memory for posterity. It was one of our last days in Paris. This is what Paris is all about . That indefinable but visible quality that is Paris has been joyfully captured by Lucien Genin in a 1925 oil painting that hangs in musee du Petit-Palais, Geneva. The same desolate '*Place du Tertre*' painted by Utrillo is now a canvas of life. There are people full of animation at cafés, the champagne bottle lies in an ice-bucket beside the table of a couple, a guitarist and an accordion-player –surely playing '*La vie en rose*' by Edith Piaf, the red-chequered table-cloth ... The vivid colours used and the vitality of life depicted cry out at us. The same Place de Tertre at night? So has Jules Granjouan painted it in pastels in 1930. It is a scene straight out of present-day Place de Tertre at night. A waiter balancing a tray enters a profusion of diners seated at candle-lit tables set under umbrellas. A most Parisian scenario.

In an effusive commentary on a Parisian visit, Mark Twain wrote, "We secured rooms at the hotel, or rather, we had three beds put into one room, so that we might be together, and then we went out to a restaurant, just after lamp-lighting, and ate a comfortable, satisfactory, lingering dinner. It was a pleasure to eat where everything was so tidy; the food so well-cooked, the waiters so polite, and the coming and departing company so moustached, so frisky, so affable, so fearfully and wonderfully Frenchy."

The only old Moulin cabaret still existing is le Moulin de la Galette. The original windmills on the hill of Montmartre were used for agricultural purposes. Over time, as the hill became more inhabited, the windmill houses were often converted for other purposes, including entertainment halls and cabarets. Started in the 1880s, cabarets were important features of *Montmartrois* haunts. Le Moulin de la Galette has been painted by any number of artists. They all wanted to capture on canvas or paper an institution and the spirit of the day. It was painted by Pierre de Belay in 1924. See it at musee du Vieux-Monmartre, Picasso painted '*Le Moulin de la Galette*' in 1900. He has depicted the warm and welcoming atmosphere of an evening-out – of debonair men in top-hats – dancing the night away. The Guggenheim Museum in New York is the proud possessor of this painting. He painted it during his first visit to Paris when he stayed three months. During his many stays in Paris, Picasso managed to sell his works of art – an infrequent event since few artists, not even Van Gogh could sell his paintings. A true *Montmartrois*, Charles Camoin lived in the area from the age of eleven. At eighty-three, he was known to have remarked, "I now appreciate the Hill. One is above the crowds, far from noise and the rumours of the city." Camoin painted in 1905 '*Le Moulin de la Galette*.'

Pierre-Auguste Renoir's '*Le Bal du Moulin de la Galette*' was painted in 1876 and it is on view at musee d'Orsay. In one of the most famous and the finest of Impressionist paintings, he captures the *joie de vivre* of couples dancing, people talking and dining in the open air. Of all the Impressionist artists, Renoir was the most *Montmartrois*. He lived at various addresses in Montmartre. While travelling in Italy with his friend, Claude Monte, Renoir nostalgically spoke of Montmartre life. "I get bored if I'm away from Montmartre," he wrote. The '*Au Moulin de la Galette*' by Renoir was sold in 1990 by the international auction-house, Christie's for $78.1 million, the second-highest price ever paid for a work of art at an auction. The title for the most expensive painting goes to van Gogh's 'Sunflowers' bought by a Japanese Insurance company for $82.5 million.

Another cabaret widely painted was Le Cabaret de Lapin Agile. Georges-Tiret-Bognet painted it in 1915 – a house on a slope in the midst of trees – a still verdant scenery early in the twentieth century. See it at musee de Vieux-Montmartre. Maurice Utrillo painted the same cabaret in the winter of 1948. It had by now lost its surrounding verdure and was surrounded by other houses – a far more urban setting. In 1906, Georges Villa painted in pastel '*A L'intérieure du Lapin Agile*'. It shows fumes clouding the interior of the Lapin Agile; as people are seated around a wooden table and a musician plays the cello. The painting is on view at musee du Vieux-Montmartre.

In 1889, a new cabaret opened in Montmatre – Bal du Moulin Rouge. All Paris came to its opening. *Le strip-trease* originated here in 1893. The best dancers of Europe performed here. The can-can dance was created here and constitutes the French national dance as far as foreigners are concerned. I recall my parents having "Can-Can" on 78 r.p.m. (a veritable antique-piece in today's market). At its entrance, a *moulin* was constructed and today the fake windmill is the most famous windmill the world over. Jules Chéret was commissioned to do a lithographic poster advertisement for Le Moulin Rouge. It can be seen at musée Carnavalet.

An invitation to Le Moulin Rouge is a memorable event. Where else can one soak in an atmosphere that comes close to the atmosphere of bygone Parisian days? Here we have a Parisian setting where we hear Maurice Chevalier singing about his beloved Paris. We sing along with Edith Piaf crooning '*La vie en rose*' and '*Non, je ne regrette rien*' and one wallows in sentiment. We see a floor-show with stunning girls in glamorous gowns. And to top-off the evening, we tap our feet to the lively can-can dance that comes to an end far too soon. On a high note, we leave the red velvet and gold hall of Le Moulin Rouge. I have to say that the performance at Lido on les Champs-Elysées is superb but less fun. It lacks the Parisian flavour. The spectacle is highly Americanised including skits at casinos in Las Vegas. There are far too many special effects and extensive use of electronics. It is all very high-tech.

Comte Henri de Toulouse-Lautrec in 1890 painted '*La Danse au Moulin Rouge*'. He has painted the two celebrated dancers of the day – Valentin-le-Désossé and '*La Goulue*'. In a triumph of atmosphere and movement, Lautrec's painting is a masterpiece. In the forty years of his lifetime, Lautrec was prolific in his output. In 1892, he immortalised the dancer, Jane Avril whom he loved in a painting that can be seen at musée d'Orsay. His portrait of Suzanne Valadon, his mistress is to be seen in Copenhagen. Lautrec's renowned poster '*Artistide Bruant dans son cabaret*' executed in 1892 shows Aristide in a black hat, black cape and a red scarf thrown around his neck. It is known the world over as characteristically *Monmartrois*, Parisian and *Français*. Wracked by pain and ill-health as a result of a physical handicap, he threw himself into the twilight world of entertainment, seeking to escape the day and reality. A sensitive film that has well-captured the bohemian atmosphere of Montmartre; its dance-halls, the artists' abodes, the lanes, the laissez-faire attitudes prevailing in the period is *Lautrec*, a French film released in 1998.

A series of foreign artists made Montmartre a stop-over, if not their home. A Japanese artist, Takanori Oguiss arrived in Paris in 1927 and never left. He painted in 1940, '*Rue des Saules a Montmartre*' which is in a private collection in Paris. Another Japanese, Kojiro Akagi came to Paris in 1963 and has also been here ever since. In 1971, he painted in minute detail

'*Le Cabaret du Lapin Agile*'. It can be seen at musee Carnavalet in Paris. Miguel Vivancos, a Spaniard came to Paris in 1944 and painted in 1958 le Sacré-Coeur and the cobbled streets of Montmartre with its houses on a vase set on a lace table-cloth. Picasso, an early resident of Montmartre told him, "Go on, pursue your artistic vocation and above all, don't imitate anyone, not even me!" The painting can be seen in Nice.

A Czech painter, Alais Lecoque arrived in Paris in 1909 at the age of seventeen. He too painted a street scene of Montmartre. The Dutch Vincent van Gogh painted '*La Guinguette*' in 1886. We see an open-terraced terrace with people seated at wooden benches and a waiter in attendance. Van Gogh was a regular at this tavern. A la Bonne Franquette. Look for it at musee d'Orsay. Pablo Picasso, a Spaniard settled himself at Montmartre in 1904. On his fourth visit to the city in 1910, he painted '*Le Sacré-Coeur*'. A beige and grey oil canvas of cones, cylinders and spheres captures the basilica. The Italian, Amedeo Modigliani reached Paris in 1906 at the age of twenty-two years. He painted a young model from Montmartre, Henriette in 1918. It remains in a private collection in Paris. Theophile Alexandre Steinlen came to Paris from Switzerland in 1881. An illustrator and cartoonist, his artistic skills were much in demand for the night-life of the day. He was commissioned to do the poster for 'Le Chat Noir' with its black cat and its phosphorescent yellow eyes in a famous *Montmartrois* art-piece for the cabaret that opened in 1882 at 84 rue de Rochechouart.

"As an artist, a man has no home in Europe save in Paris," Friedrich Nietzsche once declared.

‘Thomas Jefferson in Paris’ by Howard C. Rice, Jr.

“Ask the travelled inhabitant of any nation, In what country on earth would you rather live? – certainly in my own, where are all my friends, relations, and the earliest and sweetest affections and recollections of my life. Which would be your second choice? France.”

Thomas Jefferson, ‘Autobiography’, 1821

When good Americans die they go to Paris, thought one of Oscar Wilde’s characters. Oscar Wilde, an Irishman is buried in la Pére Lachaise cemetery in Paris. Some even made it in their lifetime.

The last book I bought in Paris was *Thomas Jefferson in Paris* at Brentano’s, the American bookstore which opened in Paris in 1895 some hundred years following Thomas Jefferson’s stay in Paris from August 1784 to September 1789. Thomas Jefferson had a diplomatic appointment to the French court as Minister at the United States Mission in Paris. These five years represented the longest period of his living outside America and importantly his longest experience of urban living for Washington DC. “was a city in name only” in the late eighteenth century.

The author, Howard C. Rice, Jr., an American scholar has spent years of research on Thomas Jefferson at Princeton University. His expertise on his subject has been combined with a lifelong interest – Paris. He writes in the Preface, “I take some satisfaction in recalling that I first saw Paris in 1925. This preface thus becomes also an *envoi* (dispatch), addressed to friends of half a century: Parisians by birth, adoption or inclination.”

Paris of the 1780s covered about half of the Paris of

today. An engraved map of 1787, shows clearly the successive rings of growth of the city from the era when Paris was the Roman Lutetia. Paris has grown in ever-expanding circles; a spiral of twenty *arrondissements* starting from the first *arrondissement* where one finds the Louvre, Tuileries gardens, Place de la Vendome…

Jefferson's Paris was the Paris of Louis XVI just prior to the cataclysmic events of 1789. Even in that period Jefferson found Paris "everyday enlarging and beautifying". Construction work was underway all over the city and if there is any truth to the French saying, "*Quand le bâtiment va, tout va*,' (When the building-trade moves, then all moves), then the Paris of the 1780s was certainly a prosperous growing city. "Sebastien Mercier's '*Tableau de Paris*' (1782-1788) remains the incomparable and inexhaustible chronicle of Louis XVI Paris," notes Rice. The 'Views of Paris' was followed by the new '*Nouveau Paris*' after the revolution in which Mercier remarked, *"l'oiseau passé, le nid demeure"* (the bird has flown but the nest remains) and "old buildings were put to new uses." While there was a pause in new constructions, there was also no widespread destruction of existing edifices.

In an interesting observation, Rice observes that, "Indeed, some appreciation of this building fever is necessary to understand the generally optimistic mood in which public opinion approached the beginning of the French Revolution. Later apologists of the *Ancien Régime*, victims of the Revolution, have looked back nostalgically to the Paris of the 1780s as the time of the only true *douceur de vivre* (quality of life). In so doing, they have transfixed the city in their own static memories and made it seem stationary and unchanging. Yet, when one attempts to live in the Paris of the 1780s with Jefferson and see it from day to day through his eyes, it is impossible not to feel it as a living, forward-looking, rapidly evolving city."

The 'old' Palais Royal opposite the Louvre on the rue de Rivoli, named after one of Napoleon's early victories became the 'new' Palais Royal in the 1780s after undergoing extensive renovation. Rue de Rivoli was the main street of the *bourgeoisie rive droite.* Mercier described the centre of the city life as follows: "The capital of Paris ... There, you can see everything, hear everything, learn everything ... There is no spot in the world comparable to it. Visit London, Amsterdam, Madrid, Vienna, you will see nothing like it: a prisoner could live here free from care for years with no thought of escape." Mercier was speaking of the 'new' Palais Royal that had regained its pivotal position in the capital.

The building and its gardens gave him some food for thought for a similar construction in America, for he discussed his ideas with a Virginian friend, a Dr. James Currie. Jefferson during his Parisian sojourn, always had in mind the Parisian-style of city planning for his home state Virginia and later Washington DC. Another example of the influence Parisian architecture had on Jefferson was his proposal that the dome covering the House of Representatives in the Capitol at Washington DC be similar to that of the Halle aux Bleds (the municipal grain market). However, problems of design led to the proposal not being implemented.

As a book-lover, Jefferson shipped home mountains of books bought from *bouquinistes* along the *quais* of the Seine to begin a Library of Congress. He donated eventually his private book collection to the Library of Congress. Jefferson wrote, "While residing in Paris I devoted every afternoon I was disengaged, for a summer of two, in examining all the principal bookstores, turning over every book with my own hands, and putting by everything related to America, and indeed whatever was rare and valuable in every science." Jefferson also had standing orders on the principal book marts of Europe–Amsterdam, Frankfurt, Madrid and London – "for such works as could not be found in Paris." His avid interest in books led him to the discovery that printing costs were considerably lower in Paris than in Philadelphia. This prompted him to have printed in Paris the manuscript of his *Notes on Virginia* written in 1781 and 1782. His order was for two hundred copies that he distributed to select friends in Europe and America.

The splendid Place de la Concorde was prior to 1789, the Place Louis XV. Where the Egyptian obelisk now stands, stood an equestrian statue of Louis XV. Work begun during Louis XV's time was completed in the reign of Louis XVI. Ironically, the square was the site where he lost his head in 1793. During the Reign of Terror, some 1300 heads rolled under the guillotine in the same place. *A Tale of Two Cities* by Charles Dickens vividly captures the rows of women knitting away while witnessing the gruesome activity. The grandiose setting for the statue "is not properly a square, but a very noble entrance to a great city," noted Arthur Young in 1787 in his *Travels in France and Italy During the Years 1787, 1788 and 1789.*

Jefferson also greatly admired the two symmetrical grand buildings facing la Place Louis XV – the current Hotel de Crillon and the present Naval Headquarters. The two buildings and the square were designed by the architect, Ange-Jacques Gabriel whose architectural legacy so enriches the Paris of today. So enamoured was Jefferson of the two façades, "celebrated fronts of modern buildings" which along with the Galerie du Louvre and the Hôtel de Salm (a predecessor of the present Palais de la Légion d'Honneur, close to the musée d'Orsay, that he cited them as worthy models for his homeland. He is known to have "sent a roll of city plans and engraved plates collected in Europe and suggested the front of the present-day Naval Headquarters as a possible model for the President's house in the new capital city of Washington DC. The Chateau de Marly in the outskirts of Paris bears some resemblance to Jefferson's design for the University of Virginia at Charlottesville, notes Rice.

Two of Jefferson's daughters attended the convent school of Pentemont in the rue de Grenelle. Martha, the older twelve- year-old wrote to an American friend after a year at the school, "and I leave you to judge my situation. I did not speak a word of French ... There are fifty or sixty pensioners in the house, so that speaking as much as I could with them, I learnt the language very soon.. At present, I am charmed with my situation." The church is today the Temple de Pentemont at 106 rue de Grenelle. One of the convent buildings is today occupied by the Ministry of War Veterans. Among the alumni of Pentemont was Josephine de Beauharnais, who later became the Empress Josephine to Napoleon I.

Jefferson had a keen interest in coinage and he closely supervised the minting of medals voted by the American Congress to commemorate persons and events of the American Revolution. "But of all the Paris-made American medals the one most truly his is the very rare 'Diplomatic Medal' conceived by him as a parting gift to retiring envoys.

Jefferson's lifelong passion was plants and he benefited considerably from his meeting with French naturalists, botanists, landscape gardeners and friends with whom he maintained common ties of the green world. A few months before his death in July 1826, Jefferson was discussing plans for the Botanical School he envisioned at the University of Virginia. According to Rice, the massive oasis of green in the heart of the metropolitan city of Paris, le Bois de Boulogne, covered much of the same area as it does today, though its general appearance has undergone transformation. "It was in the mid-nineteenth century that Napoleon III's landscape architects remodelled it and created the 'romantic' Bois known to subsequent generations. In Jefferson's day the geometric pattern of roads and lanes was still that of the traditional royal hunting ground.

Howard C. Rice, Jr. titles the final chapter of his *Jefferson in Paris* – 'Adieu to Jefferson's Paris.' Jefferson left Paris in September 1789. Abigail Adams, an American told Jefferson, "I think I have somewhere met with the observation, that nobody ever leaves Paris but with a degree of *tristeness*" (*tristesse* for sadness). She made the comment as she was leaving Paris for London. Jefferson was no exception to the same "*tristeness*" but he left Paris on leave and intended to return after a few months. As it turned out, his departure from Paris was permanent. Thus, the Paris that was imprinted in his mind and his heart forever was the Paris of the *Ancien Régime*. The *nouveau* Paris and France were to entertain new players.

Paris in 1789 was encountering a climate of change. The winter was severe. "We never had such a winter, as makes me shiver whenever I think of it," he reported to a New York correspondent. The political climate was also brewing. "The change in this country, since you left it, Jefferson wrote David Humphreys, "is such as you can form no idea of. The frivolities of conversation have given way entirely to politics – men, women and children talk of nothing else; and all, you know, talk a great deal," stated Jefferson. The composition of the Assembly of Deputies elected to represent the three orders; Nobility, Clergy and Third Estate met at Louis XVI's Versailles Palace in the spring of 1789. Jefferson was apprehensive. Twelve hundred persons of any rank and of any nation, "would with difficulty be prevented from tumult, and confusion," but when they were to compose an assembly for which no rules of debate had been established, "and to consist moreover of Frenchmen among whom there are always more speakers than listeners," he confessed he "apprehended some danger."

Jefferson received word of the tumultuous storming of the Bastille prison while he was with French friends. Rice writes that, "As an artisan of the American Revolution and author of the Declaration of Independence, he was a living authority whose counsel was eagerly sought." However, he was reluctant as a diplomat to involve himself with the intenal affairs of the host country. Nevertheless, his advice was keenly sought by Marquis de Lafayette. "I beg for liberty's sake you will break every engagement to give us a dinner tomorrow Wednesday. We shall be some members of the National Assembly – eight of us whom I want to coalise as being the only means to prevent a total dissolution and civil war ...," pleaded Lafayette.

Chaos and confusion soon followed. The optimistic beliefs Jefferson had held up to his departure from Paris in September 1789, soon gave way to disillusionment. "Years later in 1815, when reviewing with Lafayette "the crimes and cruelties" through which France had passed, he was able to rationalise his false prophecies by reaffirming his faith in democratic government while admitting that the French, at least in 1789, were unprepared for it." News of the bloody turn of events in Paris continued to reach him through French visitors and the increasing number of emigrés seeking refuge in the United States.

Jefferson went on to become Secretary of State, Vice-President and President of the United States of America. As Rice argues, "The Dialogue of the Head and the Heart continued ... (the Head) never losing sight of what he believed the true interests of the United States ... After his release from the burdens of public office – especially after 1815, when books, seeds, and wine from France could reach him without interference from the "pirates of the seas" – his Heart could have free rein. "Now that Bonaparte is put down," he told Short when the latter was contemplating taking up permanent residence abroad. "France, freed from that monster, must again become the most agreeable country on earth."

It was in such a mood that Jefferson composed his classic tribute to France, "A more benevolent people, I have never known, nor greater warmth and devotedness in their select friendships. Their kindness and accommodation to strangers is unparalleled, and the hospitality of Paris is beyond anything I had conceived to be practicable in a large city. Their eminence, too, in science, the communicative dispositions of their scientific men, the politeness of the general manners, the ease and vivacity of their conversation, give a charm to their society to be found nowhere else." A more generous tribute could not be penned.

And at his home in Monticello, Virginia he had with him "the treasures of art, science and sentiment" gathered from his years in Paris. The Parisian ambience never left him. It caused Henry Adams, the historian, when attempting to fathom the puzzling intricacies of Jefferson's personality, to remark, "with all his extraordinary versatility of character and opinions, he seemed during his entire life to breathe with perfect satisfaction nowhere except in the liberal, literary, and scientific air of Paris in 1789."

It was another American, Benjamin Franklin who had said, "Every man has two countries, his own and France."

'The Crazy Years: Paris in the Twenties' by William Wiser

"A cheerfully informal account of the Franco-American bohemia that flourished between 1920 and 1930."

'The Spectator'

This was Paris after the War – the Great War – should anyone doubt it. "The Great War was the longest adventure on the horizon, and Paris, its reconnaissance post, was the most beautiful city in the world. A passion for Paris often developed during this indoctrination tour in the besieged city, an ambulance driver's love at first sight would persist as a life time affair of the heart." Many hearts were broken in Paris – *finie l'affaire* – but not the affair with Paris. The American, William Wiser thus introduces us to *The Crazy Years: Paris in the Twenties.* These were *Les Années Folles* (The Crazy Years).

The War decimated Europe and economies were in ruin. The economy of the United States of America flourished, however, during 1914 to 1918 and in the early 1920s was the world's leading industrial power. "The critical downward spiral of the French franc was only another inducement that lured the first wave of Americans to Paris. The same day newspapers announced bread increase, January 1, 1920, the dollar stood at 26.76 francs – a single American greenback could purchase a month's supply of bread." (The franc today exchanges with the dollar at about 6 francs.) A combined environment of a low cost of living and an atmosphere of laissez-faire attracted droves of young Americans to Paris. They were drawn to the centre of creative energy which they also helped fuel. Paris was where `it' was happening. It was 'the great good place'.

This was the Paris that attracted the Irish writer, James Joyce who came at the urging of American poet, Ezra Pound in the early 1920s for two weeks and stayed twenty years. He is not the first visitor to Paris to evolve into a resident. The word on-the-grapevine was "that Paris, eternally susceptible to the miracle of rejuvenation, was entering a new golden age." Joyce wrote his masterpiece *Ulysses* in Paris at boulevard Raspail. A frequent traveller to Paris from Barcelona, Pablo Picasso in the 1920s married Olga Khoklova, a dancer with the Ballets Russes at the Russian Orthodox Church in Paris. They honeymooned at the Hotel Lutetcia whose elegant nineteenth century façade dominates boulevard Raspail in the Montparnasse district of Paris. Joan Miro, the painter also from Barcelona was hopelessly enamoured by Paris. "This Paris has shaken me from hand to foot – in the good sense … I am pierced to the marrow of my bones by all the sweetness here … Never again Barcelona, that's flat … Paris – to the day I die."

Ernest Hemingway arrived in Paris in 1921. The formidable Gertrude Stein, another Ameican-Parisian resident vetted all American literary hopefuls and literati in Paris. An invitation to her salon was an acknowledgement of acceptance into the hallowed circle. Stein advised Hemingway who had started his literary career as a newspaper journalist in USA and Canada, that if he truly intended to be a writer, he would have to give up journalism. "If you keep on doing newspaper work, you will never see things, you will only see words and that will not do…."

Sylvia Beach opened Shakespeare and Company, a bookstore and lending library of English books. A cornerstone of the Anglophone community in Paris, it continues to serve the Parisian English-speaking reader, "though possibly attracting a less celebrated roster of authors in a less celebrated literary age," writes Wiser. George Gershwin, the American composer of *An American in Paris* was in and out of Paris in the 1920s. In the summer of 1927, flamboyant American dancer, Isadora Duncan drove along the celebrated Promenade des Anglais in Nice. Picking up speed, her long, trailing scarf got caught in one of the wheels of the car and her head snapped. Visitors made a beeline for Maxim's, Café de la Paix and les Folies-Bergéres; all Parisian fixtures still attracting visiting crowds.

Charles Lindbergh made the first trans-Atlantic air-crossing in 1927. Armed with half-a-dozen sandwiches, he left Long Island saying, "If I get to Paris, I won't need any more, and if I don't get to Paris, I won't need any more either." He made it to Paris and the dazed pilot asked, "Am I here? Is this really Paris?" Wildly feted by Parisians and American-Parisians, Lindbergh was the most celebrated American-in-Paris of all time.

The Russian Revolution saw an exodus of Russian aristocratic emigrés to Paris. Lenin and Trotsky were in Paris at certain periods of their lives. However, post-1917 *emigrés* were aristocrats stripped of privileges and wealth. The only thing remaining to them were their titles. According to Wiser, "Grand dukes worked as headwaiters, czarist colonels became doormen (hoteliers thought the Russians wore their uniforms of braid and *epauletes* with such distinction) and a great many became taxi-drivers ... It was thought chic to engage a fine lady-in-waiting to the Czarina as companion to a *nouveau-riche* dowager. Russian princesses were in demand as governesses..." The mighty had fallen in Paris.

Two of the most famous Russian *emigrés* in Paris in the 1920s were the composers Sergei Prokofiev and Igor

Stravinsky. Stravinsky took to Paris like a duck to water. "Much about the west was compatible and stimulating to Stravinsky; life in Paris suited him and he became a French citizen," notes Wiser. On the other hand, "To settle in Paris does not mean that one immediately becomes Parisian," said Prokofiev. According to Wiser, "Prokofiev resisted becoming Parisian with all his Russian soul." The Russian tide included Sergei Diaghilev, the impresario who took the Ballets Russes to accolade and fame and was a prominent feature of the music and dance scenario in Paris in the 1920s. In a moment of honest self-appraisal, Diaghilev described himself as, "I am a charlatan first of all but a charlatan with style. In the second place, I am a great charmer; and thirdly, I have no end of cheek." Wiser elaborates, "Neither musician, nor dancer, nor painter, nor businessman, Diaghilev managed to be all of them, a genius in bringing all the arts together on stage and in business substituting charm for money."

The 1920s saw the advent of a woman who was to become an icon of fashion, Coco Chanel. Born in rural poverty, she came to Paris and opened in 1928 a small millinery shop in one of the most distinguished areas of real estate in Paris near the Hotel Ritz at Place de la Vendome and its well-to-do cliéntele. Observing the frills and fripperies of the ornate dress of-the-day – Chanel promised, "That can't last. I'm going to dress them simply and in black … Genius is the ability to foresee the future." So was born the quintessential 'little black dress' – the antithesis of the 'costume exotica' worn at the turn-of-the-century. She pursued in the severity of her design, *le luxe dans la simplicité* and ended with that famous "little plus" referred to by the Hungarian Georges Mikes in the 1950s in *Little Cabbages* which sets apart *la mode Française*. The

American Harriet Welty-Rochefort in "French Toast: A Humorous Tour of What Living in France is Really Like" speaks of that same "little plus" in the 1990s. She writes, "So just what is that little *je ne sais quoi* that elevates simplicity into style, an art the French have mastered not just in clothing but in almost every detail of life? After about twenty years, I'm still trying to figure it out."

Coco Chanel's astute fashion and business sense led her to embark on dressing not simply *le beau monde* (the beautiful people) but *tout le monde* (all the people). She introduced *haute couture* labels for mass-marketed items which was not quite the done thing. Fashion had to appeal to the masses rather than be restricted to the elite few. Another revolution in fashion design was the introduction of costume jewellery into the world of *haute couture*. Her legendary lengthy strands of fake pearls, set-off beautifully that 'little black dress'.

One cannot speak of Chanel without referring to that which has made her name since 1921 a byword for perfume - 'Chanel No. 5'. "Even the design for the flask was an inspiration: a simple square-edged bottle, plain in the way of a well-cut gem ... the label, 'Chanel No. 5' – in plain black letters on white – quietly announced itself a classic," remarks Wiser. So it remains to this day. 'Chanel No. 5' is the world's best-selling fragrance. According to one report, every thirty seconds, there is one bottle of 'Chanel No. 5', being sold somewhere in the world.

Coco Chanel's small boutique and apartment at 31 rue Cambon, behind the Hotel Ritz is the nucleus that since 1928, has developed into a multinational business. Chanel is today, the most powerful fashion firm in France. It is France's premier monument of style. All this is despite the death of its founder in 1971. German-born Karl Lagerfeld is the present head of the house of Chanel. Carole Bouquet, one of France's top actresses is the face of Chanel in the promotion of their products. Chanel jewellery launched its new shop at 18 Place de la Vendome, the elegant square hosting the most exclusive and prestigious jewellers of the world in 1997, in close proximity to the founder's base at 31 rue Cambon.

Another fragrance also launched in the 1920s by a French perfume house is Guerlain's 'Shalimar'. An ancestor of *gourmand* and classical perfumes, 'Shalimar' continues to be a bestseller with all generations – teenagers, their mothers and their grandmothers. Once again, Guerlain has successfully projected a French traditional image of luxury and sophistication but also a familiar world of simple pleasures and casual sensuality. The first perfume I bought this time in Paris was 'Champs-Elysées' by Guerlain from their elegant outlet on les Champs-Elysées, almost adjacent to the perfume emporium, Sephora. Guerlain products may only be bought from Guerlain boutiques. It seemed the right thing to do – to start with 'Champs Elysées' – as I inaugurated my purchase of perfumes in Paris.

The post-First World War convergence of expatriates to Paris trickled downwards at the close of the 1920s. The American Depression of the 1930s was on the horizon and rendered insolvent many of the American residents in Paris. This wave of 'the great good life' was coming to an end. Harold Stearns, an American journalist with the *Chicago Tribune* in Paris, decided to return home. "It was a useless silly life," he declared of his Paris sojourn, "and I have missed it every day since."

"The memory of each person who has lived in Paris differs from that of any other," wrote Ernest Hemingway. William Wiser's Paris is thus also unique. He first came to Paris in 1960 and today lives in the French Riviera. Revisiting the sights and places of Paris in the 1920s, Wiser writes, "A connecting thread does run through everyman's Paris; there are prototypes, touchstones: the eternal café, the central bridges (except for the sadly missing Pont des Arts), a grey changeable colouring like no other, smells and sounds, a mood due as much to the city as one's self, an alternating low fever and sometimes depression broken by sudden and unexpected delight ... Together we mourn the changes that disrupt our shared philosophy, knowing that the changes are what keep Paris alive."

The English actor, Robert Morley wrote in 'A Musing Morley, France and the French' that, "The French are a logical people, which is one reason the English dislike them so intensely. The other is that they own France, a country which we have always judged to be much too good for them." This must be the single explanation for the attraction that is France to all non-French people.

'A Moveable Feast' by Ernest Hemingway

"If you are lucky enough to have lived in Paris as a young man, then wherever you go for the rest of your life, it stays with you, for Paris is a moveable feast."

Ernest Hemingway to a friend, 1950

As a newly married young man in Paris, Hemingway's warmly evocative and poignant memories of that unique period of his life when he was young, in love and in Paris gave vent to the famous line. In *A Moveable Feast* written between 1957 and 1960, Hemingway wrote of his and his wife's years in Paris from 1921 to 1926. He married in 1921 and died in 1961. What is more remarkable is that the comment was made to a friend at the age of fifty-onc. And that too from a man who had lived life to the hilt. Yet looking back on his life, he saw fit to pay Paris this eloquent tribute – nothing less than 'A Moveable Feast'.

Hemingway was invited to *déjeuner* (lunch) at an expensive restaurant in the boulevard St.Michel *quartier* by Ernest Walsh, an American poet. They consumed plates of "expensive, flat faintly coppery oysters and a bottle of Pouilly-fuisse." In the course of a discourse, Hemingway asked, "You mean I am not marked for death?" Walsh replied, "No. You're marked for life." Hemingway then in his 20s, replied characteristically, "Give me time."

The love affair the Americans have with France has been captured, I think in the book, *Xenophobes' Guide to the French* by Nick Yapp and Michel Syrett. They observe that "though the French have long admired the Americans – for their constitution, their legal system and the fact that they too, kicked out the British – they do not admire their Americanness. The French have successfully persuaded generation after generation of Americans to fall in love with them, without reciprocating that love."

Similarly, William Pfaff writing from Paris in the *International Herald Tribune* in an article, 'Trying to Win Over the World, or Foreign Policy as Love-In', observes that, "Americans need to feel good about the countries with which they deal, in order to feel good about themselves. There has to be an affective relationship – even negative, if it can't be positive – with every major country important enough for the American public to pay it attention … The French are the other people who think their nation and civilisation a model for the world, as indeed they were in the 17th and 18th centuries, and remain for some even now. But the French don't go out to make friends and win the hearts of others … They are arrogant enough to think that the world will eventually come to them, compelled by logic to recognise France's superiority … The French have a deep confidence, often misplaced, in logic. But America seeks a conversion of the heart." A most interesting analysis on the psyche of nations!

An article in *The Economist*, 'What is it about French ideas and culture that so exasperates foreigners?' discusses Tony Judt, a scholar at New York University who has written widely on French culture and ideas. On American attitudes towards France, Judt suggests, on the one hand, there is a sure sense of political and economic superiority, for having arrived, as they see it, at a more modern, less centralised and less rule-bound way of doing things. At the same time, they are troubled by their deep and admiring conviction that 'France stands for everything they like about Europe and feel insecure about.'

Hemingway was part of *la génération perdue* (the lost generation); a term coined by Gertrude Stein in Paris after the First World War, that included herself, Scott and Zelda Fitzgerald, James Joyce, Ezra Pound, Ernest Walsh ... They and successive generations have continued to seek intellectual and artistic stimulation in *la vie Parisienne*. The contemporary English actress Charlotte Rampling had this to say of Paris, "In this city, its culture and architecture inspire creative energy as if its philosophers' ideas, its painters' colours, its writers' words have left their imprint on the atmosphere."

Reading *A Moveable Feast* in Paris this time, once again bought at my old favourite haunt, W. H. Smith on the rue de Rivoli is an absolute delight. It brings about many a silent-knowing smile to the reader as one shares the sights, smells and sounds of Hemingway's *A Moveable Feast.*

"The Café des Amateurs was the cesspool of the rue Mouffetard, that wonderful narrow crowded market street which led into the Place Contrescarpe." Remarkably, only two days earlier, on an outing with French friends to Porte Clignancourt, a massive antique market, we passed the Mouffetard market that on a Sunday morning was all hustle and bustle with Parisian shoppers.

Coming across a just-discovered *rue* on the first page of Hemingway's book certainly gives one a happy feeling and a reassuring nudge – suggesting that there was more; a most satisfying sentiment as any reader will testify. Unwittingly, the title of the book moves to a different plane - *A Moveable Feast* becomes literally a treat to savour from page to page – moving away but then coming back with associations, familiarity and recognition ... a shared Parisian experience.

"If I walked down by different streets to the Jardin du Luxembourg in the afternoon I could walk through the gardens and then go to the musee de Luxembourg where the great paintings were, that have now mostly been transferred to the Louvre and the Jeu de Paume. I went there nearly every day for the Cezannes and to see the Manets and the Monets and the other Impressionists that I had first come to know about in the Art Institute in Chicago." Today, all if not most of those paintings have been transferred to the present musee d'Orsay, the turn-of-the-century *Belle Époque* railway station, the Gare d'Orsay on *la rive gauche*. The paintings Hemingway saw in the 1920s at the musée de Luxembourg, were in the Louvre and the Jeu de Paume (where tennis was first played) museums in the 1950s and were moved to the musee d'Orsay in the 1980s where they are to be found today.

"I would walk up through the gardens and stop in at the studio apartment where Gertrude Stein lived at 27 rue de Fleurus." Today, 3 (for women) and 4 (for men) rue de Fleurus is the site of APC, a trendy favourite of young fashion design students and fashion editors. "I think Miss Stein would have liked the good Simenons – the first one I read was either *L'Écluse Numero 1*, or *La Maison du Canal* – but I am not sure because when I knew Miss Stein she did not like to read French although she loved to speak it." In our French conversation class, we read *L'Amie de Madame Maigret* (The Friend of Mrs. Maigret) by Georges Simenon, a prolific author in the order of Agatha Christie.

"Across the branch of the Seine was the Ile St-Louis with the narrow streets and the old, tall, beautiful houses, and you could go over there or you could turn left and walk along the *quai* with the length of Ile St-Louis and then Notre-Dame and Ile de la Cité opposite as you walked ... In the bookstalls along the *quais* you could sometimes find American books that had just been published for sale very cheap. Le Tour d'Argent restaurant had a few rooms above the restaurant that they rented in those days, giving the people who lived there a discount in the restaurant, and if the people who lived there left any books behind there was a bookstall not far long the *quai* where the *valet de chambre* sold them and you could buy them from the proprietress for a very few francs. She had no confidence in books written in English, paid almost nothing for them, and sold them for a small and quick profit."

On a warm, sunny day in October (in a city that beckons walkers), we had also started on L'Ile St-Louis, a Paris of the 17th century with its narrow streets, elegant *hôtels particuliers* and tree-lined *quais*. The island now has a penchant for art galleries, boutiques, cafés and restaurants. L'Ile St-Louis is also the site for the famed Berthillon icecream. Walking along *la rive gauche* of the Seine, close at the water-level, as the Bateaux Mouches sailed by us, we waved back to the sightseers on board and thought of having our portraits or caricatures done by beckoning artists near the Notre-Dame de Paris cathedral. This Parisian *memoire* is to be done on the *quais* of the Seine or at Place de Tertre in Montmartre where generations of artists have flocked. This is the Montmartre of Toulouse-Lautrec, Degas, Modigliani and Utrillo. We had ourselves sketched in front of Notre-Dame de Paris by three artists–a Cambodian, an Iraqi and an Iranian! Simply another generation of artists. The *bouquinistes* along the Seine that Hemingway refers to are still there and constitute a salient feature of picturesque Paris. The dark-green boxes that are locked-up every night, entice one to explore old books, prints and postcards and some new books, prints and postcards.

Le Tour d'Argent restaurant is there, as it was in Hemingway's days but as far as I know, without those "few rooms above the restaurant." Here, it is said, Henry IV first learnt the use of the fork. Today, Le Tour d'Argent is "a sanctuary of French cooking especially the *canard au sang* (duck in blood sauce) and it has a unique view of the Seine and Notre-Dame", says a Paris Promotion guide book. A meal there now costs two arms and two legs!

Le Tour d'Argent has featured in history. Ernst Junger, a German writer and warrior died at the age of 102 in 1997. In an obituary in *The Economist*, we are told, "After the fall of France he was posted to Paris. In what seems like a rare sample of Nazi humour, Captain Junger was given the job of censoring mail. As visitors to Paris are, he was besotted by the city, hardly able to believe that it now belonged to Germany. He lived in a grand hotel and walked the streets, guidebook in hand. He was a tourist, but not quite. During lobster in Le Tour d'Argent, he wrote in his diary of looking out at the roofs of Paris which sheltered the hungry, 'In such times, to eat, and to eat well, gives one a sensation of power.'"

"At the head of the Ile de la Cité below the Pont Neuf where there was a statue of Henri Quatre, the island ended in a point like the sharp bow of a ship and there was a small park at the water's edge with fine chestnut trees, huge and spreading, and in the currents and back waters that the Seine made flowing past, there were excellent places to fish." Nothing has changed.

"We walked back through the Tuileries in the dark and stood and looked through the Arc du Carousel up across the dark gardens with the lights of the Concorde behind the formal darkness and then the long rise of lights towards the Arc de Triomphe. Then we looked back towards the dark of the Louvre and I said, 'Do you really think that the three arches are in line? These two and the Sermione in Milano?" The two arches of the Carousel and the Arc de Triomphe have today been joined by a third – la Grande Arche de la Defénse built in 1989 during President Mitterand's term of office. It was inaugurated on the bi-centenary of the French Revolution. The three arches, the Concorde obelisk and the I.M. Pei-designed glass pyramid of 1989 in the Napoleon courtyard of the Louvre Museum today constitute the Great Paris Axis, a straight line of spectacular, inspiring and controversial-in-its-times monuments. It is an impressive architectural perspective of historical and modern alignment.

"The Closerie des Lilas was the nearest good café when we lived in the flat over the sawmill at 113 rue Notre-Dame-des-Champs, and it was one of the best cafés in Paris. It was warm inside in the winter and in the spring and fall it was very fine outside with the tables under the shade of the trees on the side where the statue of Marshal Ney was, and the square, regular table under the big awnings along the boulevard … In those days many people went to the cafés at the corner of the boulevard Montparnasse and the boulevard Raspail to be seen publicly and in a way such places anticipated the columnists as the daily substitutes for immortality." The Closerie des Lilas has now also become an expensive vintage café where you pay to be seen but where Hemingway and writers like James Joyce once dreamt of changing the world over an espresso or *un déjeuner délicieux*. This was the *café-terasse* literary crowd.

In a 1955 edition of *Little Cabbages* (a translation of *Petits Choux* which is a French diminutive word, an affectionate calling), the Hungarian writer, George Mikes writes on 'The

Art of Sitting in Cafés.' It is an art worthy of serious observation that Mikes spends considerable time on. "You sit in a café and watch people walking up and down in front of it; then you walk up and down in front of the café and give other people a chance to watch you. As a member of that strolling or surging crowd you have become one of the sights of Paris; you have become a rival of the Eiffel Tower … What the English call a café is a purely utilitarian establishment … In a French café you are both a sightseer and an object of sightseeing." How infinitely more agreeable is the second scenario. This book was also bought by my father in Paris in the late 1950s. George Mikes was a popular humorous author of the day, along the lines of Art Buchwald.

"You got very hungry when you did not eat enough in Paris because all the bakery shops had such good things in the windows and people ate outside at tables on the sidewalk so that you saw and smelled the food … The *pommes a l'huile* were firm and marinated and the olive oil delicious. I ground black pepper over the potatoes and moistened the bread in the olive oil." In a brilliant stroke of insight, Virgil Thomson, the American composer in Paris in the 1920s in 'On Life in Paris as a Young Man' said, "… if I was going to starve, I might as well starve where the food is good."

"I began my second dozen of the flat oysters, picking them from their bed of crushed ice on the silver plate, watching their unbelievably delicate brown edges react and cringe as I squeezed lemon juice on them and separated the holding muscle from the shell and lifted them to chew them carefully." Hemingway, an American, is a grand master at creating through sensual literary prose – by way of seeing, smelling, touching and finally eating – the Art of Eating *a la Française*. Paris remains a major gastronomic capital of the world, "since in France, matters of the stomach are treated with the utmost gravity," observes Peter Mayle in *Anything Considered*. *La cuisine Française* (French cooking) has raised simple eating to an art where addresses are jealously guarded from generation to generation. It was Roy Andries de Groot in an *Esquire* issue of May 1970 who found the French to be "...gourmets, eternally engaged in a never-ending search for that imaginary, perfect, unknown little back-street bistro ..."

On that unknown little back-street bistro, George Mikes has written in *Little Cabbages* a brilliant and lengthy discourse. He writes, "... everyone in Paris will tell you that he knows two or three excellent little restaurants, known exclusively to himself and an intimate circle of ten or twenty thousand other people. The address of the place is a closely guarded secret and he tells it only to all and sundry but absolutely no one else – and whenever he passes it on he does so in a whisper. To be hidden, unknown and unfrequented is the dream of every *restaurateur* in Paris. People flock to the unfrequented restaurants; they queue up before the deserted places; they storm them in their scores and hundreds. The place is sure to be full of American visitors as soon as they discover that there are no American visitors to be met there. The American visitors always fill up all the places where there are no other American visitors. A restaurant can thrive on its obscurity and lack of reputation for about a year; then it is suddenly dropped. People say: "Oh, it's just one of those fashionable places – over-crowded with tourists." As soon as the sinister word "tourist" is mentioned, the place might as well close down, and the proprietor look for another occupation. If it were simply rumoured that one could catch bubonic plague at the place, people would shrug their shoulders and murmur something about penicillin being able to cure everything nowadays. But tourists? Tourists visit the place and we should go there too? No, thank you." This attitude some fifty years later has not changed much. There is always the search for that sympathetic and unknown little place.

"To have come on all this new world of writing, with time to read in a city like Paris where there was a way of living well and working, no matter how poor you were, was like having a great treasure given to you. There is never any ending to Paris and the memory of each person who has lived in it differs from that of any other. We always returned to it no matter who we were or how it was changed or with what difficulties, or ease, it could be reached. Paris was always worth it and you received return for whatever you brought to it. But this is how Paris was in the early days when we were very poor and very happy."

Such was the Paris of Hemingway in the 1920s when he was young, poor, in love, happy writing in cafés and the place where he discovered his vocation. Yet the Parisian ambience and aura stayed with him all his life–*la expérience exceptionelle* was for Hemingway – A Moveable Feast.

A long time ago, Julie de Lespinasse in a letter dated September 19, 1774 wrote, "Paris is the place in the world where one can be poor with the least privation; it is only the tiresome and the foolish who require to be rich."

'Paris in the Fifties' by Stanley Karnow

"Karnow makes it all come alive – from Hemingway to Dior, from le tout Paris to Le Crazy Horse, from the Duchess of Windsor to the Algerian War. His eye is clear and unsentimental and his dispatches are still vivid today."

Richard Holbrook, American diplomat and writer

Here is another visitor turned resident. Stanley Karnow left Harvard to spend the summer of June 1947 in Paris. He stayed ten years.

Karnow and Anthony Lewis, his fellow friend from Harvard and future *New York Times* columnist paid fifty dollars on a coal freighter bound for Le Havre. "*Pourquoi Paris?*" ("Why Paris?") "It's name alone was magic. The city, the legendary *Ville Lumiére*, promised something for everyone – beauty, sophistication, culture, cuisine, sex, escape and that indefinable called ambience ... What was it? Perhaps, simply, Paris."

Paris in 1947 was still reeling from the effects of the Second World War. "Such essentials as milk, bread, butter, cheese and eggs were rationed, and even foreigners like me had to queue up with citizens at the *mairie* of their *arrondissement* to be issued coupons by functionaries – usually cranky old women, many of them war widows. Neglected for years, public and private buildings needed repainting and other repairs. But the French were *débrouillards*, or manipulators. They got around by bicycle, tricycle, horse carts, rickety trucks and cars, or whatever else moved ... Men in shabby suits sported *boutonniéres*, while women achieved a touch of chic by adding a *je ne sais quoi* to their threadbare dresses."

Karnow offers a perceptive account of the mood in France towards America in the 1950s. This was post-war France where a dollar went a long way and Paris attracted Americans by the thousands. The apprehension expressed by French intellectuals regarding America and moreover American culture in the 1950s, remains today in the psyche of the French; despite or because of the firm entrenchment of Americana in France. It is an ambivalent relationship on the part of the French–who thrive on it. Karnow writes, "Minimising America's role in the emancipation of Europe, they ascribed the conquest of Germany to the Soviet stand at Stalingrad. The United States, they insisted, was out to dominate Europe through the Marshall Plan, the Atlantic Alliance, German rearmament – and of course, Coca Cola, the Reader's Digest and Hollywood ... Even a moderate like Francois Mauriac (the French novelist) warned that, unless America's materialism were checked, the "cohesion of French civilisation would be jeopardised." Coca Cola made its debut in France in 1950. "It is not the drink," brooded *Le Monde*, "as much as the style of life it connotes – gigantic red trucks, garish neon signs, vulgar advertisements. At stake is the very soul of our culture." Today, the American global culture onslaught continues and so does French resistance – slowly crumble.

His first venture into academia was taking *La Cours de Civilisation Français*, a curriculum for foreigners at Sorbonne University. He fell in love with a French law student and aspiring actress, Claude Sarraute. Eventually, they married and divorced. Journalist inspirations fuelled at Harvard where he was joint editor of *Harvard Crimson News* with Anthony Lewis, led him to freelance in Paris for a Connecticut weekly. Following an unsuccessful visit to the States; still looking for a career in journalism, he and Claude returned to Paris in 1948. Soon he was contributing to a progressive news-weekly, the *National Guardian*, the *New Statesman* and the liberal French weekly, *L'Observateur.* He also graduated from the prestigious Ecole des Sciences Politiques.

Stanley Karnow's career with *Time* magazine started in Paris in 1950, "as a local employee at fifty dollars a week, with none of the benefits extended to staffers recruited in New York. The offer overwhelmed me. This was my opportunity to become ultimately a genuine foreign correspondent. His motto would be: 'Don't tell me what you think, tell me what they think.' Karnow's belief in the axiom, led him to cover Europe, Africa and Asia as a correspondent and author for forty-five years. Theodore H. White, the historian and international affairs expert called him the 'foreign affairs expert's expert on foreign affairs.' A reporter for *Time* magazine in Paris from 1950 to 1959, he was made a full-fledged correspondent for *Time* in 1955. He was reassigned to Hong Kong in 1959 as chief correspondent for Asia. He remained in Hong Kong for eleven years. He won the Pulitzer Prize for *In Our Image: America's Empire in the Philippines. Mao and China: From Revolution to Revolution* was nominated for a National Book Award. Karnow's *Vietnam: Vietnam's History* is a bestseller. His latest book, *Paris in the Fifties* (1999) is a compilation of articles he wrote as a junior journalist at the start of his career in Paris.

Time magazine's founder and editor-in-chief, Henry Luce encapsulated the approach to journalism of the twentieth century. "He had a knack of shrinking a broad canvas down to a quick sketch ... to provide *Time's* audience with the best available expertise, compressed into simple, digestible bites devoid of troublesome nuances and complexities ... He was the precursor of television news."

Luce, the media mogul was in the early twentieth century what Ted Turner is today. Both media giants have created and defined contemporary mass media.

Karnow's work site in Paris was not in a bad location. "The *Time* bureau occupied two floors above a bank in a magnificent eighteenth century building on the Place de la Concorde, one of the splendours of Paris, if not the world ... On balmy mornings, I might stroll along the *quai*, cross one of the bridges, pass the Louvre, then amble under the acacia and chestnut trees lining the Jardin des Tuileries, never ceasing to gaze at the panorama stretching beyond the Champs-Elysées to the Arc de Triomphe." Time and again, one comes across the same impact – the feeling of being bowled over. Mort Rosenblum in *The Secret Life of the Seine*, echoes similar sentiments over the same vista. Rosenblum writes, "The beauty was paralysing, and I'd never really noticed. A miniature Arc de Triomphe was lined up perfectly with Napoleon's grandiose arc at the end of the Champs-Elysées. Halfway down, past the rich Tuileries foliage, the Concorde Obelisk was centred like a gun sight. And there was all the rest. Each slate rooftop had a geometric purpose. Every scarlet tulip was a carefully placed brushstroke on a giant canvas." Elsewhere, he cautions, "In these sorts of settings, one is well advised to husband the adjectives and go easy on superlatives" – a warning he himself has failed to adhere to most of the time.

In a delightful chapter. 'The Prince of Gastronomes', Karnow treats us to Voltaire's maxim that every French person emulates while the rest of us simply entertain the thought - 'The pursuit of pleasure must be the goal of every rational person.' He elaborates, "The French had long been imbued with the belief that man, because of his superiority over all other creatures, was endowed with the gift to transform nature into pleasures ... Their obsession with gastronomy evolved out of much the same impulse ... It impressed on me the extent to which the French regarded the art of eating as one of the pillars of culture."

M.F.K. Fisher in *Serve It Forth* wrote, "France today possesses what is probably the most intelligent collective palate." The aesthetics of eating in France has been captured by Eleanor Clark in *The Oysters of Locmariaquer.* She writes, "The sign says BAR – CRÉPERIE – DÉGUSTATION D'HUITRES, and the word degustation means what it says: not 'consumption of' but 'tasting', 'savouring' ... You are in the country of the art of good food, and this degustation is very like what you do in an art gallery."

With these elevating thoughts, Karnow nose-dives into a series of culinary nuggets of information. The earliest restaurant in Paris was opened in 1765 by a certain Boulanger, undoubtedly a baker. He opened an eating-place near the Louvre. "His fortifying dishes, he guaranteed, would cure, or *restaurer*, intestinal ailments, liver trouble and other complaints – thus the genesis of the term." Louis XIV, was a "stupendous glutton ... At the king's behest, his official mistress, Madame de Maintenon, opened a school to instruct the daughters of noble families in the rudiments of cooking; they were obliged to wear blue ribbons – and *le cordon bleu* became synonymous with *haute cuisine*."

"The pre-eminent chef of his time – perhaps of all time – was Marie-Antoine Careme. Born to an impoverished Parisian family in 1783, he taught himself the art of *haute cuisine*. He once wrote, "Our culinary combinations appeal to the sense of sight and colour and, through their harmony, they are as seductive as sweet melodies." Implementing such beliefs, he caught the eye of Talleyrand, and "in 1814, took him to the Congress of Vienna, where his phenomenal dinners won key diplomatic concessions for France," notes Karnow. This probably also explains why France is such a popular venue for international conferences; both the host country and the participants profit in one way or another. The Treaty of Versailles? The Rambouillet conference on Kosovo? Well, it has always been said that `the way to a man's heart is through his stomach'.

Another French chef based in London created *cerises jubilé à la reine* for Queen Victoria's Diamond Jubilee in 1897, *pêche Melba* for the Australian soprano, Nellie Melba and *soufflé Tetrazzini* for Luisa Tetrazzini, the Italian diva. Kaiser Wilhelm, who employed Auguste Escoffier, once complimented him on his talent, saying "I may be the emperor of Germany, but you are the emperor of chefs." A young man by the name of Ho Chi Minh worked for a brief period as a pastry chef for *le grand chef.*

Le Tour d'Argent was a sixteenth century hostel before it was transformed into a restaurant in 1790. Luminaries of the day, the likes of the Maharajah of Jaipur, the Emperor of Ethiopia, the president of Argentina, Charlie Chaplin ... were diners at the frightfully expensive restaurant even in the 1950s.

What about the Parisian bistro? Karnow informs us, "according to one version, the uncouth Cossacks who rode into Paris with the Russian army after Napoleon's downfall in 1815 would storm into cafés and demand instant attention shouting 'bistro – Russian for 'quick'. A bistro offers more nourishment than a café. A bistro is the French version of a fast-food restaurant. Yet many restaurants would take offence at the very idea of 'fast-food' – a contradiction in terms.

On the other pillar of French culture, cafés, Karnow writes, "Many of them catered to distinct clientéles, for whom going elsewhere would have been treason. Or as the *fin de siècle* (end of the nineteenth century) playwright Georges Courteline once observed, "A Frenchman may change his religion, but never his café."

Who was the 'Prince of Gastronomes'? He was a Frenchman, Maurice Edmont Saillant born in the Loire valley region. His *nom de plume* was Curonsky and he consecrated himself to the French art of gastronomy, Curonsky headed "the Academie des Ecrivains Gastronomiques, a consortium of food chroniclers; the Academie Rabelais, whose members catalogued restaurants; and the Campagnons de la Bonne Tables which campaigned to beautify menus and dining rooms..." Curonsky also headed or was a member of half-a-dozen other gastronomical associations. However, his principal accomplishment was the setting up of the Academie des Gastronomes in 1928. "It was patterned on the prestigious Academie Francaise, it had forty seats, each bearing the symbolic title of an immortal gourmet, among them Epicurus ..." Every evening, Curonsky would be beseeched to partake dinner (on the house, of course) at any number of restaurants. Restaurants queued to have the Prince of Gastronomy. A word from *Son Altesse* (His Highness) and one was made.

In a lucid commentary on the French social structure, Stanley Karnow provides us with an analysis that seeks to define French society that appears quite indefinable. "Though emblematically *une et indivisible*, France was riddled with baffling and often incomprehensible contradictions. The French were simultaneously sophisticated and parochial, methodical and anarchistic, individualistic and conformist, flexible and stubborn, liberal and antediluvian, prudent and rash, puritanical and wanton, logical and wildly irrational ... Again like the Chinese, the French were imbued with an overweening sense of their superiority. They were the navel of the earth – an ethnocentric conceit ... Flaubert extolled them as *le premier people de l'univers* (the first people of the universe), and Hugo wrote, "France, *France sans toi le monde serait seul* (France, France without you the world would be alone!")

An example of the paradox – despite the credo of *egalité* and the abolishment of the aristocracy by the Revolution, "Napoleon founded the Legion of Honour as a way of rewarding services to his crown; when one of his aides protested that he was reverting to the *ançien régime*, he replied, "It is with baubles that men are led ... So to win their esteem, we have adopted such monarchic forms as titles, crosses, ribbons and trinkets." Much later, Charles de Gaulle took on the mantle of reviving *la gloire de France* in 1958. In a brilliant comment of his fellow countrymen, Jean Cocteau, the French writer and film director, once wrote, "Egotism may indeed be antithetical to civic virtue, but if it stimulates genius, discovery and that tingling electricity of creation – *alors, vive l'égosme*!" There is wisdom in that line. France's 'ego' appears to attract the 'alter-ego' within the rest of us.

Further pursuing his study of French society, Karnow observes *Le Monde* (The World) and *Le Tout Paris* (The Upper-crust of Paris). *Le Monde* consists of "a few thousand citizens, well-born, well-heeled or both – who were so convinced of their own superiority that they referred to themselves as `the world', as though they embodied everything that truly counted ... they included a highly exclusive coterie of sophisticated, clever aristocrats, politicians, authors, artists, actors, musicians, even some businessmen. They were the 'beautiful people' – the species portayed by Nancy Mitford as 'U' as opposed to the non-U' multitudes." We are talking about the 'Ins' and 'Outs'. He was told, `Unless you comprehend *Le Monde*, you cannot comprehend France.' Much of Karnow's analysis still stands today.

Monsieur de Paris is the official title of the executioner of French capital punishment – the guillotine. In 1951, Karnow attended the funeral of the Monsieur de Paris who had held the post for the past twelve years. A hereditary profession, his only son shot himself rather than follow in his father's footsteps. A cousin then succeeded him to become the new Monsieur de Paris.

The eighteenth century principles of *égalite*, *fraternité*, *liberté* which today pretty much translate into Human Rights, remain in a macabre manner *la raison d'être* of the guillotine. In 1748, Montesquieu published the classic *L'Esprit des Lois* in which he discussed inequities in the system of capital punishment. While the masses were subject to hanging, flaying, flogging, burning at the stake and many other slow forms of medieval torture, aristocrats were dealt with a swift decapitation. In the liberal-awakening spirit of the day, how could such practices of inequalities be allowed to persist?

A physician and philanthropist, Guillotin espoused the democratic cause for all. In 1789, in a debate in the assembly on penal reform, he graphically described the imaginary instrument, "The blade whistles, the head topples, blood spurts, the man ceases to exist. *Messieurs*, with my simple machine I will lop off your head in the blink of an eye, and you will feel only a slight twinge in the neck." Apparently, a magazine tagged the improved invention, *la guillotine* and the name stuck – much to the dismay of Dr. Guillotin who died in 1814 at the age of seventy-six and wanted to be remembered as a humanitarian. In a macabre twist of events, Louis XVI, Karnow informs us "was addicted to fiddling with locks, the king recommended that the blade be curved like a scythe to maximise its effectiveness; and, to clarify his point, he sketched the contrivance he contemplated. True or not, the anecdote circulated for years to come and always prefaced with the punch-line 'Little did His Majesty realise then that nine months later…"

Rural France in the 1950s as described by Karnow does not appear to be all that different from rural France of the 1990s. "Strolling around reminded me of many other desolate French towns – the crumbling houses, the sagging church and weathered tombstones, the mildewed *monuments aux morts* (monuments to the dead) in the square testifying to generations of sacrifice for *la patrie* (motherland)". It struck us as we travelled around France, that the rural landscape and rural villages and towns still appear desolate and deserted. Where are the inhabitants? All the rolling farmlands and vineyards to one's left and right, but where are the farmers and the vineyard-workers? The market-squares, shops and chain-stores in towns came alive on Saturdays. What do these shops do the rest of the week? Are all the Saturday shoppers like us, out-of-town shoppers and visitors?

In a revealing account, Karnow writes of his research into the life of Ho Chi Minh. *Time* magazine, in a blockbuster coverage of Ho Chi Minh required Karnow to investigate the years 1917 to 1923 when Ho Chi Minh had lived in Paris. Ho Chi Minh in 1954 led the Communist Vietminh into victory over the beleaguered French at Dien bien phu. It ended the six-year battle by the French to retrieve the Indo-Chine empire which dated back nearly a century. Born in 1890 to a rural gentry family in central Vietnam, Ho Chi Minh studied at a French-run Lycee. At twenty-one years, he boarded a ship to see the world. It would be thirty years before he set foot in his homeland.

Ho Chi Minh went on to Marseilles, New York, London and Paris. "At Marseilles, he applied to a new academy that prepared native auxiliaries for the French colonial administration," notes Karnow. The young man wrote, "I wish to serve France among my compatriots and also to improve myself." This was not to be – he was not accepted and he went on to do odd jobs in France and elsewhere. On his return to Paris, after his travels to the Anglophone world, Ho Chi Minh once actually, "implored President Raymond Poincare to outlaw foreign phrases from the French Press." In the early 1920s, English words were already infiltrating the French language. As a part-time sports-commentator, Ho Chi Minh lamented the intrusion of *Franglais* - '*le manager*', '*le round*', '*le knock-out*'. The French editor, Charles Brouilhet said to Karnow, "No matter what little Ho has done since then, at the time he exemplified the triumph of France's *grande mission civilisatrice*."

In another example of France's many innate paradoxes, "despite their repressive practices in their colonies, the French authorities permitted expatriate nationalists groups to ventilate their grievances in Paris. The city percolated with them– Algerian, Tunisian, Moroccan, Senegalese, Irish, Polish, Armenian, Korean. They hung out at cheap Latin Quarter cafés, where they confected propaganda, drafted petitions, organised meetings and talked earnestly about their homelands. Several young Chinese were also then in Paris, among them Chou En-Lai and Deng Xiaoping, but apparently Ho never met them." Ho Chi Minh once said, "It was patriotism, not communism, that initially inspired me." With this credo, the Francophile led his country to independence from France.

The rich and the famous regularly crop up in Paris. One of Stanley Karnow's pleasant duties was to interview them for *Time*. "A memorable if regrettably brief encounter" in 1953 was an afternoon with Audrey Hepburn. Just turned twenty-four, she was in Paris to promote *Roman Holiday*, her first American picture for which she had received an award. Karnow writes, "for all her cool composure, she was as jittery as a kitten. Little did she realise that I was so smitten by her gossamer beauty that she could do no wrong … I could have stayed with her for the rest of the day, prattling about one thing or another. But my infatuation was probably one-sided, I left, floated out of the hotel (Ritz) into the Place Vendome – and never saw her again."

In 1948, Norman Mailer was in Paris completing his first novel, *The Naked and the Dead*. James Baldwin and Karnow were café-mates. Brendan Behan, one of Ireland's future leading writers was also in town. Art Buchwald was a colleague in Paris. Karnow had in 1954 a "fleeting moment with the world's most illustrious aristocrats-in-exile", the Duke and Duchess of Windsor. He interviewed Ernest Hemingway in the Ritz bar in 1954. "Greeting me in a whisky voice … as he rattled on, I gradually felt that the icon of my youth had devolved into a caricature of himself…"

In April 1954, John Huston was in Paris. They met in the Hotel George V bar. John Huston had directed Humphrey Bogart in five films. They now rank as all-time classics - *The Maltese Falcon*, *The Treasure of Sierra Madre*, *Key Largo*, *African Queen* with Katherine Hepburn and *Beat the Devil*, also starring Peter Lorre and Robert Morley. In an interview with Orson Welles, Karnow found him cynical and depressed. The director of a score of masterpieces, amongst them the paramount *Citizen Kane*, forecast that, "I rather think the cinema will die. Look at all the gimmicks they're contriving to keep it alive; yesterday colour, today three-dimensions, tomorrow some new-fangled concoction. I don't give it another forty years." Little did he know.

In 1955, *Time* magazine was going to do a cover story on Andre Malraux, the eminent French man of letters and politicians. Stanley Karnow interviewed him for it. According to Malraux, "Our ancestors understood their environment, which was circumscribed by family, church and custom. Ours is the first generation to inherit the whole world, and we can barely grasp it. I have searched for its meaning all my life, through concrete action rather than philosophy. What have I discovered? I am not certain. Perhaps doubt. Maybe the next century will do better." Half a century later, the only thing certain is doubt. At the threshold of our leap into the twenty-first century, are we any closer to understanding the world around us? The more we know, the more there is to know.

Paris in the fifties was brimming with Left Bankers: Jean-Paul Sartre, Simone de Beauvoir, Albert Camus, André Gide, André Breton, Juliette Gréco, Françoise Sagan ... Karnow accompanied Robert Doisneau, the fabled Parisian photographer of local colour on shooting trips.

A cover story by *Time* in 1957 on Christian Dior led Karnow to explore the fashion world and the pre-eminent Parisian *haute couturier* of the day. A visitor to Paris said in 1723, "Fashion haunts this land. A fishwife can pass for a *marquise* with impunity." Louis XIV's dynamic finance minister Jean-Baptiste Colbert once remarked with great foresight, "French fashion must be France's answer to Spain's gold mines in Peru." Well, as it turns out, Spain does not have any mines in Peru but French fashion remains paramount. That line of thinking has been firmly entrenched in France as it holds the status of *la grand dame de la mode* – and more importantly, is so recognised by the rest of the world.

Christian Dior was born in 1904 to a wealthy fertiliser manufacturer. He graduated from l'Edole les Science Politiques that trained diplomats and others (Karnow's Alma Mater) much to his father's great relief. However, Dior continued not with the French civil service but entered the Parisian art world. In 1946, he presented his first collection, the 'New Look' and made fashion history. Dior said, "the hardships of the war were finished. I revived the ripe bosom, the wasp waist and soft shoulders, and moulded them to the natural curves of the feminine body. It was a nostalgic voyage back to elegance." In reply to Karnow's question – "what sustained fashion?" Dior asked, "Have you ever seen a woman enter a shop and ask for 'something just like the one I'm wearing?'"

An Anglo-American Francophile

"The best of America drifts to Paris. The American in Paris is the best American. It is more fun for an intelligent person to live in an intelligent country. France has the only two things towards which we drift as we grow older – intelligence and good manners."

F. Scott Fitzgerald, *New York World*, April 1927

Pamela Digby Churchill Hayward Harriman, Ambassador of the United States of America to France died in Paris in February 1997. Mrs. Harriman had gone from the American Embassy just off la Place de la Concorde for a swim during lunch-break to the Hotel Ritz at the nearby Place de la Vendôme. Following a cardiac arrest in the pool, she died the following day at the American Hospital in Neuilly, Paris.

"Where Ritz goes, I go," said Edward VII of England, as he came to stay, and he and all the *crème de la crème* of Europe's high society did the same. According to *The Historic Hotels of Paris: A Select Guide* by Wendy Arnold, "The Great Paris Ritz was the creation of the doyen of the world's hôteliers, César Ritz, who insisted that his hotel should have 'all the refinements of living that a prince might hope to incorporate in his own house'. At its opening in June 1898, the Ritz set the highest imaginable standards. Lit by the new electricity, it provided a spacious bathroom for each bedroom, as well as a marble fireplace, Louis XV furnishing, wall-to-wall carpets, and walls painted rather than prepared, so that everywhere could be kept spotlessly clean and fresh ... Between the World Wars, the Ritz became the meeting place of America's millionaires; but the Thirties' Depression, followed by World War II, began a long decline, ending with the sale of the hotel by the Ritz family in 1979. Thanks to its new owner, Mr. Mohammed al Fayed, the Ritz has been restored to its full glory, at a cost of many millions. Airconditioning, a splendidly elegant basement pool and health club, and a nightclub with a fashionable late-night disco have been discreetly added ... Charmingly staffed, impeccably maintained, hung with tapestries and glittering with chandeliers, its suites vast and magnificent, the Ritz is indeed once again a town house fit for a prince." Housed in the former private mansion of the Duc de Lauzan in the supremely elegant Place de la Vendôme, the hotel is today synonymous with luxury, sophistication and glitzy, ritzy glamour.

In 1997, the Hotel Ritz hit headlines the world over with the collapse of Mr. Harriman in the "splendidly elegant basement pool" and the last photographs taken of Princess Diana and Dodi al Fayed entering and leaving the Hotel Ritz which is owned by his father and where they had been staying, before they left to meet their tragic destiny.

Pamela Digby was born on March 20, 1920 in England, the eldest of four children. "Pam" as she was known in her intimate circle, was the daughter of Lord Edward Digby, an English gentleman farmer and The Honourable Constance Bruce.

Pamela began her lifelong association and love of France in 1936 when she went to stay for a year with a French family in Arcueil in South Paris. Just turned sixteen and having finished school in England, she was sent to France to "embark on a finishing process which was designed to transform uneducated aristocratic girls into marriageable young women," notes Pamela Harriman - *Life of the Party* (1994) which I bought at Brentano's, the

American bookstore. Her life-story reads like a chronicle of this century. She witnessed and participated in some of the landmark events of the period and interacted with the leading characters of the day.

Ogden writes that in the late 1930s, "French was the international language of the day and the language of culture. Paris, the capital of elegance and art, was the most popular destination. Britain was still shaking off the impact of depression in the mid-1930s but Paris was alive. Picasso was painting; Cocteau was writing and making films; Josephine Baker was singing; and Gertrude Stein, who had hosted in the twenties such 'lost generation' writers as Ernest Hemingway and F. Scott Fitzgerald, still maintained her extraordinary salon ... Everyone had a sense of style, even the lower-class French women she passed on the street. It was not only that their dresses looked smarter than anything she saw in England, but that they wore their outfits with a certain insouciance that she found very appealing. Sometimes they just added a pin or the latest fashion accessory, an artificial flower, which seemed to say, "Look at me," ... There was far more colour and verve in Paris, whether it was silk fabric draped on elegant shop window mannequins or pyramids of fancy pastries and chocolates or the strange but intriguing new smells trailing out of bistros and *boulangeries*."

Happily, such an ambience still remains.

In 1939, Pamela married Randolph Churchill, the only son of Sir Winston Churchill, then Prime Minister of Britain and Lady Clementine Churchill. Randolph Churchill had been a journalist with the *London Times* and then joined his father's regiment, the Fourth Hussars and then became a Member of Parliament. Their only child and Pamela's only child, Winston Spencer Churchill was born in 1940. Pamela and Randolph divorced in 1945.

Pamela and Averell Harriman first met in 1941 in London where he had been appointed by President Franklin Roosevelt, Lend-Lease expediter, i.e. Chief Coordinator of American-British cooperation during the ongoing Second World War. Nearly thirty years older than Pamela, then twenty-one, their close relationship ended in 1943 when Harriman was appointed Ambassador to the Soviet Union.

From 1948 to 1959, she lived once again in Paris. "The City of Light was re-lit after the war. Pamela could speak the language, had friends, knew her way around, and would have plenty of opportunity to enjoy life and expand her horizons when Gianni was not present. Paris was politically acceptable: Charles de Gaulle had organised the Free French forces while living in London during the war, occasionally dining at Downing Street with the Churchills, including their daughter-in-law," notes Ogden. Gianni Agnelli, the Italian Fiat magnate was a close friend of Pamela and he bought her a third-floor apartment near the Place de l'Alma at 4 Avenue de New York overlooking the Seine and the Eiffel Tower. Coincidentally, this apartment which she later sold, overlooks the Pont de l'Alma where a fatal car crash claimed the lives of Princess Diana and her friend Dodi in 1997.

France in the post-war period was a good time to be here. "Her decade in France was fun, profitable and offered a spectacular education. Being there fit an important criterion: from the long hemline and full skirt of Christian Dior's `New Look' to the Marshall Plan, NATO and Jean-Paul Sartre, France was the place to be, the centre of the post-war social, political and intellectual action in the late 1940s and 1950s," writes Ogden.

A number of notables of American journalism thronged to Paris in this vibrant and stimulating era. Susan Mary Alsop, the American columnist arrived in Paris in 1945, and stayed till 1961. Theodore White came to Paris in 1948. He went on to become a member of John F. Kennedy's inner circle and author of a number of books on the Kennedy era and American history. Janet Flanner described the rebirth of France post-war to *New Yorker* magazine readers in descriptive dispatches. Ben Bradlee arrived in Paris in 1951. He went on to become the editor of *The Washington Post* and took the limelight during the Watergate scandal of the Nixon presidency that *The Washington Post* first broke. Stanley Karnow reached Paris in 1947 and worked for a period as a *Time* magazine correspondent. He went on to become a Pulitzer prize winner and author of a number of acclaimed books on Vietnam and Philippines. In 1999, he wrote, *Paris in the Fifties*. Art Buchwald arrived in Paris in 1948 and became a columnist for the Paris-based *International Herald Tribune*, an honour he still holds at the close of the twentieth century. Art Buchwald went on to become a household name in journalism and a prolific writer including *I'll Always Have Paris* (1996). This was the heady Paris of the late 1940s and 1950s. An epoch where Franco-American relations were warm, friendly and ultimately left all the residents of that period enamoured for a lifetime with *la vie Parisienne*.

Pamela once again left Paris, after an eleven-year stay for New York in 1959, where she married a second time, the American film and theatre producer, Leland Hayward. Hayward was the film producer of *The Old Man and the Sea* starring Spencer Tracy; *The Spirit of Saint Louis* with James Stewart. He also produced the plays, *Gypsy*, *The Sound of Music*, *Anne of a Thousand Days*, *Mister Roberts* which he also produced as a movie with Henry Fonda, *South Pacific*, *Peter Pan* and other well-known classics. Leland Hayward died in 1971.

She threw herself into the role of producer's wife and was highly active in the film and theatre worlds. Writes Ogden, "Touring opened up a whole new world of places, close contact with creative people and non-stop action. She loved every minute." Pamela Hayward commented that, "I look on myself as a backstage person, really. But backstage people are very important. They're the ones who get the show on the road." Her self-assessment was particularly correct as time would tell.

In September 1971, Pamela and Averell Harriman both now widowed were married in New York. They had resumed a relationship after a gap of twenty-five years. She acquired American Citizenship in December 1971.

Averell Harriman in 1946 had left his post as Ambassador in Moscow to become President Harry Truman's Secretary of Commerce. In 1949, Harriman was Marshall Plan administrator for the recovery of post-war Europe. He was one-time governor of New York in 1954 and twice unsuccessful candidate for president in 1952 and 1956. In the 1960s, he was the chief negotiator for Laos neutrality, the arms control agreement between USA and the Soviet Union and the US envoy in Paris for the Vietnam peace talks. During President Carter's administration in the 1970s, Pamela and Averell Harriman represented the US government at a number of events. "In recognition of Harriman's tenacity and stature, Vance (Cyrus Vance, the Secretary of State) saw to it that he and Pamela were included on a succession of ceremonial delegations around the world. They went to Panama after the negotiation of the Canal Treaty and to Zimbabwe in 1980 to celebrate independence. They attended more state funerals than Vice-President Walter Mondale: that of Robert Menzies, their wartime blitzmate at the Dorchester, in Australia; in London for IA bomb victim Earl Mountbatten of Burma, whom Averell first met in the 1920s; Tito's in Yugoslavia," notes Ogden.

In 1980, Pamela Harriman began active participation in fund-raising for the Democratic Party – the Political Action Committee (PAC) in time to become popularly known as Pam PAC in acknowledgement of the major organiser of the committee. Averell Harriman provided moral and financial support but no active involvement. Nearing ninety, he was preoccupied in writing his memoirs. Averell Harriman died in July 1986.

Pamela and Averell Harriman hosted 'Issues Dinners'. Christopher Ogden remarks that, 'Issues Diners' became the focus of the PAC. Very quickly they evolved from being solely a means of bringing people together to discuss ideas to a method of attracting money from people inside and outside Washington who wanted the thrill of being in a Georgetown living room with big-name political players." Al Gore Jr., senator from Tennessee was one of the key speakers of the 'Issue Dinners', often on environmental matters and always a favourite. What started in a light-hearted manner "had become one of the most successful political action committees ever, having raised, by her accounting nearly $12 million from all sources in a decade," notes Ogden.

By the late 1980s and now in her late sixties, Pamela Harriman was easing off her involvement in the PAC and looking for another cause to sponsor and throw herself into. With the forthcoming 1992 presidential elections coming up, she gave her full backing to the Democratic candidate, Bill Clinton. She raised $3.2 million in a ten-thousand-dollar-a-head Day in the Country for Clinton and Gore as funds for their election campaign. "She liked Clinton very much for his brains, charm, confidence and omnivorous interest in policy. His stamina impressed her too. Clinton could talk issues for hours, down to the arcane details of welfare reform or international trade legislation, and draw out the best from other participants by incisive questioning," says Ogden.

Pamela Harriman commented on Clinton and his unsuccessful bid for re-election as Governor of Arkansas, "It's very important in life to have success, but it's even more important to have failure, and to know how to handle it." Her life experience and insight had taught her this. Harriman would never know the appropriateness of her remark – in light of the Monica Lewinsky affair.

Upon victory of the Clinton-Gore Democratic ticket to the White House in 1992, Pamela Harriman and Vernon Jordan, Bill Clinton's close friend were the two post-election dinner hosts in Washington DC. Vernon Jordan again hit headlines in the Monica Lewinsky/Bill Clinton furore.

Nothing succeeds like success. The old adage worked successfully for Pamela Harriman who was first rumoured to be appointed as US Ambassador to Great Britain. The British press went wild with speculation. The London *Times* wondered whether there was to be, "A Churchill Connection for Grosvenor Square". *The Evening Standard* wrote, "Diplomatic circles here are alive with the rumour that the queenly 72 - year-old Harriman is poised to come over to London as the United States Ambassador to the Court of St. James." If she had really wanted the post, it may have been hers. As Ogden points out, "the biggest impediment of all to Pamela's returning to Britain was that she still cannot tolerate Britain or most Britons. She dislikes the country, its pessimism and compulsion to look to the past, and the empty-headed arrogance of too many men in high position and their attitude about her. She spent her adult life avoiding the place." Her interest lay elsewhere.

At the end of January 1993, soon after Bill Clinton was inaugurated as President, Pamela Harriman was offered the post of US Ambassador to France. "The US Embassy in Paris, on the other hand, was a perfect choice. She had lived in France for a dozen years, though the Churchills knew President Charles de Gaulle, the architect of post-war political France, maintained good cultural and social contacts, spoke the language and knew well – and adored – Paris itself. The post met her standards: it was big, luxurious, in the middle of Europe and, in the post-Cold War shakedown, plenty substantive," remarks Ogden.

Her nomination made headlines both sides of the Atlantic. Reaction to the nomination was generally favourable, if not effusive." At 73, the most powerful kingmaker of the Democratic Party has retained the allure and the charm that made her, in half a century, a legend on both sides of the Atlantic, A veritable heroine from a novel," wrote *Le Figaro*. *Paris Match* headlined, "Pamela, the Enchantress, this woman of exceptional destiny". *Le Point* noted, "Clinton's gift to Pamela', *France Soir* described her as "The iron lady in the silk suit." France's Consul General in New York, Benoit d'Abonville observed, "An excellent choice. She knows France, is certainly well-connected to the Clinton administration, and will be, I am certain, a splendid representative."

At her confirmation before the Senate Committee on Foreign Relations, she remarked, "I came before you today conscious of one great difference between us and one great similarity. Unlike you, I was not born in this country. I am an American by choice. But, like all of you, I have a deep love for this land that has long been my home and I am proud to serve it in any way I can."

Pamela Digby Churchill Hayward Harriman moved to 41 rue du Faubourg St. Honoré, Paris as US Ambassador to France in 1993 at the age of seventy-three. It was a long road from her first trip to Paris in 1937 as a sixteen-year-old school girl.

At a reception at the Hotel Ritz, I was talking to an Ambassador of an East European country and I was telling him that I had just finished reading this biography on Pamela Harriman who had died at the Ritz. He then related the following anecdote. He had met Ambassador Pamela Harriman and in the course of the conversation, she asked him what he did when he faced some problem in the course of his work. He replied that he contacted the relevant person at the Quai d'Orsay (Ministry of Foreign Affairs) desk in-charge of his country. Harriman replied that she chatted over the fence with her next-door neighbour. That neighbour happens to be the President of the Republic of France! The woman had *panache* and a sense of humour.

With her death in office in Paris, Mrs. Harriman's personal possessions at the American Embassy residence at Faubourg du St. Honoré, beside the Elysée Palace, the residence of President Jacques Chirac and her properties in Washington DC and Virginia in the United States were put up for auction. Sotheby's New York sold the private collection of paintings, furniture and objects of art of Pamela Harriman in May 1997. The collected estimated at $5.9

million fetched $8.7 million. A painting done in the 1930s by Winston Churchill, her then father-in-law of a jug and two bottles estimated at $30,000 sold for $18,000. A pair of palm trees of Russian origin in crystal, white marble and gilt bronze sold for $46,000. A painting, the 'House of Flaubert at Croisset' by Paul César Helleu who had a brilliant career in France and North America sold for close to $1 million.

As noted in Demeures et Châteaux, "it is clear that, as for the auction sale of the 1996 collection of Jacqueline Kennedy Onassis, the extraordinary personality of Pamela Harriman incited amateurs to raise the prices." This was an exceptional sale for an exceptional destiny.

It was George Moore in *Confessions of a Young Man* in 1888 who said, "Whoever seems a little more distinguished than another has been to France."

Death of a Princess

"She was born a lady, became a princess and died a saint."

L *'Express,* 9 a.m. Sunday, August 31, 1997.

While gathering to go on an outing to Deauville in Normandy, a North Sea resort town also renowned for its horse-racing, horse-breeding and casinos, someone had seen the news on television early this morning. Stunned with disbelief, we switched on immediately the car radio. We tuned into a French radio station and then BBC radio news. And so passed the week, as we alternated between CNN and BBC televsion coverage of the fatal car accident in the tunnel under Place de l'Alma, close to the Seine river and in view of the Eiffel Tower. The dead included Diana, Princess of Wales; Dodi (Emad) al-Fayed, her companion and Henri-Paul, the driver. The sole survivor, Trevor-Rees Jones, Princess Diana's bodyguard returned to London following a month's stay at a Paris hospital in October 1997. Suffering from amnesia, he was unable to fully account for the events of the tragic night.

A situation *déjà vu*? Yes. On November 22, 1963; thirty-four years ago, in Washington DC we had passed a similar week glued to the television when President John F. Kennedy was assassinated. Then at Alice Deal Junior School in Washington DC, we were let out of school early that 22nd November afternoon.

Where were you on November 22, 1963? Where were you on August 31, 1997? Global mass communication, both the electronic and print media have imprinted these two dates in people's minds unlike few other events of the past fifty years. The deaths of two individuals whom very few of us have known constitute a memory milestone and a time reference in our lives.

A gold-painted sculpture of the Statue of Liberty's flaming torch erected by the *International Herald Tribune* newspaper in Paris in 1987, commemorates Franco-American relations on the occasion of the hundred year anniversary of the newspaper. The sculpture is located at Place de l'Alma, above the tunnel of Alma. This site has today become a memorial site to Diana, Princess of Wales. The actual tragic spot is inside the tunnel of Alma. In the two weeks following the fatal crash, there were floral bouquets at the two spots inside the tunnel where the car first hit the thirteenth pillar on the left side and then the right wall where the mangled remains of the car wreck were found. The base of the flaming torch sculpture was plastered with pictures of Diana, Dodi, Diana and Dodi; letters, cards and floral bouquets. The international presence of mourners was evident with flags of countries accompanying the bouquets, letters and cards. Many have signed their names and given names of their countries. The grassy mounds at the side of the tunnel were strewn with flowers even six weeks after the accident. Our daughter also paid her floral respects.

As a hundred days of the fatal accident passed, French television screened on December 10, 1997, a French-produced documentary titled, *All You Need is Love.* It analysed Diana, Princess of Wales' role in the British monarchy and her place in society. The same evening, another French-produced programme, *La Vie à l'Endroit* (With Regard to Life) was screened on France 2. The particular programme, 'The Orphans of Lady Di' presented by Mireille Dumas was an original and intelligent treatment of a much-media-exposed individual. Both documentaries dealt with the concept of Myth, for which essential ingredients are beauty, suffering, love and death and both spoke of Diana's unique and exceptional destiny.

More than one hundred days following the crash, the situation has not changed all that much. There are still fresh flowers being placed at the base of the sculpture. Pictures, cards and letters and candles are still to be seen. There is a lot of graffiti on the base and the column of the flaming torch and on the bridgehead of the Pont Alma. There are now also remarks pertaining to the Conspiracy Theory.

While talking to a Sudanese friend about the large number of visitors to Paris, he noted that "in addition, they all want to see the Tunnel." I, for an instant, thought of the Euro Tunnel, the Channel crossing between England and France through which the Euro train passes. This tunnel has considerably eased travel between London and Paris and added to the number of visitors from London. I, then realised, that he was referring to the tunnel at Place de L'Alma. The spot is now crowded with tourist buses and on the must-see-in-Paris list.

There is also a suggestion on a piece of paper on the base of the flaming torch statue that the Place de l'Alma be renamed Place Diana, Princesse de Galles (Place Diana, Princess of Wales). In fact, Place de l'Alma was to have been renamed Place Maria Callas in September 1997, Maria Callas, the Greek opera singer; the Diva, Voice of the Century died in Paris twenty years ago. However, since August 31, 1997, such is the sentimental association of Place de l'Alma now connected with Diana that the naming ceremony was postponed. Sadly, in life too - Maria Callas lost out. Aristotle Onassis, the Greek shipping tycoon with whom she had a long-term relationship, left her for Jacqueline Kennedy whom he married.

Interestingly enough, the residence of the Ambassador of Thailand in the Meutte area of Paris, 16th *arrondissement* is an imposing property Onasis was about to purchase for Callas in the early 1960s; but neither the purchase nor the relationship matured. He bought her an apartment on the prestigious avenue Georges Mandel, Number 30 on the double tree-lined boulevard connecting the Eiffel Tower and le Bois de Boulogne. She died there in 1977, it is said of a broken heart. One evening while my husband and I were out for our evening walk along avenue Georges Mandel, we came across a card and a bouquet of yellow flowers tied to the small gate at Number 30. We could not read the card as the ink had run. It was a touching sight.

I saw a poignant exhibition, *L'Éternelle Maria Callas* at the Hotel de Ville. The woman, the voice, the myth were celebrated in this exhibition of some of her famous opera performances supported by many personal items. There were evening dresses by Christian Dior and Jacques Fath. There were furniture, shoes, jewels, fans and many other possessions depicting the fashion of another era of style and glamour. Many of the photographs and personal correspondence on show were made public for the first time.

Paris was also the city for another grand romantic legend of the 20th century – the historical love affair of the Duke and Duchess of Windsor. Following, King Edward VII's abdication in 1936 in order to marry American, Wallis Simpson in 1937; the former king now reduced to Duke of Windsor and the Duchess of Windsor went into exile in various places. In 1953, they settled permanently at 4, route du Champs-d'Entrainement, a sumptuous mansion in the west of le Bois de Boulogne placed at their disposal by the city of Paris.

The Duke of Windsor died in Paris in 1972 and the Duchess of Windsor passed away in 1986. History abounds in coincidences. The same regal residence of the couple-in-exile was subsequently bought by Mohamed al-Fayed, the Egyptian businessman millionaire and father of Dodi al-Fayed, Princess Diana's companion. There has been much speculation in the French newspapers if that very residence would have become the home of Diana and Dodi – if they had married. We will now never know. Press reports wrote of a brief visit to the secluded residence by the couple – en route from le Bourget airport to the Hotel Ritz on the afternoon of the accident. The British-French connection started by one ex-king of England would have been continued to another ex-future Queen of England. Was it Fate? Was it Destiny?

The priceless and historical contents of the former residence of the Duke and Duchess of Windsor were to have been auctioned in September 1997 by Sotheby's, the renowned international auctioneers. Following the deaths of Diana, Princess of Wales and Dodi al-Fayed, Mohamed al-Fayed, owner of the historical residence postponed auction of the contents of the mansion. Today, the future of the residence remains unknown. The auction was then rescheduled for February 1998. I saw the catalogue in two volumes entitled, 'The Private Collection' and 'The Public Collection' at Harrods (also owned by Mohamed al-Fayed) in London. The more than 40,000 objects including paintings, photographs, carpets, furniture, objects of art, clothes and personal belongings were presented in 3,200 lots of sale.

What might have been also plagues the ring Dodi al-Fayed supposedly ordered for Diana at Alberto Repossi jewellers in Monte Carlo during their idyllic summer vacation in the French Riviera. Press reports write of his crossing la Place de la Vendome from the Hotel Ritz (owned by Mohamed al-Fayed) where they were staying, in order to collect the diamond ring worth 1.2 million French francs from Alberto Repossi at Place de la Vendôme, the very afternoon of the fatal crash. The ring is one out of an exclusive series named - 'Dis-moi Oui' (Say Yes)'. The ring was later found in the ill-fated car.

In the poignant events of the year, there were certainly many facts which beat fiction. And so a summer of personal triumph and collective tragedy came to a close on August 31 1997.

Two Historical Auctions

"France, it is often said, is a huge attic that from time to time empties itself of some of its contents."

Popular quote

"Going...going...gone. Sold at...French francs." And the auctioneer hit hard his hammer. So proceeded the auction of lock, stock and barrel of the entire contents of the Hotel George V at 31 avenue George V in Paris in November 1997. The super-prestigious hotel changed hands. The new owner, Prince al-Waleed bin Talal bin Abdul Aziz al-Saud, a nephew of King Fahd of Saudi Arabia, ordered the George V to close its doors on November 1, 1997 for a period of total restoration and refurbishment at an estimated 300 million francs (some $50 million).

The Hotel George V opened in 1928 to the public (in a matter of speaking only), since its clientele were always the rich and famous; largely princes, princesses, sheikhs, other royalty, actors, actresses, media personalities ... Its interior is of the turn-of-the-century style, l'Art Déco – sumptuous furnishings, plenty of light – all in all, *une magnifique et grande intérieure.* Marlene Dietrich and Cary Grant in earlier days and Harrison Ford in more recent times have graced its rooms. Only the bare walls of the Hotel George V with the nineteenth century front-façade of the building are to remain. The entire interior is to be gutted and redone from floor to ceiling which entails a clearing out of the building from bottom to top.

On auction are objects of art and furniture; paintings, frames, carpets, lights, curtains, chandeliers, crockery, cutlery, glassware, kitchen utensils, door grills, curtain pelmets, door knobs, clocks and anything else any luxurious hotel in Paris is equipped with. Buyers have a choice of some ten thousand articles. The sale was assigned to Etude Tajan, noted Parisian auctioneers. Etude Tajan had, in fact, been conducting their prestigious auctions at the premises of the hotel for the past twenty years.

Having arrived at 31 avenue George V some thirty minutes early, I joined a queue of already some two hundred people. Through the grapevine, I heard that there was a bomb alert in the building. Do I stay or do I go? No one moved, the queue continued to lengthen and after a prayer, I shuffled along in the queue. Following considerable pushing and shoving by surprisingly some elegant and elderly men and women, and a bag security check – we were in. There was a run down the stairs by some agile prospective buyers and a dash to grab seats. This was a no-holds barred situation. Everyone for oneself. I spotted a front row seat and promptly deposited myself. For a first time attendant at an auction, this in itself was good fortune. Bienvenue en France (Welcome to France), an organisation for diplomatic women hosted by the Quai d'Orsay, the French Ministry of Foreign Affairs had arranged this invitation. I was a member of the group, *Les Antiquités et les Objets d'art* and this was one of the many fascinating events I had the tremendous pleasure of enjoying with the organisation.

As Harriet W. Rochefort writes in *French Toast: A Humorous Tour of What Living in France is Really Like:* "The Silent Pusher is an endemic Parisian phenomenon. He or she is generally someone who is unhappy about not being in front of you but is afraid to tell you directly … In the market, at the bakery, but especially at the post office and banks where you could easily fossilise if you don't catch on to the great game of queue-hopping, you must concentrate all your forces on defending your place in line."

The auction started. Two Louis XV arm-chairs were hoisted on to a table. The evaluator said 1000 francs. The auctioneer rattled off "1100, 1200 by the woman in red, 1400 says the woman to the left, 1800 by the woman with the shawl, 2000 by the young girl with the brown hair, 2500, 3000? Yes, sold at 3000 francs to the happy lady with the red shawl !"

A box of ten early twentieth century sidelight glass shades went from an estimated 500 francs to be bought by a lady for 700 francs. Another similar box, auctioned later in the afternoon, started at 200 francs and went finally for 500 francs. Buyer's luck. Four ivory coloured, doubly-lined brocade curtains went for 2500 francs, *un bon marché* (a good buy). Even a pair of badly stained curtains were sold. A five seater Louis XV sofa set went from an estimated 2000 francs to a sale at 12,500 francs. A ghastly 8 foot high chrome light-stand sold for 2,500 francs, *Chacun son goût* (everyman to his taste). And so it went. After all, a short-term-bargain theory always has a glimmer of a long-term-investment excuse at the end of it. Some items were interesting and in good condition and many items looked somewhat shabby and out of place in a luxurious hotel. Perhaps *la crème de la crème* of the sale items had already been sold. Maybe, it was a good thing that Hotel George V was undertaking a top-to-bottom refurbishment.

When it rains, it pours.

My second visit to an auction occurred just two days later. Having experienced one, I went off to the second armed with an abundance of enthusiasm and as before, no chequebook. As observed at the George V auction, no cash appeared exchanged. Auction practice and etiquette perhaps demands no 'cash on sale'.

In my observer status, I had the good fortune to be invited to a historic auction of 'Important Drawings and Paintings of the Impressionist and Modern Period.' It was organised by the renowned French auctioneers, Druout and held at their prestigious premises at Druout-Montaigne on avenue Montaigne, where are also to be found the haute *couture fashion* houses, such as Dior, Gucci and Givenchy.

I once again pushed my way in and in my thoughts, thanked my friend for providing excellent reserved seats. In the upstairs balcony was an international press of some 50 people, armed with TV cameras and video recorders. On the platform before us were seated twenty-three persons, many of them with telephones placed before them. The auctioneer stood on the platform behind a microphone. Behind him on the back wall, was a digital board listing French Francs, US $, Pound Sterling, Swiss Francs and Japanese Yen. It was explained to me that there would be immediate conversion of the quoted prices into the above-quoted international currencies. It was an awesome sight.

I sat with my hands clenched tight. Any untoward movement and I could be in an immensely grave situation. It was Peter Mayle, the author of the immensely popular *A Year in Provence* who cautioned in *Anything Considered*, "If you should decide out of curiosity, to be a spectator at one of these million-dollar orgies, the golden rule is to sit on your hands. One absent-minded scratch of your ear might catch the auctioneer's eye and you could find yourself with a twelfth-century bleeding cup and a bill the size of a mortgage."

Promptly at 9 p.m. the auction of the private collection of the late Madame Julien Rouart started. She was the wife of the grandson of Berthe Morisot, one of the few women painters of the Impressionist period. To be sold at this auction were twenty Berthe Morisot paintings, two Degas, two Renoirs, a Gauguin, a Boudin, a Monet and other works of art of the Impressionist period. A rare and stunning collection was now to be sold individually to international buyers. The musee Marmottan in the 16th *arrondissement* of Paris houses another Rouart art collection. This collection, a donation, however, remains intact. The auctioneer prefaced the start of the sale with a few remarks on the rare and historic nature of this particular auction.

The first Berthe Morisot painting estimated at 10,000 French francs sold at 92,000 francs. (Conversion 5.75 French francs = $1). 'Autumn in Bois de Boulogne' by Berthe Morisot estimated at 150,000 francs sold at 750,000 francs. Her 'Seaside' in oil estimated at 820,000 francs sold for over 2 million francs. Another Berthe Morisot, 'Two Women Seated' estimated at 220,000 francs was sold at 2,250,000 francs. Even an unsigned Berthe Morisot sold at 1,550,000 francs. Breathtaking.

Most buyers were not in the packed room, nor in the adjacent rooms with gigantic screens carrying live the sale. Most of the bids made were over the telephone – probably a billionaire in Tokyo or Los Angeles or a museum in New York. A most remarkable sight was to see the offers made by the Druout representative on the platform over the telephone to the prospective buyer, maybe some three thousand miles away and in a second committing $1000...$2000 over the top. And the digital currency conversion was taking place instantly on the board. Each time a painting crossed the million francs mark, there was a grand round of applause.. Six out of the twenty Berthe Morisot paintings crossed the million franc mark. The evening's sale exceeded twice the estimated sale price for the paintings.

Edgar Degas' pastel painting of 'Two Girls' sold close to $5 million. Gauguin's oil painting, 'Horses in the Countryside' sold for over $4 million. Auguste-Renoir's portrait of his son sold for 1,880,000 francs after a nerve-wracking battle between two absentee buyers. The auctioneer looked and waved his hand to the left for a telephone bid and immediately switched to the right as another desperate buyer bid over the telephone. We were switching our heads in time as well.

Souren Melikian in her reporting of 'A New Golden Age of Old Masters', in the *International Herald Tribune* similarly noted, "The impact of combined rarity and availability, enhanced by the freshness of works which had been out of the market for many years, or, in some cases, decades, stung collectors and dealers into bidding matches as rarely before ... This left Green (the winning bidder) with a huge 2.2 million Pound Sterling bill, more than double the highest estimate ... That evening, it became clearer than ever that professionals of his calibre and financial resources now feel that time has come when an opportunity, if missed, is unlikely to repeat itself."

The French auction market is closed to foreign auctioneers, i.e. international auction houses are unable to conduct sales in France. The practice changed in 1998 when Christie's, Sotheby's and others extended their already exsting presence to conducting sales themselves. In *Demeures et Châteaux*, a magazine devoted to the international arena of art, auctions and architecture, the president of Sotheby's, France, Princesse de Beauvau-Craon observes that, "Paris can recover its reputation as the leading international market place for art, which was formerly the case up until the 50s.

(New York is now the centre stage for auctions) … in this sector, Paris can and must reassert itself as the historical and geographical centre of Europe. Fifty per cent of the pieces put up for auction in the world are French."

At the close of the evening, I trooped out quite spellbound. So this is how 'those things' happen; 'those things' we often read about in the paper the next day. 'Those things' include the auction sale of Begum Salimah Aga Khan's jewellery by Christie's in 1996, the sale of the belongings of Pamela Harriman, the former American Ambassador to France in 1997; auction of Princess Diana's dresses in New York in June 1997 and the February 1998 sale of the contents of the Duke and Duchess of Windsor's residence in Paris.

According to *Demeures et Châteaux*, "for an object to be an object of value, it should combine harmony with style, the quality of the work, the originality of the subject and the quality of the materials have to have more or less a degree of uniqueness, of rarity. The value of the object can also double or triple, etc. if it benefits from famous reminiscences, historical or sentimental." I had the privilege of witnessing the practice behind the theory.

How to 'Do' the Louvre in Forty-five Minutes

"Four hours more at the Louvre, that exhaustless mine of art and interest: in paintings and sculpture at all events most other collections pale beside it."

Martin F. Tupper, 'Paterfamilias Diary of Everybody's Tour', 1856

One of the many hats *les étrangerés* (the foreigners) wear in Paris is that of a tour-guide operator. My organisational capacity and repository of information were keenly tested one autumn afternoon. I was coordinating three groups of visitors – all on a tight schedule – to the City of Wonders. A couple familiar with Paris wanted to do their 'own thing' – which included a repeat visit to the perfume emporium, Sephora. My brother and sister-in-law with two small children were somewhat limited in their range of activities. The third party, a friend on her first visit to Paris and that too for a day – just had to see the Louvre Museum. You must be joking. A day? There in fact, was less than half the day left; in fact, we could fit in about an hour; in fact, forty-five minutes to be precise. This was truly throwing in the gauntlet. Yet what is a challenge if it is not to be tested?

In 1981, the late President Francois Mitterand declared that the Louvre Museum was to become "the world's biggest museum" and so was launched another of *Les Grands Travaux* (The Grand Works) of the Mitterand era. In all probability, that distinction now lies with the Getty Centre in Los Angeles which opened in December 1997. Its six buildings covering a space of 92,000 square metres cost a cool $1 billion. The endowment funds in terms of their purchasing power of art are second to none. The Getty Centre's architect, Richard Meir remarked, "Think of it as a small college campus with different departments … not a museum but an institution in which art predominates." Meir is also the architect of the French Canal+television station headquarters on *la rive gauche* of the Seine – a stunning glass and chrome complex.

Another museum making news in 1997 was the Guggenheim Museum in Bilbao, in the Basque region of Spain. It opened in October 1997 on some 23,000 square metres of floor space and is estimated to have cost some $100 million. Frank Gehry, the architect spoke of, "Connecting the urban fabric of a fairly dense city to the river's edge with a place for modern art is my idea of heaven." The Guggenheim Museum has been described as, "an architectural meteorite … Nineteenth century streets and then POW!"

A resounding succcss the Guggenheim Museum eighteen months later, has been credited with adding $160 million to the local economy in twelve months and for the creation of 3,800 jobs. T.R. Reid writing in the *International Herald Tribune* says, "For cities around the world, it has become the classic case study of economic revival based on culture." The commerce minister of the Basque provincial government exclaims, "Normally, you couldn't say that a single building saved a city. But this building – it's magic!" This sort of credibility and enthusiasm must be the dream of every architect.

Once upon a time, churches and cathedrals were prime buildings in communities. It was a centre for communication with a Greater Being and also a centre for communication with one's fellow beings. Religious centres were richly endowed both by the state and individuals. The best in art and architecture were sought and got. It was a means of achieving immortality by mortals. In time, academia received such investments and people also sought society's recognition and thereby social status. Providing the means to enrich other people's minds is surely regarded as exceedingly noble. One has only to see today's endowment of chairs and foundations at universities. Anthony Lewis in an article in the *International Herald Tribune* writes, "In the developed world today, people want at the same time to be part of the global society and to be attached to local roots. The museum is a symbol of both: an institution of international standing with a strong local attachment. From ancient Athens to Angkor Wat and the great cathedrals of Europe, architecture has expressed the highest aspirations of the human spirit."

The twentieth century has seen the museum come into the forefront. An article categorically states, "Museums– the temple of art has gradually replaced the church as the emblematic focus of civil self-esteem." The lure of a focus museum considerably adds to a city's attraction and prestige. A journal, *Museum International* refers to the museum as a temple of knowledge, repository of heritage and cultural academy. Claus Kapplinger in an article 'Architecture and the Marketing of the Museum' in the journal writes, "The fact that more and more members of the public today want not only to buy postcards of the art works that they have seen, but of the building itself as a souvenir of their visit, points to a changed concept of a museum. Twenty years ago, few visitors would have considered buying a photograph of the museum building. But in recent decades, museum architecture has become a central symbol, representing the site and the image of the museum." So it is with the Glass Pyramid at the Louvre Museum. T.R. Reid in writing about the Guggenheim Museum at Bilbao also observes, "A magnet for architects from around the world,

Mr. Gehry's seemingly chaotic twisting sculpture of a building is one of the few museums anywhere where the architecture students on the outside sketching the building outnumber the art students of the inside sketching the paintings."

The mission of the 'New' Louvre according to 'The Grand Louvre: The Palace, The Collections, The New Areas', (1996), a Beaux Arts magazine, was to transform what was basically a nineteenth century museum into a modern museum – a museum that would take the Louvre into the new millennium. It involved relocating the Finance Ministry which was housed in the Richelieu wing of the Louvre since 1871 and which runs alongside the rue de Rivoli to a new site at Bercy – an ultra modern mega-complex along the Seine.

The transformation increases the exhibition floor space from 31,000 square metres to more then 60,000 square metres creating kilometres of galleries and "from now on in possession of all necessary scientific, cultural and technical equipment for the conservation of the exhibits and for the reception of an ever more demanding public ... The saga of the Grand Louvre is written with superlatives: 6 hectares of land have been dug by archaeologists, 11 hectares of façades and 7 of roofing have been renovated, thousands of works of art have been restored and cleaned, the reception areas for the public have been multiplied by ten. The Louvre has become the Louvre City which hums with the activities of its 1500 employees and the to-ing and fro-ing within its walls of five million visitors," notes the Beaux Arts issue.

And we had forty-five minutes.

With the opening of the Grand Louvre in 1994, the Louvre Museum was organised into three wings – the Sully enclosing the Cour Carrée, the Denon running parallel to the Seine and the now vacant Richelieu alongside the rue de Rivoli. The three wings house the Department of Oriental Antiquities and Islamic Art; Egyptian Antiquities; Greek, Etruscan and Roman Antiquities; Objects of Art; Sculptures; Prints and Drawings; Paintings and Medieval Louvre and History of the Louvre rooms. Yet each department constitutes a museum within a museum.

Given a time constraint of forty-five minutes to achieve the impossible, I took my friend in hand and ran her through itinerary I had chosen. The basis of my criteria? I, by now, knew of the mega-attractions at the Louvre; written in italics in the official 'Handbook in English: Louvre' (Venus de Milo, Michelangelo's Slaves, Mona Lisa) and another reference, 'Paris: User's Guide' which advises visitors, "without forgetting, of course, the most famous of masterpieces which continue to amaze visitors from all over the world: the Venus de Milo, the Victory of Samothrace, the Mona Lisa by Leonardo da Vinci, and many other great works of human genius."

To the "other great works of human genius", I added – an eye-opener – Napoleon III apartment. We first dashed to the Napoleon III rooms fitted out between 1857 and 1861 and which today constitute the only example of Second Empire interior decoration preserved in its original state in Paris. We first entered a room with shelves of French porcelain china from Limoges and Sevres, then two ante-chambers and two grandiose, spectacular salons – the last two all in gold and glitter. Here one finds colossal wall-mirrors, massive crystal chandeliers, red velvet upholstery for the ornate designed chairs and sofas and curious almost x-shaped three-seaters, ornate fireplaces on two facing walls, the roof covered in paintings and friezes, all marked with the emblem of Napoleon III. It's a breathtaking sight due to its magnificence. An adjacent rectangular dining room seats some forty people (if I recall correctly) – a gigantic table set out with massive ornate candlesticks and the walls and ceiling painted with gory hunting scenes – dogs, deer, horses ... (perhaps, not everyone's idea of an ideal dining ambience). These rooms give the visitor a glimpse of the opulence of royalty's lifestyle in the second half of the nineteenth century.

One down, four more to go. I looked at my watch, thirty-five minutes left. We walked fast, with me walking faster than my friend and thus almost leading her by the nose – we made it to the long corridor in the Greek, Etruscan and Roman Antiquities at which end stands in all her glory – the Venus de Milo. This Hellenistic piece of sculpture was discovered in 1820 by a Greek peasant on the island of Milo in the Cyclades. The Venus de Milo was donated to the Louvre by the Marquis de Riviére. "This statue has come to be considered the prototype of Greek feminine beauty. Somewhat more than 6 feet hig, with its arms broken off ... it belongs to the end of the second century ... critics and art lovers have long gazed on the slender nude body of the goddess emerging from the heavy cloth of her cloak which is slipping towards the ground," notes *Places and History: Paris.*

There was a thick pack of amateur paparazzi taking photographs for posterity. I duly took one of my friends and recalled that I first 'saw' the Venus de Milo in an album of my parents – my late father had photographed my mother gazing at the epitome of beauty – way back in the early 1950s. Venus de Milo has looked upon generations of humanity – all captivated by the sheer beauty of the human form on stone. Enough, we had to run on.

By now, I had given up consulting the *Handbook* and questioned instead the museum attendants for direction to the next target, the next sight. And so we made it to a crossroad of grand staircases in the Louvre whereupon one is struck by another sublime sculpture of Hellenistic art. The nine-foot high Winged Victory Parian marble female-form statue was found in 1863 at Samothrace. It dates about 190 BC. "The Victory figure stands erect on the prow of the ship which she will guide to victory: the sea wind hits her with all its force, tearing at her clothing and pressing it to her body … It vibrates in contact with the Victory's body and in turn pushes the Victory's arms violently backwards," exalts *Places and History: Paris*. The Winged Victory stands rightly majestically in its grandeur overlooking the multitudes at her feet.

Three down, two more to go. We were now pushed for time. My lecture was briefer at site and conducted more while we were shuffling fast on the glistening marble floor between masterpieces. We came across Michelangelo's statue of Slaves more by chance than design. Created in Florence early in the sixteenth century, it is a moving and inspiring piece of creativity. It was meant to decorate the tomb of Pope Jules II. 'Slaves' signifies the soul that is shackled by its earthly body.

Finally, if the world knows one item at the Louvre – that is the Mona Lisa. It is the Louvre's *piéce de résistance.* People are known to enter the Louvre to see the Mona Lisa and having seen, it, turn around looking for the exit. Admittedly, they are a small minority. On the other hand, the Louvre receives annually some six million visitors. Should even a small percentage of them enter the museum principally to see the Mona Lisa – Well! Thus an international jury has picked a French architect Lorenzo

Piqueras to turn the Salle des Etats, where Leonardo da Vinci's masterpiece now hangs, into two galleries, one for the large oils of the Venetian Renaissance, the other exclusively for Mona Lisa. The $4.5 million conversion is to be paid for by the Japanese Nippon Television and should be ready in 2002. This filter-system will permit the 'quickie' visitors to 'Do' the Louvre in Five Minutes!

The Mona Lisa or La Gioconda painted by Leonardo da Vinci in the early sixteenth century in Florence is a portrait of a young Florentine woman, Monna Lisa who married Francesco del Gioconda, which accounts for the other reference to the Mona Lisa. Leonardo da Vinci himself loved the painting. How it came to be sold to Francis I of France is not known. It came to be considered the prototype of a Renaissance portrait. A sixteenth century writer, Firenzuola wrote in his essay, 'on the perfect beauty of a woman', that the slight opening of the lips at the corners of the mouth was considered in that period as a sign of elegance. "A real portrait or an image of beauty? The changed patterns of light with the juxtaposition of nature and the human body, create an ideal of eternal grace," marvels *The Grand Louvre: The Palace, The Collections, The New Areas*. In another description, "Mona Lisa has the slight smile that enters into the gentle, delicate atmosphere pervading the whole painting," writes *Places and History: Paris*. The eyes too are uniquely famous – in that they appear to follow the viewer from whichever angle one gazes at the painting.

A glance at my watch, told me that our forty-five minutes were up and we made it back to the massive foyer under the Glass Pyramid, up the packed escalator and out of the Glass Pyramid into the sunshine and my niece and nephew running around the Cour Napoléon with its centre court statue of Louis XIV. A.E.V. Lucas in *Wanderings and*

Diversions written in 1926 observed that, "The French never allow a distinguished son of France to lack a statue." And what would Paris be without its innumerable magnificent statues?

We had made the Louvre in forty-five minutes – a feat and a physical accomplishment too. We were both breathless; perhaps in more ways than one – the mind boggles at the sheer breath of human genius and creativity.

It was with a sense of amazement and amusement when I came across much later, the following piece which I have reproduced in full, while reading *I'll Always Have Paris: A Memoir* (1996) by Art Buchwald. What it proves is that, however, unimaginable, ludicrous and unique an endeavour or experience may be, there may well be someone else who had the same incredulous idea. The trick lies in locating the 'great minds think alike' and foregoing the 'fools only differ' category.

With every credit to Art Buchwald:

"Over the years, the Louvre and I became familiar companions. Whenever someone came to Paris, it was a regular stop. One Sunday, I went to the museum with a young struggling American writer named Peter Stone, who also lived in Paris. While we were walking around, Peter said, "I wonder what the record is for going through the Louvre."

"You mean taking in everything?"

"No, just looking at the three things everybody comes to see – the Winged Victory, the Mona Lisa and the Venus de Milo. It's no secret that many tourists whiz through glancing at the three works of art, and then go out shopping again. What do you think the record for doing that is?"

I pretended to look in a guidebook, and said, "It says here that the track record for the Louvre is six minutes and twelve seconds. It is held by a man known as the Swedish Cannonball, who, paced by his Welsh wife, did it on November 23, 1937."

"Let's try to beat it," Peter said.

"No one can break a six-minute Louvre," I declared.

"That's what people said about the four-minute mile," Peter replied.

We had nothing to lose, so the following Sunday Peter showed up, and I made a show of firing of a starting pistol. He dashed in around the Venus de Milo, then up the stairs past the Winged Victory, down to the Mona Lisa – and you always have to say something when you look at the Mona Lisa, and Peter said, "I know the guy who has the original." Peter than dashed out into a waiting taxi. I timed him at five minutes and fifty-six seconds. That record still stands.

Years later, the Louvre hired I.M. Pei to build an entrance in the form of a glass pyramid, which makes it impossible for a tourist to enter in less than three hours, thus preventing anyone from breaking the old record."

No, it does not take that long to enter the Louvre. Yes, the old record still stands.

A Little-Known Gem

"Crushing display of showy wealth."

Emile Zola

Everyone but everyone has been to the Louvre. Almost everyone has been to musée d'Orsay. Yet few even know of the musée Jacquemart-André. The comment of Emile Zola, the French writer on the sumptuous Parisian mansion of Edouard André and Nélie Jacquemart built late in the nineteenth century is all that and more. It is an enchanting and dazzling architectural gem.

Once again the vision of Napoleon III and the genius of Baron Haussmann combined to extend the aristocratic residential quartiers of *la rive droite* (the 6th and the 7th *arrondissements*) to the newly-developed areas of the 8th. The new road system radiating from l'Étoile became part of the Napoleonic legend. Leading Parisian political and financial figures constructed palatial residences along these broad avenues. The inhabitants of these sumptuous mansions were known as *Napoléonides* to use the expression of the day. A large number of the owners of the opulent buildings were members of the imperial aristocracy. It was a matter of social prestige as the opening of each new mansion became a major Parisian social event.

In 1868, Edouard André bought the property at 158 Boulevard Haussmann for his future home and construction was completed in 1875. The project was assigned to a popular architect of the day, Henri Parent. He created an aristocratic residence in a modern city; not simply reviving past styles but incorporating a contemporary lifestyle. The building is one of the finest examples of Napoleon III empire architecture – a harmonious symmetrical façade in pure classical style. The location of the building itself is unique. It stands on elevated ground and thus the front elevation is visible to all passing by. The entrance to the mansion is through a gate that follows a ramp into a driveway and an inner courtyard facing the inner façade of the building. A stone and cast iron porch greeted people as another gate at the other end of the driveway saw them out. Moving partition walls operated by hydraulic jacks concealed in the basement allowed for small intimate gatherings as well as grand balls.

The *piéce de résistance* is the innovative and magnificent staircase. At the far end of the salons, the monumental stairway occupies a small space set against the wall. A tightly-knit double 'S'-shaped staircase in intricate black and gold wrought-iron railings soars to the upper floor. Parent's creativity bore fruit in this masterpiece after he was not selected for the design of the new opera house. His rival, Charles Garnier won that prestigious honour. Garnier's opera house and its stairway are architectural landmarks. Private rooms are located upstairs and the public salons are at ground floor level at the musée Jacquemart-André. The private mansion was hailed the day after it was inaugurated. "The press unanimously applauded the residence as an unrivalled masterpiece." The *International Herald* Tribune has attributed French style to the following : "Elegance is achieved through simplicity, discretion, a touch of eccentricity and a respect for history ... Atmospheric rather than correct, not so much decoration as personal expression." That just about sums it up.

Edouard Andre, the son of a Protestant banker and heir to a vast fortune was a member of Napoleon III's imperial guards. Further advancement in a military career was closed to him due to his poor health. Materially endowed, he became a patron of the arts and an avid art collector. In 1881, he married Nélie Jacquemart, a Catholic artist from a middle-class family. The union of different backgrounds resulted in an extraordinary union of a passion for the arts. Edouard André died in 1894 and Nélie Jacquemart in 1912. They had no children. Upon her death, she bequeathed their superb mansion and its priceless contents to the Institut de France. After three years of extensive renovation and restoration work in the early 1990s, the musée Jacquemart-André reopened to the public.

So armed with an audio-guide, I started the tour. The autumn day I visited the museum, there was hardly anyone around. In a short while, I realised I was often the only one in a room. One could, almost, imagine being an occupant of such exquisite surroundings. A perfectly polished parquet floor, warm and inviting wall-colours, non-intimidating décor and non-intimidating-sized rooms, every priceless item well-placed and the furniture and furnishings 'all-just-so-right', creates a luxurious yet cosy ambience. One can imagine people actually living here.

In an article, 'All That Glittered' by Dominick Dunne in an issue of Vanity Fair, Dunne wrote about the auction sale of the contents of the Château de Groussay near Paris. In his visit to the Château, he felt as I did on my visit to the musée Jacquemart-André. He wrote, "Rarely have the sensations of 'grand' and 'cosy' been so artfully united. The place is a masterpiece of comfort, inviting you to linger in each room, sit in all the chairs (hardly) and stare at the pictures on the walls, hung one above the other from floor to ceiling ..."

The immense collection of works of art is testimony to the husband and wife joint venture. Here are paintings by Rembrandt, Van Dyck, Watteau, Fragonard, Prud'hon, Joshua Reynolds, Delacroix, Ingres and others; Greek and Roman sculptures; Limoges porcelain; and Italian Renaissance works of art by Boticelli, Bellini, Donatello, Tiepolo and others. A smoking-room is filled with oriental pieces of art – Chinese porcelain jars and furniture, Korean cloisonné enamel urns, Moroccan tables, a mosque enamel lamp. Not all purchases at the time were recognised works. Many were simply buys of a 'good eye' – like all good collectors – and today, are treasures.

The famed ceiling fresco by the Italian artist Tiepolo adorning the upper section of the main staircase of the musee Jacquemart-André was acquired by the French connoisseurs of Italian art in 1894. They bought the fresco for 30,000 Italian liras, a handsome sum in the day. It had originally adorned the villa Contarini in Venice. The fresco by Tiepolo depicts Henri III being received at the villa Contarini. Another Tiepolo fresco graces the ceiling of the present-day café Jacquemart-André. The Louvre Museum held a lecture in early 1999 on the restoration of these frescoes of Giambattista Tiepolo that had been executed in 1745. These two frescoes are the only works of the master artist in France.

The Institut de France rents the venue for 'prestigious cocktails and receptions'. We had the good fortune to be invited to such a reception at the musée Jacquemart-André. Not often do Commerce and Arts collaborate so successfully. We were invited for an evening of 'amusements of the eighteenth century'. (The building itself was only built late in the nineteenth century – but never mind). As we entered the portico, there were men and women dressed in period costumes welcoming us. Inside, a more admirable setting cannot be imagined. The warmth and richness of the décor was illuminated by the many candelabra and chandeliers. A bewigged violin player here and an imperial couple danced there. There was gaiety and glamour all around. We were transported to another century – a period of *la finesse et la beauté*. It was a magical evening. The French spirit includes a love of the decorative arts and a passion for the art of living. The fruit of such a spirit can be found at the musée Jacquemart-André.

It was an American, Henry James in *Parisian Sketches* who remarked, "The French have always flattered themselves that they gave gone further in the art of living, in what they call *l'entente de la vie*, than any other people."

Egyptomania

"For a French person, nothing that is Egyptian should appear strange – and the reverse is without doubt equally true."

Jean Leclant, Egyptologist and Permanent Secretary of the French Academy of Literature

If Paris has perennially been a source of fascination for foreigners, that ardour has been reciprocated by Parisians for other cultures. The year 1998 was the year of Egypt in Paris. Two hundred years (1798-1998) of cultural and scientific co-operation between Egypt and France were celebrated under the title '*La France-Egypte Horizons Partagés*' ('Shared Horizons'). The celebration marked the two centuries since the Napoleonic expedition to Egypt in 1798. Napoleon exclaimed, "Remember that from the top of these monuments, you are seeing forty centuries." This declaration was made at the French victory over the Mamlukes at the Battle of the Pyramids and was the beginning of France's never-ending Egyptomania.

I too have a keen interest in the culture of ancient Egypt. I first visited Egypt in 1959, following the completion of my father's posting in Paris. En route to Bangkok, the ocean liner stopped at Port Said on the Suez Canal and on a trip to Cairo, I saw for the first time the Wonder of Wonders, the Pyramids. The next visit was some ten years later in 1969 when we stopped in Cairo while moving from Dar-es-Salaam, Tanzania to Beirut. My husband and I were posted to Cairo from 1993 to 1996, before moving to Paris. I there succumbed to the global passion for the Pharaonic civilisation.

The Parisians' love for the Egyptian civilisation is deep and it is real. Its strength was demonstrated in the incredible range of activities presented in their '*Horizons Partagés*'. The year of Egypt in Paris saw Egyptomania reach a peak. It appears that the more Parisians (and others) come to know, the more they are fascinated. Discoveries are being made all the time and as knowledge increases, the passion grows even more. It is an endless source of discoveries and enthralment. This is the strange and eternal magic of Egypt.

What is the root of the unending fascination, the universal admiration for the valley of the Nile? Jean Leclant in an article '*La Fascination de l'éternité*' in *Le Figaro* on the opening of the expanded department of Egyptian antiquities at Louvre writes, "Egyptomania, Egyptophile, Egyptology – all these nuances of expression converge towards the same theme: the immense prestige of the Pharaonic culture. The beauty of the works is certainly stunning: richness of materials, perfection of techniques, the charm of forms and colours, the multiple variations of the grandeur of the gods and the kings but also of the surprising vivacity of scenes from daily life."

Ancient Egyptians also produced art and architecture not for self-expression, in the artist's sense; but for self-perpetuation into eternity. Aesthetic values were not meant for this world but for the next – a triumph over death and the certainty of eternity. And with this objective, the legacy of the ancient Egyptians has truly become eternal. The Egyptian rooms at any museum in the world are the most visited by the young and not-so-young. Egyptology is as fascinating and potent today as it was when I first came across pyramids, pharaohs, mummies, the Nile, the Valley of Kings and the Valley of Queens, Tutankhamun ... in history at school. Time has not lessened its magic. As I write this, I am told that my niece and nephew aged six and four, in a visit to the New York Metropolitan Museum were fascinated by the Egyptian department of antiquities. She is into hieroglyphics and creating her own and he has a keen interest in mummies. *Plus ça change, plus c'est la même chose.*

The department of Egyptian antiquities, the oldest at the Louvre was founded in 1826 by Jean-Francois Champollion. He had deciphered the Egyptian hieroglyphics on the Rosetta Stone in 1822. As a French officer of the Egyptian army, he discovered a stele in black basalt stone that had engraved on it inscriptions in three scripts and they appeared to be the same text. Reading the Greek inscription, Champollion was able to translate the Demotic writings, the ancient Egyptian language and subsequently deciphered the up-to-now secret hieroglyphic writings of the Pharoahs. He discovered that hieroglyphics were phonetic and ideographic (idea of an object without naming it). He tested his deciphering from Alexandria to Abu Simbel and it worked. Charles X signed an edict for the creation of a Division of Egyptian Monuments within the Royal Museum of the Louvre in 1826. Champollion, the father of French Egyptology was the first curator of the Division of Egyptian antiquities. He is buried in the Père Lachaise cemetery in Paris under an Egyptian monument.

The second key person in the French involvement in Egyptology was Auguste Mariette, a professor at Boulogne who was sent by the Louvre to Egypt in 1850 to purchase some papyrus. He succumbed to the irresistible temptation of archaeological excavations. He discovered at Saqqara, the Serapeum – burial grounds of the Apis bulls. This was the beginning of French archaeological work in Egypt. He worked hard to stem the illegal export of Egyptian antiquities and is one of the founding fathers of the Cairo Museum and the Egyptian Antiquities Organisation (EAO), a central body to coordinate and monitor archaeology. Mariette accompanied Empress Eugenie to the opening ceremonies of the Suez Canal. In a recent book, *L'Egypte Ancienne: Sauvée des Sables* ('Ancient Egypt: Saved by the Sands'), Gilles Lambert points out that it was Mariette who contributed early to the Egyptian fever among Parisians by creating the Egyptian park at the Universal Exposition in Paris in 1867. Mariette is the writer of the libretto, 'Aida'. The celebrated opera set in Egypt was composed by the Italian Guiseppe Verdi. Mariette also designed the costumes, the sets and set guidelines for the direction of the opera.

The third giant of Franco-Egyptian archaeology is Gaston Maspero. In 1880, he founded L'Institut Français d'Archaéologie Orientale (IFAO). It initiated extensive excavations at Deir el-Bahari, the Pyramids at Giza, the temple at Luxor and the identification of the mummy of Ramses II. Ramses the Great even travelled to Paris for a 'check-up' and restoration work on his mummified remains at the Louvre.

Any wish to study hieroglyphics? Well, Paris has something to offer everyone. 'Kheops' offers from October to June every year for 2,800 francs, an intensive course on hieroglyphics. Some six hundred apprentice-scribers are enrolled annually. The most dedicated of them obtain a certificate in the language of Egyptology following a study-period of three years. Some fifteen professors, the majority of them young Egyptologists from the Louvre school teach aspiring language students the meaning of picture-drawings.

The halls hosting the Egyptian antiquities closed for a period of two years and reopened in December 1997. The floor space allocated to the highly popular department increased two-fold with 4,500 square metres now at its disposal. More than a thousand pieces of artwork in reserve were put on display. Costing? A mere 43 million francs. It is worth every franc. Given the crowds, the financial investment should be recovered in no time. I was told that in order to avoid the long queues, we should be there at the time the doors of the Louvre open in the morning at 9 a.m. We were there at 10 a.m. and a good portion of the masses had preceded us. We joined the invasion of Egypt.

The invasion of the Louvre is via Egypt. The entrance to the Louvre is through the Glass Pyramid. An ancient Egyptian form, the Pyramid screens almost every visitor. It forms the entrance to the 'new' Louvre. The Glass Pyramid is also symbolically and factually the umbrella of the immense new underground space of the 'new' Louvre.

In its expansion, the new department has revolutionised presentation of its collection. Traditionally, artifacts on display are arranged chronologically – in historical order – usually following the reign of successive rulers. This was the practice at the Louvre and is the general routine at most museums both sides of the Atlantic. A conceptually advanced approach has split the Egyptian collection. On the ground floor, in nineteen halls, a thematic presentation of art history covers the daily life of ancient Egyptians; covering diverse areas such as agriculture, clothes, furniture, habitat, writing, death, gods, mummies, religion, temples ... Upstairs, over eleven halls is a chronological presentation of some of the finest relics of the ancient civilisation. According to Christiane Ziegler, head curator of the department of Egyptian antiquities, "Today's presentation policy hopes to meet the demands of a very faithful and broad public, ranging from the neophyte to the connoisseur, from the university professor to the traveller making preparations for a cruise down the Nile, not forgetting the thousands of children drawn by the demands of school curricula and the lure of mystery…".

Christian Jacq, the incredibly prolific and immensely popular French novelist has published more than sixty essays and novels on Egypt. He selected 'top ten' masterpieces of the empire on the Nile at the expanded department of Egyptian antiquities at the Louvre with great difficulty. He said, "I have chosen ten objects – an impossible choice truly speaking – in order to evoke many fundamental dimensions of a civilisation that is our spiritual mother."

Number One is the magnificent Sphinx of the Crypt found at Tanis in the Nile Delta some 2600 BC. Number Two is the fine stele of the serpent king found at Abydos some 300 BC. It shows a falcon perched on a rectangle in which the serpent hovers over an edifice. Number Three is a massive sculpture of a seated Amon with the Pharaoh Tutankhamun seated between Amon's legs in a symbol of protection. Amon is a cosmic deity and king of the gods. He is usually depicted as a man wearing a head-dress adorned with two tall fathers. He can also be shown as a man with a ram's head or as a ram. The Fourth selection is a detailed bas-relief of Sethi I and Hathor, the goddess of love and joy, music and dance. She is represented as a woman wearing a head-dress with a cow's horns encircling a solar disc. It was found in the Valley of the Kings dated 1200 BC. The Fifth choice is a superb bronze statuette of Karomame, the grand priestess to the god Amon. It was found at Thebes dated 900 BC. Champollion, the discoverer wrote on December 27, 1829, "It is this which I bring to Louvre, the most beautiful bronze that has ever been discovered in Egypt." Jacq's Sixth preference is for a small stele in brilliant colours in wood also dating some 900 BC. It depicts an Egyptian woman of the day. Number Seven is an impressive statue of a man of letters, a scribe seated cross-legged. It was discovered in Saqqara near the Giza Pyramids dated 2500 BC. The Eighth wonder is a stele found at Abydos in 2030 BC. Covered in hieroglyphics, it speaks of the art and science of spirituality. His Ninth choice is the mammoth sarcophagus in rose granite of Ramses III, found in his tomb in the Valley of the Kings in Upper Egypt. Finally, Number 10 is the famous Zodiac of Dendera dedicated to the goddess Hathor from the Greco-Roman era, first century BC. Amongst the zodiac signs, writings and symbols speak of the Pharaoh who lives eternally in the sky in the form of a star.

Other museums with a rich collection of Egyptian antiquities are museums in Cairo, London, Berlin, New York and Turin. There is an Egyptian *piéce de resistance* in each of the above international museums. Cairo has the spell-binding mega-discovery by Howard Carter of the tomb of Tutankhamun. The British Museum in London possesses the Rosetta stone from the Ptolemaic period. The breathtaking beauty of Nefertiti can be seen in Berlin. The pride of the Egyptian department at the Metropolitan Museum in New York is the totally reconstructed – stone-by-stone – temple of Dendera. The temple was saved from the engulfing waters of Lake Nasser upon the building of the Aswan Dam. Turin is the host of a pair of extremely well-reserved and poignant mummies – the mummies of the architect Kha and his wife and their worldly belongings that were found in a tomb in Deir el-Medina in Upper Egypt. Except for the Egyptian collection in Turin, I have had the good fortune of seeing all the other precious Pharaonic artefacts.

Following his return from the successful Italian campaign in 1797, Napoleon Bonaparte set out for Egypt in 1798. This time his army was accompanied by one hundred and fifty *savants* (scholars); archaeologists, architects, artists, astronomers, botanists, chemists, doctors, engineers, geographers, historians, mathematicians, musicians, pharmacists, writers ... A motley of hard-nosed French military campaigners, ivory-tower academicians and field scientists formed the Napoleonic expedition to Egypt. Napoleon had just been elected to l'Academie and he took along with him some of his new colleagues. He had just turned thirty. Many of the others were twice his age and the youngest was just fifteen. Sailing from Toulon, were two hundred sailors, forty thousand soldiers, scientific instruments and amongst other things, a printing press. The destination remained unknown and only divulged when approaching the island of Malta. It was then proclaimed that the first country to be sighted was founded by Alexander. And so did the Napoleonic expedition set foot on the legendary land of the Pharaohs.

The work of the *savants* during the Egyptian campaign of three years resulted in an extraordinary repository of documents and research. The monumental '*Description de l'Égypte*' is the fruit of their labour. The publishing of this landmark masterpiece of research occupied first the French imperial and then the royal printers for a quarter of a century. The illustrations and text are infinitely detailed, ranging from the very fine drawings of the temples at Karnak, to the citadel of Cairo, to the often desolate and other times fertile landscape along the Nile, to the intensive studies of the flora and fauna of Egypt.

The most distinguished and adventurous of the *savants* who accompanied Napoleon Bonaparte was Dominique V. Denon. His splendid and classic book *Voyage dans le Base et le Haute Égypte* (Travels in Lower and Upper Egypt) was published in 1802. The book established him as an Egyptologist and an artist. *The Discovery of the Nile* by Gianni Guidalipi carries detailed and evocative drawings by Denon. Denon later became the director of museums in France. One of the three wings of the Louvre Museum bears his name.

One of the earliest Egyptian Francophiles was strangely enough, Mohammed Ali Pasha, the Ottoman general of Turkish-Albanian origin who was despatched to Égypt by Selim III to battle Napoleon's army. Driven by the same need for domination; energetic, ambitious and intelligent as his foe; Mohammed Ali Pasha has been titled '*Le Dernier Pasha*' (The Last Pasha) by the French author Gilbert Sinoue. Thirty centuries after the greatest of great pharaohs Ramses II, Egypt was once again an empire, stretching from the Persian Gulf to the deserts of Libya and Sudan and to the Mediterranean Sea. He even sent Egyptian scholars for further studies to Paris in 1826. The ultimate gesture? The Pharaonic obelisk that Mohammed Ali Pasha offered to France in 1830. The French reciprocated the most generous of gestures by placing it in 1836, in the most beautiful heart of Paris, la Place de la Concorde.

On the other hand, David Roberts, the intrepid traveller, landscape painter and lithographer of the Middle East, "deplored this pillage, and would probably have been pleased to hear that the French government officially renounced its right to ownership of the second obelisk (in front of the temple of Amun in Luxor) in 1980", notes Fabio Bourbon in *Egypt: Yesterday and Today – Lithographs and Diaries* by David Roberts.

One hundred and sixty-eight years later, the French continue to lavish attention on the slender monument. In

May 1998, during the year-long celebration of '*La France-Égypte Horizons Partagés*', the coned-tip of the obelisk was crowned with two thousand leaves of gold that weigh six hundred kilos. The brilliance of the gold cone glimmers in the sun and radiates down les Champs-Elysées and around la Place de la Concorde. The 'crown of gold' has restored the obelisk to its original grandeur that it had lost some 2400 BC. Once upon a time, the cone at the top had been covered in gold but not surprisingly it went missing down the ages. The 'crown of gold' has been called the symbol cementing Franco-Egyptian relations. It is no exaggeration, for there stands in all its glory – the most overt symbol of the ties. The gold capping of the obelisk had always been the dream of the French father of Egyptology, Champollion. The dream came true and the love affair continues.

Ferdinand de Lesseps was the French engineer behind the Suez Canal. At its opening in 1869, Empress Eugenie of France inaugurated with Khedive Ismail of Egypt, the Canal. The engineering feat furthered Occidental and Oriental commercial and other ties. Two palaces with rich interiors, presently five star hotels in Cairo; the Marriott Hotel on the Zamalek island along the Nile and the Mena House Oberoi beside the Pyramids at Giza were built for the imperial visit to Egypt. Egypt remains one of the foremost destinations of French tourists. *La langue Francaise* can be heard inside the Giza Pyramids anywhere in the Khan-e-Khalili *souk* (bazaar) in Cairo, on the cruise down the Nile from Luxor to Axwan and even deep down a royal tomb in the Valley of the Kings and the Valley of the Queens in Luxor.

Egyptology and French cooperation is as extensive today as it was in the nineteenth century. Commerce continues to maintain close links with ancient Egypt. A major sponsor of the cooperation is the Fondation Electricité de France (EDF). The sponsorship of EDF towards Egyptian archaeology started in 1984, when the 'Orient', flagship of France's first expedition to Egypt sunk by the English admiral, Horatio Nelson, was discovered off Aboukir in the Mediterranean. EDF offered its technical expertise to salvage objects located around the wreck. In 1986, a canon from the 'Patriote', another French ship that sank off Alexandria underwent similar EDF expertise. The French take care of their past.

A range of state-of-the-art engineering technology has been put to use in the pursuit of greater knowledge of ancient Egypt. The panoply of techniques includes electrolysis, geographic surveying, anastylosis software. The last item "enables them to manipulate the different fragments on a computer screen and to put forth various hypotheses for its reconstruction unimpeded by the real weight (several tons each of these fragments)," explains an article on Egyptology and Patronage in 'Egyptian Art at the Louvre'. The Ptolemaic colossus found in the waters off Alexandria has been subject to such computer-generated images. Two French archaeologists had a hypothesis about the existence of an unknown cavity within the Pyramid of Cheops at Giza. EDF resorted "to the microgravimetry it uses to study the ground beneath its future industrial plants. This technique measures the tiniest variations of gravity and thus detects the presence of possible cavities. The experiment undertaken at Giza was a world premiére, since this technique had never been tried on a building before ... enabled us to pinpoint the internal structure of the pyramids and to establish through our calculations, the existence of unknown cavities." Phenomenal. The 'new' can be so brilliantly used to understand the 'old'.

At Karnak for the temple of Amon, computer-aided designs are producing computer-generated images of the temple at different styles of its existence and in collaboration with Egyptologists recreating its past. The oldest vestiges found on the site date back to twenty centuries BC! Artificial Intelligence (AI) was suggested by EDG engineers for the reassembling of *talatat* (engraved and painted sandstone blocks) found scattered in bits and pieces. Like a jigsaw puzzle, they were reassembled by AI and corroborated by Egyptologists.

Extensive excavations are being conducted at Tanis near the Nile Delta and at Saqqara near Cairo. While Egyptian and French archaeologists were searching for the two pyramids of the wives of Pepy I at Saqqara, EDF proposed, "the simultaneous use of several geophysical surveying techniques so as to compare results: electromagnetism, short-line electric surroundings, low frequency monitoring, measuring variations in the earth's magnetic field with a protonic magnotemeter." It yielded success. As a bonus treat, tombs of his other wives whose existence were hereto unknown, were also found. Similar excavations at Tanis have yielded impressive vestiges of colossal statues and established the presence of Tanis as the New Kingdom's northern equivalence to Thebes (Luxor) in the south.

Since 1996, EDF has been assisting the extraordinary underwater excavations headed by Jean-Yves Empereur, the director of the Centre of Alexandrian Studies in collaboration with the renamed French Institute of Ancient Near Eastern Archaeology (IFAO). This is the same body founded by Maspero in 1880. In the waters lapping the ancient city of Alexandria, Empereur has moved marine archaeology to new depths. Armed with the latest gadgets and techniques, Empereur and his team discovered a colossus of the Ptolemaic period dating 300 BC in the Mediterranean Sea. They believe this colossus of Ptolemy II weighing twenty-three tons, the head alone weighs more than thirteen tons and an arm weighs seven hundred kilos, is one of the pair of three couples of Ptolemaic rulers who supported the super-structure that is known as the Lighthouse of Alexandria, one of the Seven Wonders of the World. It disappeared in the course of the fourteenth century as a result of a series of earthquakes. And so long lay the ruins embedded in the Mediterranean waters till modern technology retrieved them. The reconstructed colossus of Ptolemy II was a star of the Franco-Egyptian year. He made the cover of almost every magazine devoted to the celebrations. Guarding the front façade of Le Petit Palais, the Ptolemaic colossus loomed over us while welcoming us to one of the major events of '*La France-Egypte Horizon Partagés*', '*La Gloire d'Alexandrie*' exhibition.

Other ongoing underwater explorations and excavations include vestiges of the ancient port of Alexandria, the palace of Cleopatra and literally a sea of ancient Egyptian artefacts await identification. There is talk by the Egyptian authorities of creating an underwater museum so that these centuries-old remains can rest in peace and yet also benefit posterity. Howard Carter and Lord Carnavon discovered in 1922, the hereto unopened tomb of Tutankhamun in the Valley of the Kings in Upper Egypt and made the greatest archaeological discovery of the twentieth century. Seventy-five years later, a French archaeologist, Alain Zivie and his team found the tomb of 'Maya', Tutankhamun's wet-nurse. Her tomb was discovered in Saqqara in Northern Egypt. It raises questions about the origins of Tutankhamun and as always adds further mystery to an entity already captivating. Zivie has been working on this site for seventeen years. Jean Leclant is also working here on the study of pyramids in various texts. Also at Saqqara, the ninety-five- year-old Jean-Philippe Lauer has devoted his entire life to the reconstruction of a funeral complex.

The merger of old objects and new technology keeps Egyptology up-front and yields surprises regularly. The hitherto unknown becomes known, maybe partially known; however, the mysterious void is somehow routinely pierced and a little more knowledge further coaxes and incites further the passion. The never-ending supply of fascination and mystery perpetuates the eternal mania. This mania also prompts the necessary funding required for lengthy archaeological research work. Not every dig yields headlines, yet investment in Egyptology appears to yield returns; judging from the evidence of global Egyptomania. If I was thirty years younger, I would have studied Egyptology and followed in the shadow of, and not the footsteps of Egyptologists who have contributed to the most current of past civilisations.

In the February 1998 issue of *Paris Capitale*, the magazine covers the crossroads of Egypt in Paris under a clever article titled, '*Sur les Traces de Pharaohs: Par Isis*!' ('On the Trial of the Pharaohs: By Isis!'). Isis is the goddess that watched over the process of mummification and protected the mummy. Paris has found something in common even with a key deity of ancient Egypt!

The trilogy of obelisks, pyramids and sphinxes abound in the city of Paris as demonstrated in a fascinating exhibition organised by the Mayor of the Tenth *arrondissement* and the musée de la Légion de'Honneur in April-May 1998.

Next time you are in Paris, take a look around; here is an obelisk as the centre-piece of a square, there are a pair of sphinxes guarding the entrance to a *hôtel particulier* and here is a gate decorated with hieroglyphics – excluding two of Paris' ultimate symbols – the Glass Pyramid at Louvre and the obelisk at Place de la Concorde.

In a brilliant piece of research, *Paris Capitale* has meticulously located at least one piece of evidence of the influence of Egypt on Parisian architecture in each and every one of the twenty *arrondissements* in Paris. Incredible but true. The first *arrondissement* possesses the maximum. There are listed eight venues that portray some Egyptian influence, with the Louvre having the lion's share. The second *arrondissement* lists two and includes the House of Egypt at 2, place du Caire. The third *arrondissement* has three buildings including the Picasso Museum that displays sphinxes in its courtyard. The fourth *arrondissement* also has two sites where sphinxes have been constructed. The fifth *arrondissement* hosts a painting of the island of Philae at Sorbonne University. Philae, a gem of an island that we have visited, was moved to higher ground during the massive relocation of temples by UNESCO in the 1970s. A statue of Champollion by Frédéric-Auguste Bartholdi stands in the main courtyard of the College de France. The sixth *arrondissement* has listed six venues including a frieze with hieroglyphics at L'Institut d'art et de'archéologie. At the seventh *arrondissement*, one can see seven listed venues including a pyramid mausoleum at les Invalides and a bronze sculpture l'Afrique made in 1878 at musee d'Orsay. In the eighth *arrondissement*, there is the pyramid in the Parc Monceau built in 1779, the battles of Aboukir and Alexandria are listed on the Arc de Triomphe and any number of artefacts are to be found at le Grand Palais. The ninth *arrondissement* hosts an obelisk in the courtyard of the Paris Opera and a café-restaurant, Le Pharaon opened in 1938 and it was redecorated in 1993. The tenth *arrondissement* has listed four buildings including Cinéma Louxor.

There is a *boulangerie* at 149 boulevard de Charonne that displays an Egyptian frieze in the Eleventh *arrondissement.* The twelfth *arrondissement* boasts two obelisk columns in the Bois de Vincennes. The thirteenth *arrondissement* gives us three obelisks. The fourteenth *arrondissement* provides us with the Montparnasse cemetery in which there are any number of Egyptian influenced tomb-designs as there are at the Montmartre cemetery in the eighteenth *arrondissement.* A 1996 wall-painting of an Egyptian hippopotamus can be found in the fifteenth *arrondissement.* Our sixteenth *arrondissement* has listed four sites; a pair of sphinxes can be found in the Bagatelle *parc* of the Bois de Boulogne, two more sphinxes guard the musée Marmottan that houses some Impressionist paintings, particularly, a large collection of Claude Monet's paintings including the mega-canvasses of his 'Water-lilies.' Musée Blazac also has sphinxes in its garden. Place d'Auteuil erected an obelisk to the memory of Chancellor d'Aguesseau in 1753.

Even hi-tech audio entertainment complexes have adopted Egyptomania. The FNAC Etoile in the Seventeenth *arrondissement* has an Egyptian column in the centre of its escalators. The eighteenth *arrondissement* in addition to the Montmartre cemetery, boasts two more places depicting Egypt. The nineteenth *arrondissement* hosts columns on rue de Crimee and a lion-fountain at the Grande Halle de la Villette. Finally, in the twentieth *arrondissement*, there are once again numerous tombs with Egyptian designs at the Pére-Lachaise cemetery. All this is ample evidence of an Egyptian presence in Paris that is both historical and contemporary.

The 1998 Year of Egypt in Paris would be incomplete without covering some of the amazing number of exhibitions, films, seminars put forth in order to ignite a new generation and further stoke the enthusiasm of an older generation for Egyptomania. '*Il y a 200 ans … les savants en Égypte*' ('Two hundred years ago … the scholars in Egypt') was the name of the exhibition at the musée Nationale d'Historie Naturelle. It retraced the voyage of the scholars who accompanied Napoleon I on his Egyptian campaign from 1798 to 1801 and their intellectual and human adventure in Égypt. One write-up asks, "Who invented Indiana Jones? Spielberg? No. Napoleon!"

'*Photographies d'Égypte*' at musee d'Orsay displayed some fifty prints of photographs taken in the 1850s in Egypt. '*Visions d'Égypte*' at l'Institut du Monde Arabe (Institute of the Arab World) and Centre Pompidou screened for children a series of Egyptian documentaries, cartoons, films. '*L'Égypte, mille et une images*' ('Egypt, thousand and one images') at l'Institut du Monde Arabe, screened films on Egypt and films by Egyptian directors, the most famous in France being Youssef Chahine who has been recognised by the Cannes Film Festial. '*L'Egypte Fatimid: son art et son histoire*' was a lecture presented at the Fondation Singer-Polignac. '*Les Fatimides: la fascination de l'Orient*' at l'Institut du Monde Arabe organised an exhibition for the first time in Paris of the immense variety and history of Fatimid works of art (969-1171). '*Malmaison et l'Égypte*' presented the strong influence of Egypt on Parisian architecture, décor, furniture and fashion during Napoleon I and Josephine's reign. Empress Josephine shared his passion for all things Egyptian.

The Louvre Museum presented an exhibition on the 'Mummies of Roman Egypt and their Adornments'.

L'Hôtel Scribe was built in 1860 during Napoleon III's reign by the Peréire banking brothers who helped finance the construction of the Suez Canal. Napoleon following his return from Egypt cultivated Egypt in dress and décor. Turbans, harem pants and cashmere shawls were à *la mode.* During 1998, l'Hôtel Scribe hosted lectures, food festivals, musical *soirées*, a photographic exhibition – all, most naturally, on Egypt. At the Mona Bismarck Foundation, one hundred and fifty photographs dating from 1948 to 1998 document the fathomless fascination that Egypt holds for the West. From Paris to Boston, from London to Warsaw – the aesthetics of Egypt have influenced the West. Public buildings, private homes, parks, libraries, factories, Masonic temples, cinemas, restaurants, monuments, casinos, funeral décor, interior décor … Egyptomania remains a phenomenon five thousand years on.

The year that celebrated '*La France-Egypte Horizons Partagés*' was a monumental conception and event. Egypt, like Paris was not created in a day. Human endeavour has successfully combined two rich cultures into a harmonious blend of creativity.

Stadium of France

"There is nothing better than what the French do well, and nothing worse than what they do badly."

Pope Benedict XIV

"Gleaming with lights on a winter's day at dusk, the gigantic national stadium that France has built for the 1998 World Cup soccer tournament looks like an ocean liner about to glide out to sea. The elliptical roof of metal and glass, suspended from 18 soaring steel masts, floats above the cityscape between Montmartre to the south and the ancient cathedral of Saint-Denis to the north – so ethereal that it is difficult to imagine it covers an area as large as the Place de la Concorde in Paris," writes the *International Herald Tribune* on the eve of opening of Le Stade de France (The Stadium of France) on January 28, 1998; built for La Coupe Mondiale 98 extravaganza due to start on June 10, 1998.

President Jacques Chirac of France accompanied by Prime Minister José Maria Aznar of Spain graced the opening friendly match between France and Spain. Happily for France, the inaugural match ended in a score of France 1 and Spain 0. The *International Herald Tribune* had headlined one of its on-the-eve articles, 'France Despearately Needs a Scorer to Inaugurate Its Stadium.' The hero of the match was Zinedine Zidane who scored the victorious goal. According to *Le Figaro* headlines, "The Blues inaugurated the Stadium of France by a Success against Spain: A Victory for History."

"The mission of the architects, Costantini, Macary, Regembal and Zublena was to create a dramatic public space calling to mind the stadiums of the ancient world. It is intended to be more than a sports stadium: a civic centre as the Colosseum was to Rome," notes the *International Herald Tribune.* "It has everything except the gladiators," says a spokesman. Today's entertainers, in the form of the ageing British Rolling Stones appeared in concert in 1998 as well as Johnny Halliday, the French ageing rock n'roller. Celine Dion the mega-voice of the 90s performed in 1999.

Le Stade France has a seating capacity of 80,000, making it the largest in France. The cost is put at a phenomenal $445 million. France continues its endeavours in *Les Grands Travaux* that so characterises architectural projects particularly, in Paris. "Its elliptical grandeur is a brilliant monument to French ambition ... The stadium is part of a national tradition of building big for the greater glory of France, no matter what the cost. Even before the foot first touches the ball, Le Stade seems certain to become a cultural and architectural success," notes the *International Herald Tribune.* Other *Grands Travaux* launched by the late President Francois Mitterand include the soaring Grande Arche de la Defénse, the massive Bastille Opera, the Bibliothéque Nationale de France in the form of four L-shaped glass towers and the expanded and renovated Louvre Museum.

The opening game of the World Cup 1998 on June 10, 1998 is between Brazil and Scotland.

Extra-terrestrial Extravaganza

"A country where the impossible always happens and the inevitable never does."

Anon

On the evening and into the night of June 9, 1998; Ho, Mousa, Pablo and Romeo lumbered into la Place de la Concorde in the heart of Paris creating a supernatural scenario – a fantasy from science-fiction. The six-floor high (420 metres high) four giants represent the four participating continents of Asia, Africa, Americas and Europe in the last global mega-sports event of the twentieth century – La Coupe Mondiale 98, the sixteenth football World Cup 1998 held in France from June 10 to July 12, 1998.

On the eve of the opening of the matches, Paris staged a spell-binding spectacle, an impression of being transported to another planet. Some 4,200 volunteers performed dances, acrobatics, processions to pulsating ethno music and the irresistible drum-beat of African sound, techno music and the heavy metal electronic sound. Witnessing the event was to embark on an extra-terrestrial voyage to the tune of world music, where Time became irrelevant – as one crossed between the Paris of the eighteenth, nineteenth and twentieth centuries – and then again into some indeterminate Time in the future.

There were Martians dressed in silver; there were scurrying mice; there were fishes on roller-blades; there were striding ostriches; there were walking baobabs and pine trees; there were mobile exotic plants. There were multitudes of children with footballs. There were celestial women dressed in fluid-like gowns by Yves Saint Laurent, *le grand haute couturier* who will also do a presentation with some three hundred models on the day of the final match on July 12, 1998.

Michel Platini, the French soccer legend and president of the World Cup organising committee had 2.4 billion francs ($ 400 million) at his disposal for the staging of La Coupe Mondiale 98. Jean-Pascal Levy-Trumet, the creator of the four giants, envisioned them as symbols of opening, ambassadors of the world population, reminders of fairy tales." The construction of the giants involved a balloon-like inflatable exterior which covered the internal mechanical structure. Jean-Batiste, the director of the extravaganza deserves accolades for the brilliance and vision of his design. Batiste was also the choreographer behind the two hundred year anniversary in 1989 of the French Revolution when he covered the famed les Champs-Elysées into its original site – a field of wheat sheaves.

The giants were to be found standing in Paris' most recognised venues. Ho, from Asia stood at Pont Neuf, Le Pont Neuf almost touches the Louvre Museum which Ho passed by on his slow march down the rue de Rivoli, the elegant-arcaded avenue of the nineteenth century and into la Place de la Concorde which was now transformed into the Square for the Encounter of the Giants. La Place de la Concorde, surely the most magical of any square in the world has as its centrepiece the obelisk of Ramses II of Egypt which was transported to Paris in the 1830s.

On the occasion of the World Cup 98, the obelisk was transformed into a model of the football trophy – the World Cup. We saw the obelisk being surrounded by scaffolding – a frame around which a plastic-like covering resulted in the creation of the gigantic golden-coloured

World Cup trophy. The metamorphoses of the obelisk commissioned by Ramses II some 3200 years ago would surely give him cause to turn in his sarcophagus. The transformation at the close of the twentieth century is an apt symbol of the harmony of humanity – a professed ideal of the World Cup.

The vast arena of la Place de la Concorde has played an important role in French history. It was commissioned by Louis XV and of course, carried his name – Place Louis XV. Following the French Revolution in 1789, it was renamed to symbolise the concord reached between the state and its people. Louis XVI and his Queen Marie Antoinette met their deaths at the guillotine at the site. Danton and Robespierre of the French Commune also shared the same fate in the 1790s.

Mousa, the giant representing Africa which had Cameroun, Morocco, Nigeria and Tunisia participating in the World Cup stood gloriously in the Champ de Mars, the open garden expanse behind the Eiffel Tower. Mousa slow marched along the Seine that rightfully can claim to be the site of the longest library in the world, due to the presence of the *bouquinistes.* These are the second-hand booksellers managing the green-boxed quay-side book-stalls who have been on site since the seventeenth century. The name, 'bouquinistes' is derived from *bouc* in French referring to the odour of leather and mouldy paper that emanated from the book containers.

The African giant, Mousa trotted past les Invalides best known as the final resting place of Napoleon and crossed the Seine at the magnificent Pont Alexander III, the most grandiose of all Parisian bridges. Pont Alexandre III commemorates Franco-Russian friendship. Four gold-painted superb sculptures grace the corners of the bridge. And so Mousa crossed into la Place de la Concorde.

Pablo, representing the Americas – Latin America and the United States of America stood in all his immense height in front of the majestic l'Arc de Triomphe facing the penultimate of paths – les Champs-Elysées. It was started by Napoleon in 1806 to commemorate his military victories and finished in 1836, long after his fall from power. Perhaps there was a message to be read in the placing of Pablo at this particular site. Les Champs-Elysées has traditionally welcomed winners and favourite sons – Napoleon en route to his final burial at les Invalides, Charles de Gaulle after the liberation of Paris in 1945, all Bastille day (14 July) celebration parades and all heads of states on official visits to Paris are honoured here. Were favourites and four-time winner Brazil being honoured?

Pablo passed Lido, the well-known Parisian floor-show, *C'est Magique* (It is magic), performed by the Bluebell Girls. He then went past the luxurious Louis Vuitton store, selling their legendary bags, suitcases and trunks. Royalty and stars have always been favoured clients. Today, one sees young Japanese and Korean women on buying sprees as if Louis Vuitton had no tomorrow. He also walked by the audio music mega-stores of FNAC and Virgin Megastores, a favourite place for music lovers, past the Rond Point with its fountains and seasonal floral displays and the Grand and Petit Palais built for the 1900 Paris exhibition. They are now venues for top-class, solo or thematic exhibitions – such as the Eugéne Delacroix exhibition at the Grand Palais of one of the most romantic French painters of the nineteenth century.

The Petit Palais on the Avenue Winston Churchill is

the venue for the highly-acclaimed 'Glory of Alexandria' exhibition. On show are the fruits of recent Franco-Egyptian underwater archaeological discoveries off the Mediterranean coast of Alexandria in northern Egypt. The now drowned city of former Alexandria founded by Alexander the Great in 332 BC was at its zenith, a mega-city of Greek culture. The *piece de resistance* at the exhibition is the massive twelve-tonne statue of Ptolemy II excavated from the waters of the port of Alexandria on view in front of the Petit Palais – another manifestation of Egypt in Paris. In a triumphal march down les Champs-Elysées, Pablo joined his compatriot giants from the other three continents in la Place de la Concorde.

Romeo, representing Europe stood in front of the neo-Baroque Opera of Paris, a masterpiece of Second Empire mid-nineteenth century architectural grandeur by Charles Garnier. Napoleon III commissioned its construction in 1858 after he narrowly escaped an assassination attempt in Le Peletier and decided a new opera house in a more secure area was desirable. We saw 'Don Quoxote', a ballet choreographed by Rudolph Nureyev and performed by the Ballet of the National Opéra of Paris at the Opéra Garnier – a building of breathtaking dimensions. The central chandelier in the interior of the opera hall is alone the size of a small-sized room. The ceiling, in total contrast to the gilt and gold ornate opulence of the nineteenth century opera house, is painted with multi-coloured angels – a very twentieth century artwork done by Marc Chagall at the persuasion of André Malraux.

The twentieth century giant also walked by the Café de la Paix, a well-known stop for refreshments that had in the past attracted the likes of Guy de Maupassant and Emile Zola as noteworthy clients. He passed down the boulevard des Capucines (named after a religious order who used to inhabit the street) and in front of the Greek-inspird fifty-two columned Madeleine church where we had seen performers dressed as angels rehearsing on the steps for the forthcoming spectacle on our way home from the 'Don Quixote' ballet performance. Romeo could have window-shopped the exclusive outlets of French crystal, table-ware and fashion on the rue Royale while passing the famed Maxim restaurant on his right before entering la Place de la Concorde.

As the four giants driven by hidden cars at their feet, converged on the Square of the Giants, nightfall had fallen. In a superb spectacle of *son et lumiére* (sound and light), there was electricity in the air – a mixture of sheer surprise, joy and emotional climax. The dark sky twinkled with stars as cameras flashed in thousands. Surely a surrealistic scenario. The four friendly giants were now given a number, 9, 1, 8 and 9. In an embrace of global fraternity – the global giants: Ho, Mousa, Pablo and Romeo stood side by side. And they stood for 1998. It was impressive. It was "Paris as we have never seen it and may never see again", commented a TV5 French commentator – almost speechless at the explosion of *la grande finale*.

We were told that forty television cameras were installed in la Place de la Concorde to capture the show. Two cameras were placed in the artistic twin fountains on either side of the obelisk. Two more cameras were located atop the famed Hotel Crillon and the headquarters of the French navy.

The Paris of grand monuments was miniatured by the presence of the four six-floor high giants. The innumerable Parisian monuments along the paths of the giants were illuminated and thus were active participants in the greatest show Paris had ever staged. The French flair for combining tradition and the *avant-garde* resulted in an extra-terrestrial extravaganza in which eyes confirmed the presence of the unimaginable. A spectacle in which the past, present and future – all rolled into one span of time – at the threshold of the third millennium.

Agony and Ecstasy

'Patriotism takes the place of religion in France. In the service of la patrie (the country) the doing of one's duty is elevated into the sphere of exalted emotion."

William C. Brownell, *French Traits*, 1889

On the eve of the final encounter between the 'hots' and the hosts, the feeling within us was one of pure ecstasy for the winner – since we wanted both Brazil and France to win the last Coupe Mondiale of the twentieth century. Hand in hand and heart to heart were also feelings of sheer agony for the vanquished – since we wanted neither to lose. But *ce n'est pas la vie* (but such is not life) and France trail-blazed into a stunning 3-0 victory over Brazil.

The French team was slowly picking up momentum as it crossed hurdle after hurdle. And so too did the French public. For even the official programme of the World Cup notes that, "France is a paradox. A land of footballers rather than of football, the country has some of the best training facilities in Europe, and French players are exported with great success ... and yet, the public is despairingly quiet when it comes to supporting and encouraging the national team. Critical and virulent towards their national stars, the French are generally only chauvinistic when a television screen is between them and the field ... Will the public provide the warmth and support necessary to encourage their national players...?"

What was a lukewarm and undemonstrative French public was slowly and surely wooed by the momentum of success and when France qualified for the semi-final against Italy – it exploded. The outpour of emotion; shrieks and shouts, joy and disbelief, claxon of horns and furling of the *tricolores* (the red, white and blue French flag) on les Champs-Elysées on the night of the semi-final qualification was a sight France had never seen. The celebrated first avenue of France became an impasse of humanity and tooting vehicles. The Mexican Wave by the public seated on les Champ-Elysées and then rising and raising their arms in unison was a sight to behold. Had France already smelt victory?

Within twenty-five minutes of the final whistle on le Stade de France, thousands and then millions poured into les Champ-Elysées and every large expanse and narrow streets of Paris and every other city of France. The friendly festivity of frenzy overtook France by storm and surprise. L'Arc de Triomphe was crowned in light – a crown of victory. On it were flashed Champions de la Monde (Champions of the World) and 'France 3-Brazil 0'. On the façade of the monumental heart of Paris was screened the picture of Zinedine Zidane, the twenty-six-year-old Algerian-born scorer of two of the three French goals who plays for the top Italian club Juventus Turin.

France stunned the world and itself with the victory.

The key question? Have I seen any match live? No. My husband had four tickets for four matches (a qualifying match, a quarter-final, a semi-final and the final). He reluctantly offered me a ticket. I graciously declined. I figured this was ammunition to use as a bargaining-point in the future. I was a television-couch viewer and a street-spectator throughout.

En route to Charles de Gaulle airport at 3 p.m. on the day of the final, I saw the crowds already heading for le Stade de France for the match scheduled for 9 p.m. The fan-fare of festivities following victory was still to be heard at 3:30 am, the following morning. The morning saw a downpour of rainfall – perhaps Nature's way of dampening the euphoria which nevertheless exploded once again as the victorious French team received the adulation of the nation and the ultimate honour – a triumphal march down les Champs-Elysées on the 13th of July. Even Nature turned sympathetic. For the afternoon march was held under a brilliant blue Parisian sky. "My God! This is like it was at the Liberation", (of France from German occupation in 1945), said two World War Two veterans in tears. From her balcony on the fourth floor of a building on les Champs-Elysées, 83-year-old Maria Jeanne Larriot swore that she has never seen les Champs-Elysées this way. And she has lived at this address since 1939.

The renowned Champs-Elysées traditionally always received the victorious and the beloved of France. This may have been the reason why Pablo, the giant representing the Americans (including Brazil, the favourites and four-time cup winners) was selected to start off from l'Arc de Triomphe and trot down less Champs-Elysées in the extravagant ceremony staged prior to the start of La Coupe Mondiale. Le Tour de France (the cycle-race), the traditionally favourite sporting event in France ends here too.

This time, it was not the favourites, Brazil who took honour, but for the first time ever – France – carried the 4.98 kgs. La Coupe Mondiale 98 trophy of gold and malachite down the avenue of victory. It was also a Frenchman, Jules Rimet who first conceived the World Cup in 1928. However, it took France another seventy years to possess it.

There has been much analysis and discussion on television, in the newspapers and magazines of the social significance of this sporting event. The almost unanimous voice is one of cohesion and fraternity that this victory has created within the nation. Much has been made of the multi-ethnic composition of the French team, with winners whose roots go back to Algeria, Antilles, New Caledonia and Africa. Michel Wieviorka, sociologist and author spoke of the "real image" the French team represented of France. He also remarked that the multi-racial makeup of the team is the triumph of republican integration." Fate could not have dealt France a greater gift in timing than this victorious sporting event on the eve of 14th July. Its repercussions were felt far and wide within the country's social fabric. Is not the demolishing of the Bastille prison, the symbol of royalty and privileges by the marginalised masses in the 1789 French Revolution the *raison d'être* for the 14th July celebration of the event? In commemorating today the past, France appears to have renewed its commitment to *Liberté, Egalité et Fraternité.*

And on the 14th of July – celebrating the Bastille event, President Jacque Chirac of France royally received *l'equipe Français, les bleus* (the French team, the blues) at the presidential palace, Elysées Palais for a garden party. We saw Zinedine Zidane, the darling of the French public enter the Elysées amongst cries and shrieks. To the cries of "*Et un! Et deux! Et trios zero!*" (And One! And Two! And three zéro!) the singing of 'Champions of the World' (in English within the bastion of the French presidency!) within the sumptuous splendour of the Elysées Palais; the French team, their wives and children were introduced by a visibly thrilled President Chirac flanked by Prime Minister Lionel Jospin and members of the French cabinet to a rapturous crowd of invitees. For the next elections, President Chirac has the vote of French women in his pocket. He made a marvellous gesture by particularly thanking the wives of the victorious team. Aime Jacquet, the coach of *les bleus* was bestowed the highest French civilian honour. He was given the Legion of Honour medal.

As the host-country winner of La Coupe Mondiale 98, the last major sporting event of the twentieth century, France in its first-time victory with a score of 3-0 cut a milestone in French history.

It was Charles de Gaulle who once said, "France was created either for complete success or exemplary misfortunes. France cannot be France without grandeur." It is all or nothing. And France went out for all.

'Le Testament Francais' by Andrei Makine

"It was Charlotte who had taught me to pick out Parisian silhouettes in the midst of a great industrial city on the Volga; it was she who had imprisoned me in this fantasy of the past, from whence I cast absent-minded glances at real life."

Andrei Makine

A literary panorama sweeping over the empire of the imperial Romanovs, the communist Soviet Union and a now-professed capitalist Russia intersperses with memories of a Paris of *la Belle Époque.* The reminiscences of a Parisian grandmother, Charlotte in the plains of Siberia to her grandson, Andrei Makine, create a mesmerising tale of a nostalgic Parisian past and a harsh Russian reality.

Andrei Makine born in Siberia in 1957 sought political asylum in Paris in 1987 and has lived in Paris since. *Le Testament Français*, written in French is Makiné's fourth novel and has the unique and unprecedented distinction of having won both the Prix Goncourt and the Prix Médecis, two of France's most prestigious literary prizes. *Le Testament Français* was published in 1995 and the English translation in 1997. Having sold close to a million copies in France, it is now being published in translation in twenty-six other countries.

His is a veritable fairy-tale of rags-to-riches, of ignominy-to-fame. Andrei Makiné having arrived in Paris, at first, "lived rough and wrote by day on park benches. Eventually he found work teaching part-time, but could not get his first novel accepted by a publisher until he pretended that he had translated it from a Russian writer's original. His third novel was published under his own name." Foreign authors writing in French face considerable obstacles. Their achieving literary recognition is thus a double feat. Alphonse Daudet wrote in *Trente Ans à Paris* (Thirty Years in Paris), "I questioned the Russian writer about his method of work and was astonished that he did not do his own translations, for he spoke a very pure French, with just a hint of hesitation, owing to the subtlety of his mind. He confessed to me that the Académie and its dictionary paralysed him." The Académie Française, the bastion and caretaker of the French language, is a formidable institution.

In one of his many sessions with his grandmother, Makine and Charlotte discuss the French poet, Baudelaire, his poetry and the Russian translation. Referring to different translations of Baudelaire's poems, Charlotte remarks, "… you see: the translator of prose is the slave of the author and the translator of poetry is his rival." There is plenty of food for thought in this one line and such are the thoughts which have so enriched the book.

Makiné's lyrical and poetic way with words reveals itself exquisitely when he writes of the French his grandmother spoke and the image and significance that language had on him throughout his childhood. He writes, "As for the French language, we basically regarded it as our family dialect. After, all, every family has its little verbal whims, its ties of language, and its nicknames that never cross the threshold of the house, its private slang … Language, that mysterious substance, invisible and omnipresent, whose sonorous essence reached into every corner of the universe we were in the process of exploring. This language that shaped men; moulded objects; rippled in verse; bellowed in streets invaded by crowds … But, above all, throbbed within us, like a magical graft implanted in our hearts, already bringing forth leaves and flowers, bearing within it the fruit of a whole civilisation. Yes, this implant, the French language."

Yet this fascination, love and knowledge – "this implant" – of the French language drove him to despair when his novels written in French were rejected by publishers and he was forced to invent a French translator of his work. He writes bitterly, "All this was the fruit of a pure and simple literary hoax on my part. For the novels had been written directly in French and rejected by publishers. I was 'some funny little Russian who thought he could write in French.' In a gesture of despair I had then invented a translator and submitted the manuscript, presenting it as translated from the Russian. It had been accepted, published and hailed for the quality of the translation. I told myself, at first bitterly, later with a smile, that my Franco-Russian curse was still upon me. But whereas in childhood I had been obliged to conceal my French graft, now it was my Russianness which failed to find favour." In an interview, Makine said that in his opinion, the Russian novel is written to be lived. And the French novel is written to be understood. Another food for thought ... Living versus thinking? Is one a Russian experience and another a French intellectual exercise?

Le Testament Français has been variously acclaimed. *Le Nouvel Observateur* lauds the novel thus: "Every so often in literary life's routine, a miracle happens that makes up for a hundred disappointments. This year that miracle is Andrei Makine." *Le Figaro Litteraire* says, "Astonishing ... a novel of great beauty." *Le Journal de Dimanche* notes, "Bewitching ... a beautiful, profound novel." *The Irish Times* exults, "Superb ... one of the many fascinating facets of this sad, beautiful, old-world novel, which has echoes of Alain-Fournier's *Le Grand Meaulnes*, in its merging of contemporary French fiction with the 19th century Russian novel." *The Literary Review* states, "He communicates brilliantly the exquisite agony of nostalgia." It has been hailed as the most breathtaking ode to memory since Marcel Proust's *Remembrance of Things Past* writes *Newsweek*.

The novel is the awakening and growing-up odyssey of a boy in Siberia. The paramount person in his first twenty-five years, is his French-born grandmother, Charlotte who came to Siberia in 1922, "half, or may be a third of that journey, you know, I made on foot." Makiné writes of his grandmother, "there was this Frenchwoman with the calm gaze of her grey eyes, elegant, despite the simplicity of her dress, slim and so different from the women of her generation, the *babushkas* (Russian grandmothers). In Moscow or Leningrad everything would have turned out otherwise. The motley humanity of the big city would have eclipsed what was different about Charlotte. But she had found herself in this little Saranza, ideal for living out endless days, each one like the last. Her past life remained intensely present to her, as if lived only yesterday."

During the holidays, Andrei and his sister spent long stretches of time with their grandmother. She would reminisce, recall an anecdote, an individual, a road or a place in Paris and leave its vivid imprint on the adoring and growing Andrei. These memories were often supported by old sepia-coloured photographs or newspaper-cuttings that she would extract from a battered suitcase which within it, contained sweet memories of a place and a time. "The France of our grandmother like a misty Atlantis was emerging from the waves … France-Atlantis was revealing itself as a whole gamut of sounds, colours and smells. As we followed our guides, we were discovering the different elements which made up this mysterious French essence."

Glimpses of a Paris of bygone days is recreated for Andrei Makiné and for the reader. Charlotte recollects that, "At that time I must have been almost your age. It was the winter of 1910. The Seine had turned into a real sea. The people of Paris travelled around by boat. The streets were like rivers, the squares like great lakes. And what astonished me most was the silence..." Neuilly-sur-Seine (today, a central part of Paris) was composed of a dozen log cabins. "Oh! At that time Neuilly was just a village...". Of the Elysée Palace, Makiné writes, "The Elysée Palace appeared in the glitter of chandeliers and the shimmering of mirrors. The opéra dazzled us with the nakedness of women's shoulders and made us drunk with the perfume exhaled by the magnificent hair styles. For us Notre-Dame was a sensation of cold stone under a stormy sky. Yes, we could almost touch the rough, porous walls – a gigantic rock, shaped over the centuries, it seemed to us, by ingenious erosion ... We could not picture the Eiffel Tower without seeing the mad Austrian who had jumped from this serrated steeple, whose parachute had failed him and who crashed in the midst of a gawping crowd."

The association and significance of a café is memorably conveyed by Charlotte to Andrei. "We came upon a quiet little bistro, the name of which Charlotte spelled out to us smilingly as she recalled it : *Au Ratafia de Neuilly*. 'This *ratafia*, she would elaborate, the patron served it in silver scallop dishes ...' So the people of our Atlantis could feel sentimental attachment to a café, love its name and discern an atmosphere that was special to it. And for their whole lives retain the memory that it was there, at the corner of a street, that one drank *ratafia* from silver scallop dishes. Yes, not from thick tumblers nor from goblets but from these fine dishes. It was our new discovery: this occult science which linked the place of refreshment, the ritual of the meal and its psychological tonality. 'In their minds, do their favourite bistros have a soul,' we wondered, `or at least a face of their own?' There was only one café in Saranza. Despite its pretty name Snowflake, it did not arouse any special emotion in us, any more than the furniture shop next door or the savings bank opposite." A delightful and meaningful exposé on "this occult science ... the ritual of the meal." Makiné discovered early in childhood the total fascination of the French for the institution of the café and the entirely pleasant preoccupation with gourmet culinary living.

It was Rabelais, the French writer who said, "Appetite comes with eating." In the same philosophical tone, the gravity of the ritual of the French meal is best expressed by the following declaration, "The French palate is the rampart of the most prestigious socio-cultural heritage of humanity and it deserves a more effective fate than the Maginot line." This sombre note was found in an editorial in *L'Evénement du Jeudi*, deploring the fall in standards.

It was another grandmother who influenced the course of another writer's life. Harriet Welty Rochefort, in *French Toast: A Humorous Tour of What Living in France is Really Like*! writes about her twenty years experience of living in France and being married to a Frenchman. She tells us, "...my grandfather remarried a woman who was a professor of French at Grinnell College. She was to have a capital influence on my life, telling me all about France, where she had lived for a time, even marrying a Frenchman whom she eventually divorced. She bought me books about France, taught me French words. With her beautiful white hair and blue eyes and the breath of foreign air she bought with her, she totally won me over. From age eight, I knew I had to go to France, if only to have a look and come right back home ... I loved Paris. It was all my 'aunt' had told me, and more. The first night I was here I boarded a Bateau Mouche to cruise down the Seine; the air was soft and warm; a man spoke some unintelligible words to me in French and I was conquered, by the sound of the language, the way people walked and moved, even the air which seemed different. I felt I had walked into a Toulouse-Lautrec painting. Later, I would find Paris too noisy, too traffic-filled. But that first heady moment was a strong one. Actually, though, I felt I should savour that moment, leave Paris in my mind as a beautiful memory, and head for a new destination – South America. I was on my way when I met Philippe." And the rest is history.

I read that Andrei Makine was discussing the possibility of *Le Testament Français* being made into a film. If it does happen, the film will be on the scale of *Doctor Zhivago*, based on Boris Pasternak's novel – a vast scenic panorama and larger-than-life characters so vividly portrayed. Charlotte's voyage from Paris to Siberia and Andrei's imaginary accompaniment on this voyage of discovery would make a beautiful and memorable film.

'Paris in August' by Adrian George

"I have known Paris through every season, in every month. The August days are distinct. Much of Paris closes down. Parisians take their holidays; the streets, away from the Grand Boulevards and tourist sites, empty. A sunlit, echoing, ghostly town .. It is always enchanting and consoling to walk these streets. Through this stone, lead and iron landscape, melancholy but beautiful, traced with the history of wars and revolutions and the extraordinary art, ideas and legends of the people who have lived here. Everyone of course, has their own Paris; this is a portion of mine. Reading it now I see how the moods of the days change, as do the pictures with their various methods and mediums. This book is a remnant of the larger, yellowing medium, time."

Preface, Paris in August, Adrian George

If you want to doze off – pick up *Paris in August.* High on observation and low on action, Adrian George leisurely strolls one through his account of Paris in the month of August 1993. In the form of a diary, British artist, Adrian George wrote this account of his month in Paris combining text and charcoal drawings "to portray the city that acts as his muse." He maintains studios in London and Paris.

"Paris with its filigreed lace iron balconies, is once again the most southerly of northern cities … Paris is emptied. Parisians pack their cars with their wives, children, grandparents, dogs and cosmetics and drive to the sea or the mountains or the great rich countryside … It is Sunday and one must make an act of faith. Mine is to go to the bookstalls on the banks of the river Seine. Lining the parapets and pavements above the river bank are the *bouquinistes,* second-hand booksellers, who have been there as long as printing … He (the Mayor of Paris) usually tries to prove his fitness to accede to the Presidency by his mastery of this old and crumbling city. (President Jacques Chirac was Mayor of Paris for many years). Yet it is beautiful, one can see the architectural follies, the intricate intimacies of the buildings, which are signed and dated with pride by their creators. There are mysterious de Chirico shadows and vanishing points, *cul-de-sac* ... Walking is much the best way to move around Paris; one can cross the city in an hour, and have all senses delighted." Such are samples of his nuggets of observation of a city he is intrigued by and obviously loves.

The artist's verbal depiction of a canvas that visually presents itself to any discerning observer of Paris has been divinely captured by George. He writes, "I crossed the Pont des Arts in the morning sunlight. The prow of the island just upstream, Notre-Dame could be seen above the green candy-floss of trees on the Vert-Galant. Through the Pont-Neuf one could see the Pont au Change, through that, the Pont Note-Dame evaporating in the yellow haze. The distressed golden dome of the Mazarine is topped by a little turret fit to contain a princess. The stonework of the Louvre is engraved with patterns like human brains. The Samaritaine department store as *Déco* as a glass liner, the fairytale towers of the Conciergerie that contain cruel memories of torture. A fly-blown *bateau-mouche*, a barge like a suburban house, with geraniums, trees in tubs, washing lines, and a motorcar on deck..."

Adrian George in describing the Sacré-Coeur church perched on top of the Montmartre hill notes, "The tarmac is melting on the rue Montmartre. It is silent, still, like a plague city. In the heat flocks of pigeons fly above, leaving moving shadows on the road as if of fish swimming in a grey river ... The streets, once empty as a film set, are now crowded with extras dressed as tourists. The sugar-white Byzantine basilica of Sacré-Coeur lies painted on the powder-blue sky." The only crowds to be seen in Paris in August are non-Parisians.

One such non-Parisian is the American writer, Henry James. He writes in *Parisian Sketches*, "Of all the great cities, Paris is the most tolerable in hot weather. It is true that the asphalt has a way of liquefying to about the consistency and the temperature of molten lava ... But... the boulevards are a long chain of cafés, each one with its little promontory of chairs and tables projecting into the sea of asphalt ... Then you may dine in the Champs-Elysées at a table spread under the trees, beside an ivied wall, and almost believe you are in the country." For the French remain global leaders in matters of *l'art de vivre* (art of living).

Following everyone's appetite for food, George has us drooling over his account of his visit to his neighbouring *marché* (open market). "Food, the Buci market has glorious food. To step into the streets lined with these stalls is to enter into a living, bursting cornucopia. An enormous *ratatouille* of vegetables, a flocculation of poultry, chicken, quails, partridges, turkeys ... An intricate collocation of cheeses from all those little farms all over France ... A patchwork of *pates* like house bricks ... oven-loads of country breads. A frivolity of fish, an ostentation of oysters, crabs and lobsters and an endless fandango of fruit." The language is music to the ears.

His appreciation of the old and beautiful and a parochial sense of humour is apparent when he describes a *hôtel particulier* on the island, Ile Saint Louis. "It is forever being repeated that when good Americans die they come to Paris. I think they would have to be very good indeed to live in the Hôtel de Lauzun. The Hôtel de Lauzun is a seventeenth-century town house on the Quai d'Anjou. Unpredictbaly opening to the public, it has been restored to wonderful effect. Floors, walls, ceilings, furniture, all carved and painted and encrusted with golden fruits and cherubs, with an Italianate sumptuousness. A fairy-tale, for once made real."

The French respect for age and continuity manifests itself also in forms other than classical culture. What about the role of the magazine *Paris Match*? As so aptly observed by Adrian George, "Jeanne Moreau, Brigitte Bardot, Johnny Halliday, the French never let go of their stars. The covers of *Paris Match* bear continuing witness to their lives, adventures, readers measure their own aging against them. The British equivalents are of course the Kay twins, Myrah Kindly and Ronnie Biggs." However, the British did have Princess Diana, an international icon. One can often see a 1950s copy of *Paris Match* displayed at the *bouquinistes* along the Seine. On the cover is a wedding picture of a radiant Grace Kelly (now deceased) and her debonair husband, Prince Rainier of Monaco (later portly and grey-haired). *Paris Match* vividly captures the passage of time.

Paris by night. *Ah oui.* Scores of writers have written of the sheer beauty and magic of it. The artist within George sees, "Paris by night, the city of light, red and white stripes of car lights run the length of the Champs-Elysées. They should have blue street lighting to make a tricolour up to the Arc de Triomphe. What triumph is this?" He then sees elements of tawdriness, vulgarity and degeneration along the Champs-Elysées. However, he remarks, "All cities have a version of this. Not all have the Place de la Concorde at the end of the tunnel, and its compensating fountains, monuments and light ... It is said that due to some meteorological quirk, the atmosphere is thinner above Paris and that is why it has such sparkling light."

On the day of his departure, August 31, 1993, as he closes his window shutters, he observes the return to normalcy and routine. "The shutters are being opened in other apartment buildings, brown paper is being stripped from shop windows, which are being washed and cleaned. Elaborate displays are made of the wares; Parisians are natural decorators. Fresh food and flowers are arriving from the countryside. All the people with normal lives return – tomorrow is the day that the new year begins, the new season, the new fashions."

And in his last entry after his August stay in Paris is over, he writes, "And I feel the sadness, as I always do, because Paris, being feminine, always looks especially beautiful the day you leave her."

Tea and Tattered Pages, a tiny cavern of second-hand literary delights is where I came across *Paris in August* by Adrian George. And at 40 francs a real buy. Tea and Tattered Pages is where one has a hard time locating an inviting read because of the resident wolf-whistling parrot. I am serious.

The lazy, hazy days of August in Paris are calm and still – warm days and long and balmy nights. The cobbled streets resound with the passing of a few cars as compared to the bumper-to-bumper grind of in-season traffic. Parisian streets are cleaner as much of the dog population has accompanied the human population to *la maison en la campagne* (country-home) or *au bord de la mer* (seaside). Much of the canine population has migrated to the French Riviera. There are also fewer children in Paris; probably attending the vacationing dogs. France is officially on holiday.

The Lamartine *boucherie* (butchery) opposite our apartment on avenue Victor Hugo is closed in the month of August. A little note is posted on the door informing its valued clients of the shutdown. Our local restaurant, the Brasserie Stella with its delicious *foie gras* (goose-liver paste) and mouth-watering chocolate profiteroles dessert has all its chairs perched on the tables. The deserted look is Paris in August. The inviting waft of French cheese – a runny brie or a strong-smelling *roquefort* cheese no longer permeates the air as one walks by the neighbourhood *fromagerie*. The classic tribute to French cheese was made by Charles de Gaulle. He declared, "How can you be expected to govern a country that has two hundred and forty-six kinds of cheese?" He should know. The nearest *boulangerie* and *pâtisserie* (bakery and pastry shop) has its shutters down. No more warm *baguettes* to munch the top off on the way home. No more temptations to resist in the windows – trays and trays of glazed strawberry and cherry tarts, inviting chocolate and coffee éclairs and feathery *mille feuilles* pastries. The few remaining open shops stock chic Parisian clothing and shoes. And all announce that this is the second and third markdown or closing sale. Fortunate are those who are extra-*petite* or extra-*grande*.

The Mairie de Paris (Mayor of Paris) offers discount film tickets for those less than twenty-five years old at 25 francs. All the informative and thus important French magazines, *Paris Match*, *Gala* and *Point de Vue* which concentrate on the lives of jet-setters, media personalities, royalty and other such celebrities have on their covers and promising more inside, pictures of *les Bleus en vacances* often in the French Riviera. The Blues are the 1998 World Cup football heroes. Media-coverage gratefully suggests that *les Bleus* have earned their days in the sun, sand and sea. Paris in August will always be remembered as the tragic site of the fatal accident that claimed the lives of Princess Diana, Dodi al-Fayed and Henri Paul, the driver.

The digital display on the Eiffel Tower that is a countdown of the number of days left before the year 2000 screened 500 days left on August 19, 1998. It started in April 1997 with 1000 days till the year 2000. Five hundred days have just zoomed by. As we approach the autumn months of the year and into winter, so too does Paris in August announce that the twentieth century too is closing to an end.

'I'll Always Have Paris: A Memoir' by Art Buchwald

"Paris is not an easy city to leave."

Art Buchwald

I first came across the name, Art Buchwald in the mid-50s during my first stay in Paris with my parents. His articles appeared regularly in the *Herald Tribune* published in Paris. However, I read neither the Art Buchwald column nor the contents of the paper itself. What was of sole interest to me as a child were the cartoons for which I flipped the pages of *Herald Tribune* daily. Some four decades later, in the late 1990s, once again in Paris, now with my husband, I pick up daily the now *International Herald Tribune*. My interests have extended and diversified over the long span of time to include the news coverage and the Art Buchwald column. And I remain faithful to the cartoon page. However, of my literary heritage of bygone days, I recollect only 'Dennis the Menace', 'Blondie' and 'Beetle Bailey'. Dennis remains the loveable rascal; Blondie now has a catering career and Dagwood remains the easy-going layabout; and Beetle Bailey as always continues to be the unwitting victim of Sarge's manipulations.

History repeats itself for I have introduced the *International Herald Tribune* – via cartoons – now to our daughter. Four decades ago, there was no 'Garfield', 'Peanuts', or 'Doonesbury. But there was and still is Art Buchwald. Who has not heard of Art Buchwald? Today, Art Buchwald is a syndicated columnist and writes from Washington for 550 newspapers. He is a Pulitzer Prize winner and a member of the prestigious American Academy of Arts and Letters.

Art Buchwald in *I'll Always Have Paris: A Memoir* published in 1996 writes of his years in Paris from 1948 to 1962. Typically Buchwald, the title is probably a twist on the famous line between Ingrid Bergman and Humphrey Bogart in the all-time classic film *Casablanca*. Bidding adieu to Bergman, Bogart says, "We'll always have Paris." The book is dedicated to his wife, Ann, "because Paris belonged to both of us. The book was our story – not just mine." *The New York Times Book Review* comments, "Honest and moving … A consummate storyteller." The magazine *People* states, "Buchwald is an enthusiastic, generous raconteur and makes his Paris ours as well." *Publishers Weekly* notes, "Both irreverently funny and deeply touching, this golden memoir gloriously recreates the adventurous, liberated spirit of expatriate Paris … which magically makes the reader feel young and hopeful."

It is all that and more; for Art Buchwald evokes an era, recollects personalities and reminisces of a Paris that both no longer exists and yet at the same time, recalls a city that has not changed. Once again, a case is made for a city – Paris – where '*Plus ca change, plus c'est la méme chose.*'

Having docked at the port, Le Havre in France in the spring of 1948, Buchwald remarks, "We were about to claim our chairs in sidewalk cafés in one of the loveliest and most civilised cities in the world. We would never be the same again. The memories of the years, months, or even weeks we spent here would remain with us all our lives. Even those who could not speak the language would absorb the culture and learn a way of life that was unlike anything we had ever experienced."

Within a few months of his arrival in Paris, he started his life-long association with *Herald Tribune* by writing a column. One of his early columns was titled, "*Garçon*, my *café* won't *filtre*" (Waiter, my coffee won't filter)." "It was about an ugly American who didn't have the patience to wait for the water to penetrate the coffee grounds." He recollects that, "French coffee was also one of the mainstay of our café lives. It was served as "*filtre*". Hot water was poured over coffee grounds, and in ten or fifteen minutes the coffee dripped into the cup … Choosing a café was like choosing a home. You knew that you would be returning again and again as long as you remained in Paris. Your social life revolved around the café of your choice. You left messages with the bartender, you began a love affair or ended one over a drink. Hours were spent rating poets and writers and speaking with contempt about any new writer who had become a success." It took an Englishman, Adrian George to note in *Paris in August* that, there was one eating-place for every twelve of its population in Paris.

In his extensive observation and appreciation of *la gastronomie française*, Buchwald aptly attributes the finest accolade to the oh-so-French of all French objects – the celebrated *baguette*. "It is impossible to spend time in France without becoming attached to the French loaf of bread. Bread is to the French what the umbrella is to the British. It is carried at all times, rain or shine, and has many functions. You can hail a taxi with a loaf of bread, use it as a weapon if you are attacked, signal a friend across the street, or present arms when the President of France goes by." It was Buchwald who commented on the paramount importance of *la cuisine française* and its aftermath. He said, "A bad liver is to a Frenchman what a nervous breakdown is to an American. Everyone has had one and everyone wants to talk about it."

Buchwald finally met his idol and the idol of a

generation of aspiring American writers, the 'Great One', Ernest Hemingway at the bar (which today, is named 'Hemingway Bar') of the Hotel Ritz. Buchwald wrote an article making fun of Hemingway's book. *Across the River and into the Trees*. "Years later, a friend showed me a letter he'd received from Hemingway, in which the Great One called me "a smart-assed son of a bitch." I was very happy, because this meant he was reading me in *Herald Tribune*."

About the *International Herald Tribune*, he writes, "Every young journalist's dream was to work on the *Trib*. As far as I know, it still is … I yearned to work on the paper more than anything I had ever wanted in my life … All of my luck in writing since has been the result of my landing that job in the *Trib* in Paris."

In the 1950s, the *International Herlad Tribune* offices were located at 21 rue de Berri, off les Champs-Elysées. Close by was the Lancaster Hotel at 7 rue de Berri where notes Buchwald, stayed Elizabeth Taylor, Audrey Hepburn and John Huston. According to *The Historic Hotels of Paris: A Select Guide*, by Wendy Arnold, the Lancaster Hotel, "built as a private residence in 1896 by a Monsieur Santiago Drake del Castillo, the Lancaster was sold in 1925 by his heirs, the Comte and Comtesse Ferrent, to a Swiss *hôtelier*, Emile Wolf. He added a further four floors to the mansion, and filled it with a splendid collection of genuine and reproduction antiques, creating a highly idiosyncratic hotel which attracted the great personalities of the time: King Umberto of Italy, the Nizam of Hyderabad, Noel Coward, Clark Gable, Greta Garbo and Marlene Dietrich – after whom a favourite suite was named."

The *International Herald Tribune* offices have since moved to 181 avenue Charles-de-Gaulle at Neuilly-sur-Seine, Paris where they are still to be found "in a grim steel building amongst other unappealing buildings .. anyone who worked on the rue de Berri thinks of the present building as a pile of *nouveau* junk." Buchwald's eventual jurisdiction of journalistic territory was such that, "I was given leeway to travel anywhere, and so I covered Rome, Venice, Vienna, Berlin and even Sicily. The varied datelines gave the reader the sense that the *Trib* was truly covering the Continent. Paris was the hub and all the major capitals were the spokes of the wheel."

In 1950, Art Buchwald met his future wife, Ann McGarry, an Irish-American visiting Paris in order to learn the business of *haute couture*. They married in London in Westminster Cathedral in October 1952. He a Jew and she a Catholic had their wedding reception at Claridge's Hotel, "the snootiest hotel in the city ... We went to Majorca for our honeymoon and finally returned to Paris, where for fourteen years we lived happily ever after." Ann Buchwald too wrote a book on their life in Paris, *Seems like Yesterday*.

After forty years of marriage and three children, Art and Ann Buchwald separated in 1992. Before divorce proceedings started, Ann was diagnosed with lung cancer and died in 1994. "Ann allowed me to come back into her life and I was there every day. I discovered she was happiest talking about our days in Paris ... Those last days were very precious. Paris brought us together in the beginning and it brought us together at the end... We could not have survived the way we were, but the years in Paris had been good – very, very good – and I wouldn't trade them for anything. When we were making arrangements for her funeral in 1994, our son Joel suggested that since Paris had played such a significant role in Ann's life, we ask the church soloist to sing *La Marseillaise* at the end of the service. She did. It was the perfect tribute to Ann, and to Paris, which had given both of us so many glorious years." An infinitely moving gesture to the woman and the city they loved.

What makes *I'll Always Have Paris*, such a delightful read is the sense one has of identifying with the writer in 'also-experienced situations,' places and people. For example, he writes, "Over the years, the Louvre and I became familiar companions. Whenever someone came to Paris, it was a regular stop." That sounds familiar.

In a manner so ringing true – Buchwald writes, "A large portion of our Paris life was spent entertaining visiting firemen, mostly from the United States. It seemed that as soon as someone announced he or she or both were going to Paris, someone said, "You have to look up our good friends, the Buchwalds," even though they weren't good friends of ours at all." Yes, we have all come across the long-lost close friend of an acquaintance of a passer-by!

At a supposedly quiet dinner with his wife and visiting mother-in-law at the Hôtel Plaza-Athenée, he met Ingrid Bergman, Gary Gooper, Anatole Litvak, the Hollywood producer and Bettina, the model and last girlfriend of Prince Aly Khan. His mother-in-law was thrilled to bits and the son-in-law came off very well. At a dinner at the same venue with Greek friends, we were pleasantly surprised to meet an Egyptian industrialist friend.

Buchwald often sat at Fouquet's which was patronised by movie stars. A typically Buchwald line goes like this. "Shall we have asparagus at Fouquet's or shall we send Harry to college?" After all, fame does not come cheap. Fouquet's, I recall existed in the 1950s at the same location. Today, it is still the quintessential French restaurant renowned for its film, music and theatre associations. There are plaques which note the famous personalities who frequented/frequent the restaurant ... Juliette Greco, Yves Montand, Simone Signoret, Brigitte Bardot, Isabelle Adjani, Charles Aznavour (whom I saw at Orly airport), Marcel Marceau (whom we saw perform at Espace Pierre Cardin off les Champs-Elysées).

In 1956, the Buchwalds were living at 52 rue de Monceau across from the Parc Monceau that featured prominently in the memorable film, *Gigi* starring Leslie Caron and Maurice Chevalier. The same Parc Monceau was also used in 1997 in a film, *A Soldier's Daughter Never Cries* directed by James Ivory. Mary Blume writing in the *International Herald Tribune*, in an article titled 'Merchant Ivory on Growing Up in France', observes that, "The day's shooting was at a private school, the Ecole Active Bilingue on the edge of the Parc Monceau, where children of many nations were being initiated into the obscure rites of Halloween." Our daughter attends the same Ecole Active Bilingue.

A unique anecdote related by Buchwald refers to, "one of my best friends during those years was a French doctor named Jean Dax, who took care of many Americans in Paris. Jean was not only our doctor, but a buddy." As I came across this sentence in his book, I immediately told my husband, "I am sure this Dr. Jean Dax is our Dr. Jean Dax!" The next day, I called our Dr. Jean Dax whom I had seen two weeks earlier. I thanked him for the good his prescription had done me and then enquired if he had read Art Buchwald's memoirs, *I'll Always Have Paris*? He was surprised and amused at my query and replied, "yes, Buchwald had been his patient for many years in Paris and had been kind enough to send him a copy of the book."

Buchwald writes of the Paris of the 1950s where Brigitte Bardot, Sophia Loren and Gina Lollobrigida ("I was the love of her life, though she'd never admit it") appeared regularly at the annual Cannes Film Festival. He met the likes of the Greek shipping tycoons, Aristotle Onassis and his rival and one-time brother-in-law, Stravros Niarchos. He wined and dined with Somerset Maugham. He was a close friend of Audrey Hepburn, David Niven and Ingrid Bergman ("I was also in love with her, and hoped after she got bored with Rossellini, (the Italian film director) she would turn to me.")

Doing the right thing at the right time, landed him with "the toast of London." Buchwald was once at a show of Marlene Dietrich at the Café de Paris in London, at which Princess Margaret was present. After the show, "all those fans and friends were gone. Nobody had bothered to ask Marlene if she had plans after the show. I finally said, "Would you like to go to supper with me?" She said, she'd love to, and after her evening to remember, I wound up alone with the toast of London."

In 1962, when they decided to return to the United States, Buchwald writes, "At the Gare St. Lazare, we sat on our luggage, waiting for the boat train to take us to the Queen Mary at Le Havre and home. There were six of us, Ann and myself, the three children, and our Irish nurse, Kay. We had fifteen pieces of luggage. When Ann and I had arrived separately fourteen years earlier, we had each had one bag and hardly any money. Paris had been extremely kind to us and would leave its mark on us forever."

In 1948, when he had boarded the battered World War II troopship for Le Havre, France, he "bid farewell to my father and sisters, promising them that when I returned from France, I would be the most important writer in our country, or its equivalent." He kept his word!

He knew they had made an irrevocable decision. "I knew in my heart that I would never go back to being a Parisian columnist... emotions of an impending loss welled up." This pained him immensely and he writes with tremendous feeling and poignancy of his and Ann's sense of loss and heartache in the final chapter of his book, *The Road Back*. "Every time I went to Fouquet's or another café, I felt it was for the last time. The Champs-Elysées, which I had taken for granted, was now an old friend on whom I was turning my back. There wasn't a park or building that I didn't make a mental image of in my head." He went from *quartier* to *quartier*, Montparnasse, avenue George V, Quai d'Orsay, rue de Monceau – exploring the areas where he had lived through the years 1948 to 1962 – years where he had moved from being a struggling journalist to an established household name in journalism. "The last two months for me were the toughest. Paris is not an easy city to leave."

Anyone who has ever lived in Paris and then left Paris will be able to identify with Buchwald's account of that painful period of *au revoir*. Yes, it is a situation *déjà vu*.

"I will always go back, but I know that a beautiful city like Paris has to be enjoyed with someone you love. There is so much to do and so much to see that the magic must be shared. I shared my Paris history almost exclusively with Ann. It is painful to revisit, because I want to turn to her and say … The ghosts are everywhere – the memories remain vivid, sometimes painful and sometimes exploding, making me want to cry."

Art Buchwald's celebrated and lifelong association

with the *International Herald Tribune* came to an emotional peak in 1987 at the one hundred years anniversary celebration of the paper in Paris. Buchwald was the grand guest of honour. "I loved the idea that I was looked upon as the Rip van Winkle of the paper." The banquet was held in a specially constructed tent at the Palais de Chaillot with its spectacular view of the Eiffel Tower across the Seine. There were 1600 guests. "I gave my speech, and because the occasion was so meaningful to me, I delivered it with great feeling. I don't think that anything could compare to that week in Paris. The combination of time, the place, the people – in my heart I knew there would never be another celebration like this, because there would never be another occasion like this one."

Now in his seventies, Buchwald reminisces about his years in Paris–largely the 1950s–with punch and humour as expected, but also enchantment, appreciation, poignancy and nostalgia. Art Buchwald, the world-class humorist ends his account of *I'll Always Have Paris* with a lump in his throat.

Last Month

Visited the Rodin Museum for the first time. Gazed at the 'Thinker' and the 'Kiss'. Strolled in the gardens and took in the day over *un café*. I thought I would take the Métro home but nearing the Varenne station besides les Invalides, I thought I should take in the front-view. Looking at the splendid view of the wide-bodied building, I looked across and there was the magnificent Pont Alexandre III inviting one to cross it. So I did. The shimmering Seine lay below me serene. Ahead was le Petit Palais, the museum where I had seen '*La Gloire d'Alexandrie*'. Now I would take the Métro on les Champs-Elysées that lay just ahead. Having reached the avenue, how could I disappear underground? The finest avenue in the world stood before me and I could not turn away. I walked the length of les Champs-Elysées with appreciation for what it represents – life and living. Having reached l'Étoile, like countless occasions before, I turned into our avenue Victor Hugo and took in the superb and imaginative window-displays at Céline with their autumn collection of chic clothes and luxurious leather goods, the *chocalatier* of Marquise de Sévigné and beckoning baked products at our corner *boulangerie*. And so I reached home. I had covered some three and a half kilometres and I could have walked on and on …

Visited the Louvre Museum for the last time. Walked through some of the rooms hosting French painters; Boucher, Chardin, Delacroix, Fragonard, Georges de la Tour, Le Brun, Watteau … Also visited the Khorsabad courtyard with its exceptional Assyrian sculptures of winged bulls and the rooms containing antiquities from Mesopotamia and Ancient Iran. We were moving on to Iran.

Scanned the richly-stocked boutiques of the Louvre Museum and the musée d'Orsay. Too late to buy more art books and books on Paris.

Toured the Bienniale of International Antique-dealers at the Carousel du Louvre. They are the top-of-the-range in their profession. Such works of art displayed in such an imaginative setting–each antique-dealer recreated 'an interior of a shop'. *Mais quel intérieure et quel shop*. This was my last activity with 'Bienvenue en France'. I am deeply grateful to its dedicated members for greatly enriching my stay in Paris. They opened doors that I never would have found.

Roamed to our heart's content in Parc Floral de Paris at Bois de Vincennes for their bi-annual antiques exhibition and sale. Fatigued, we sat down to the most succulent *poulet rôti* (roast chicken) and *tart tarte aux pommes* (apple-pie) this side in Paris.

Invited to a concert at l'Hotel de Ville by the Mayor of Paris, Jean Tiberis. The city hall of Paris is no ordinary Mayor's seat. It rivals any palace. While listening to the orchestra playing, one had to marvel at the opulence and grandeur of the exquisite frescoed-ceiling, the massive glittering chandeliers and the thick marble columns. Not bad at all for a municipal office.

Also gràce à 'Bienvenue en France', I attended my last fashion-show. I saw the Autumn-Winter Collection *Haute-Couture* of 1998/1999 of Louis Feraud at their salon on rue Faubourg du Saint-Honoré.

On a rainy, grey afternoon, I saw in a tiny basement art-cinema hall the 1997 film, *Le Leçon de Tango*, set in Paris and Buenos Aires.

We gorged on *brie, camembert* and *roquefort* cheeses and Japanese sushi at every chance.

We lingered at cafés and had a farewell meal at Stella's, our neighbourhood *brasserie* on avenue Victo Hugo.

On our last day, I fitted in two visits to Sephora, my favourite haunt. A morning visit to their flagship outlet on les Champs-Elysées was followed by a flying visit in the afternoon to their branch at Passy, my favourite shopping area. *Quelle tristesse.*

On our last night in Paris, we attended the banquet at Aiglemont, outside Paris, that was hosted by Their Highnesses the Aga Khan and the Begum Aga Khan to celebrate their recent marriage. Prince Karim Aga Khan had remarried in the summer of 1998, a German countess. This was an occasion one reads about. Extraordinary fairyland setting, fireworks unlike anything we have ever seen before, lines of buffet of international cuisine, designer dresses ... I told my husband that all these years of investing in *Paris Match* had finally yielded a return. There were any number of royalties, ex-royalties, dignitaries, jet-setters from all over the world, international stars, the rich and the famous, the bold and the beautiful, the important and the used-to-be-important ... There was the King and Queen of Spain, the ex-Empress of Iran, the could-have-been Queen Fadila of Egypt, the Foreign Secretary Robin Cook, Madame Claude Pompidou, members of the old French aristocracy, the Pretender to the French throne Duc d'Orleans, Javier Perez de Cuellar, Prince Sadruddin Aga Khan.. and us. I thought I spotted Clint Eastwood on our way out but my husband was not convinced. And why should he not be here? On a previous such fortunate occasion, we were also invited to the celebratory dinner the Aga Khan hosted for his brother, Prince Amyn Aga Khan. That evening, we saw the step-mother of Princess Diana, Countess Raine Spencer, Anouk Aimée, the star of the 1960s masterpiece film *A Man and a Woman*; Prince Hassan and Princess Sarvath of Jordan, Shaikh Yamani of Saudi Arabia and his wife. I sat at a dinner table between an Italian contessa and a German member of the Board of Volkswagen, Deutsche Bank and a few other major German institutions. There was also an Italian Prince von Furstenberg at the table. A most charming conversationalist, he was a member of the ex-Egyptian royalty whose grandfather had served on the board of the Suez Canal.

It was now well into the early morning hours of our last day in Paris. It was an unforgettable last evening in Paris. We literally left Paris with a bang – with the fireworks at Aiglemont resounding in our ears.

A Bientôt Paris

We left Paris on October 3, 1998, after a stay of a year and nine months. This time, I did not wear the red coat.

The countdown on the Eiffel Tower showed 456 days before the year 2000.

In the film, *Casablanca*, Humphrey Bogart says in a farewell to Ingrid Bergman, "We'll always have Paris." Art Buchwald's book is *I'll Always Have Paris.* Stanley Karnow's last chapter in *Paris in the Fifties* is 'Toujours Paris' ('Always Paris').

Despite similar sentiments, *A Bientôt* Paris! (So long Paris!)

Postscript

Summer 1999

Nine months later, my daughter and I were crossing Champs-Elysées – once again charmed by our surroundings.

Summer 2002

Here we were in the domain of Retail Therapy - the Shopping Capital of the World. No city can match the offerings of Parisian window-shopping - elegantly simple in set-up and sensually aesthetic. Not having visited Bon Marche, the oldest department store in Paris for sometime, I made a dash to the left bank by metro. It was partly designed by Gustave Eiffel of the Tour Eiffel fame. An 'Icon of Flair' in a select neighbourhood, Bon Marche disapproves the local dictum 'literature on the left bank, luxury on the right'. After all, is not Paris the place where fashion is passion? Customers here believe in discretion in consumer consumption. It is in this low-key neighbourhood that speaks of hidden wealth, that one comes across a manifestation of *luxe populaire.* The up-market contemporary dress code is defined as 'popular luxury'. That translates into jeans accompanied by a Chanel or Louis Vuitton bag.

The Mother of all Parisian Grand Magazins of Large Department Stores has to be the Galeries Lafayette on Boulevard Haussmann on the Right Bank. A sprawling nineteenth century shopping city it is complete with a spectacular stained-glass central dome that hovers above the hedonistic Beauty and Perfume Department. No one would dispute that the Mother of all Perfume Stores in Paris is the retail giant Sephora on Champs Elysées. Is not Paris the fragrance capital of the world? We duly paid our homage to perfume at this ultimate beauty utopia site and came away both financially lighter and light in the head with the profusion of smells permeating every pore. Here is an altar to fine fragrance. I reckon that there are few visitors to Paris who have not ventured into this tunnel of olfactory delight.

Another visual delight can be sourced at the little-known Musee de Mode on the Rue de Rivoli. My daughter and I have enjoyed many afternoons at this temple to fashion. Retrospective collections by Christian Dior and Coco Channel have been beautifully presented. British, French, Japanese designers have all been honoured in this tranquil setting that offers them an opportunity to showcase elegance and luxury. Paris does rule the fashion industry.

The Musee Guimet that had been closed for five years was open for business. Located on the Place d'Iena, 'the foremost museum on Asian Arts in the world' states *Newsweek* magazine, now fully-restored was our destination. We had just missed the exhibition hosting the Heritage of Afghanistan. Maintaining the 19th century facade, the interior was entirely gutted to create an expanse of space and light. One cannot but be inspired and envy the investment and delight that goes into the creation of such an exquisite backdrop for what are treasures and masterpieces from distant shores. Once again, the perennial dilemma of foreign heritage items in alien exhibition sites came to mind. One has the contents and the other provides the form. One provides substance and the other style. Some 50,000 works of art from 17 Asian countries are housed here including objects of art from Southeast Asia, India, Afghanistan, Central Asia, Korea and Japan. Khmer, Ming and Mughal mingle in harmony. Many of the exhibits from the private collection of industrialist Emile Guimet who left it to the state in the late 1880s. An enigmatic declaration provides the origin of what constitutes a priceless collection- 'art treasures gathered during scientific missions to the Far East studying world religions.' Other donors include Jean and Krishna Riboud. Their fabulous collection includes Mughal textiles to Maharajahs' jewellery and other Indian decorative sumptuous pieces.

Five years have elapsed and a small crowd and some bouquets of flowers can still be seen at the Place de I'Alma. This is the location of a gold-painted sculpture of the Statue of Liberty's flaming torch that was erected by the *International Herald Tribune* newspaper in 1987 to commemorate 100 years of Franco-American relations. Few people are aware of this fact. People frequent this site believing it to be a memorial to Princess Diana who died in a car accident in the tunnel below. It seems like only yesterday (1997) that while living in Paris, we witnessed thc massive outpouring of shock and grief that accompanied the death of the 36-year-old Princess of Wales.

Summer 2003

"The last time I was in Paris, fifteen years ago..." The voice of an American woman floated across - as her group of six and our family of three sat familiarly close together in the outdoor area of 'Le Restaurant de Passy', just off rue Passy in the 16th *arrondissement* area of Paris. The French are unique in their fondness for spacious, grand and magnificent public buildings and places: note every French avenue, *chateau*, museum, monument, park and square. On the other hand, note every French private item: living area, eating space at a cafe or restaurant and of course, bathrooms. We are now talking about manoeurving gingerly for space to move, sit or stand. Cramped quarters and limbs are the order of the day. Is it any wonder that I overheard the American diner

at the restaurant? This refrain is common to scores of visitors to Paris from the world over... that category of Parisians - not by birth but by adoption... Parisians by choice.

The hotel we stayed in, Les Hauts de Passy, had us three in a room in which you could not swing a mouse, let alone a cat. We took it in turns to get up, use the terribly cramped bathroom, dress and move downstairs for an unhurried cafe and *croissant* breakfast at a roadside café. Heading out meant strolling down the cobble-stoned lane lined with creamy and chocolate-filled pastries and freshly baked *baguettes* at the *boulangerie*, succulent strawberries, dark green avocadoes and floral artichokes that beckon you from the greengrocer's, the strong aroma of a runny *brie* and a forceful *roquefort* cheese that follows one down the path, stimulating the senses. This is known as running the gauntlet of atmospheric shops. Of course, we need not have stayed on in this miniscule hotel room and its dwarf-size bathroom. However, hotels in the heart of Paris do not come cheap and that too in the peak summer season. Also, being in the 16th *arrondissement* is about as central as you can get. After all, the room was only for sleeping, for Paris is a city in which the streets are made for walking. In addition, this is the *quartier* I have always lived in and familiarly love.

For Paris, despite all its *glorie* and grandeur is also an amalgamation of villages. Each *arrondissement* has its own character and support structure. Thus Passy within the 16th area creates its own ambience with parks and profusion of shops, boutiques, cafes and restaurants. The Marmottan Museum with its magnificent collection of paintings by Monet, namely his many-faceted 'Water Lilies', the sudden glimpse of the slender top of le Tour Eiffel that peeks at you between nineteenth century Haussmannian buildings and the sighting of the commanding and monumental "I,

Arc de Triomphe down Avenue Victor Hugo (a thoroughfare that is a 'must' for even the most widely travelled and seasoned window-shopper for its artistic and aesthetic showcasing) are also some of the visual treats this chic habitat offers.

During our posting in Paris in the late 1990s, we had lived at 179 Avenue Victor Hugo. I located this apartment one winter morning while strolling down the avenue and having entered an *immobilier* real estate office, was shown this classic-appointed apartment the next morning. The 1910-built building in pure nineteenth-century Haussmannian architectural style with its seasoned wooden parquet floor, well-proportioned accommodation and grand sweping staircase had me in awe. Funnily enough, I had also lived in the same 16th *arrondissement* as a child many decades back.

Paris, the City of Light and the most beautiful city in the world, is an oft-repeated cliche. However, like all cliches, there is some if not absolute truth to it. For Paris remains Paris; not only for its obvious external splendour that combines irresistible glitz and glamour with allure - but also for its unexpected depths and novelties. The known and familiar is there to greet you - every time. Yet, the magic sustains itself, for there is always something new and marvellous just around the corner. Boredom never sets in.

Towering above the City of Light is le Tour Eiffel. Here is the 'Iron Lady of Paris' and the veritable symbol of both the city and the country. It draws some 6 million visitors a year, making it the world's most popular-paying tourist attraction. The city of Paris alone attracts some 25 million visitors annually. Yet its population is put at 2.15 million only. A nation of 60 million inhabitants was visited by some 77 million in 2002 according to government figures

- thus ranking France as the premier global tourist destination. Built in 1989 on the occasion of the World Exposition held in Paris, its construction was slammed by the Parisian press. "A gigantic garish iron chimney piercing the Parisian sky... A hollow candlestick... what is this horror that the French have found to celebrate their much vaunted good taste... A ridiculously vertiginous tower overshadowing Paris like some gigantic black factory chimney." Well, all one can say is that Time heals wounds inflicted by even the most vicious verbal onslaught.

The same Parisians now have bejewelled le Tour Eiffel in a stunning fashion. On June 20, 2003 the slender and majestic 'Iron Lady' made her renewed debut, bedecked in 20,000 sparkling lights. It took nine months of preparation for the host of lights to shine at 11.30 p.m. and then every night on the hour for ten minutes - through the night. We were at dinner in the Montmartre district when suddenly, looking out of the window of this shoebox-sized apartment, we saw this most elegant and sparkling jewel - exquisitely beautiful in the backdrop of a clear Parisian night. *Oui, la Grande Dame* remains radiant. Just like the Mother City.

Many credit Mayor Bertrand Delanoe for aggressively improving the quality of life and the beautification of the French capital. I must confess that on this visit to Paris, the avenues and *rues* were much less littered with dog turd - otherwise, a blot on the Parisian cityscape. 'Paris Plage' is yet another testimony to the fertile imagination of Parisians. A Brainchild of Monsieur Delanoe, Paris now has an artificial beach without a sea. Importing sand, palm trees and sun-beds, the right bank of the Seine has been transported into the Riviera in the South of France. Sun-worshippers throng the man - made beach on weekends, once again proving that a small idea can bring in big returns.

The novelty has been reproduced in Brussels and Brooklyn, New York. Mayor Delanoe is on record for saying that "Paris is a museum, and that is a privilege. But if it wants to be loyal to its history, it needs to innovate, to dare - it needs to move into the 21st century." Tradition moves hand-in-glove with innovation. It is this constant consciousness of the need for economic dynamism and cultural innovation that keeps the City of Light on its toes.

We, however, simply took in the crowded sight en route to an old literary haunt. I must pay a visit to the bookshop W. H. Smith on the rue de Rivoli, whenever I am in Paris. It has been described as 'an institution to English-speaking travellers in Paris since 1903'. I am in possession of what should be classified as 'an antique book', *Little Women* by Lousia M. Alcott - purchased for 8 shillings and 6 pence in 1958 at the same shop. In those days, there was a *salon de the* (tea-room) on the upper floor. As children, for a treat following our book-purchases, we would indulge in scones with cream and strawberries - in the heart of Paris. It ceased to exist in 1989.

W. H. Smith/Paris mercifully, still retains its old world charm in its interior unlike the drugstore look of its London counterpart. When I mentioned to the young salesgirl that I was an old customer of theirs since I noticed that there were banners proclaiming 100 areas of presence, she most generously did not believe me. She yet offered me a discount card as a small token of appreciation for being a loyal customer over decades. I was most happy to buy books for my dauther - a third-generation customer - using the card. She also mentioned that all newly-recruited salespeople are told of the former tearoom upstairs, since they still get some twenty queries a week about the *salon de the* from former customers of this legendary Anglo-establishment.

Memories and new times came together beautifully as I read of the forthcoming grand spectacle of Johnny Hallyday appearing on stage in celebration of his sixtieth birthday. Here is a living institution of Frnce and the French-speaking world. He is the French Elvis Presley, the icon of French rock 'n' roll who first hit the French music scene in 1960. Hallyday has outlived elvis by decades and has witnessed six Presidents occupy the Elysée, the French presidential palace. The ever-young French rock 'n' roller (like his English counterpart Mick Jagger) brings energy and hope to a generation of ageing fans. Johnny Hallyday is the all-American rock 'n' roll crooner on stage complete with flowing locks (earlier), a bandanna tied across his forehead, the Harley Davidson motorbike on stage... yet, he has always been and remains quintessentially French.

Spring 2005

April in Paris; a moment of seasonal splendour. A week in Paris and we were privy to the glorious sight of soft green tender leaves maturing fully to cloak perfectly lined up trees along the quays of the glistening Seine. An abundance of blossoms delighted one's view-including flaming forsythias-furiously yellow. A saunter through Parc Bagatelle, behind the Bois de Boulogne revealed Wordsworth's dancing daffodils, trees laden with soft pink peonies whose fallen petals carpeted the ground below and in the distance, green fields dotted with multi-coloured tulips and orange-red poppies. The sweet-smelling fragrance of white, purple and pink pansies wafted through the air. All is well in the world. This must be the 'sense of sublime' that Alain de Botton refers to in his enriching and enchanting book *The Art of Travel.* It appears appropriate to quote here Thomas Gray from his 'Letters' (1739). "There are certain scenes that would awe an atheist into belief without the help of any other argument."

We had better luck this time. Here we had a good-sized room and a respectable bathroom and the entrance to the metro station la Motte Picquent Grenelle outside the front door. Tourisme Hotel in the 8th *arrondissement* was near the Tour Eiffel and the large expanse of Champ de Mars. just around the corner is the Café du Commerce. This restaurant was originally built as a fabric store. In 1921, it was tranformed into a restaurant frequented by automobile workers. It has flourished since then and retains its *Belle Epoque* charm and authenticity. It was in 1929 that George Orwell worked at a restaurant as a dish-washer on rue du Commerce. He wrote about his experience in this demanding occupation in *Down and Out in Paris and London.* The imposing les Invalides built by Napoleon I lay at the other end of Champ de Mars. One evening after a dinner of gorging ourselves on succulent *'fruits de mer'* (literally translates into 'fruits of the sea' or sea-food), we walked to the Champ de Mars. We seated ourselves at the feet of the Tour Eiffel - on the steps of the Peace Memorial - that has on its walls inscribed 'Peace' in any number of languages. At the stroke of midnight, the softly illuminated Tour Eiffel came to life with thousands of sparkling white lights. Here was the majestic Grande Dame in all her bejewelled finery. Someone once said - Paris is a theatre and all the city a stage.

Another late night after dinner, we took a drop at Boulevard St. Michel and walked over to the Notre Dame de Paris. I was mobile television vans parked in the square before the cathedral and remarked that they must be covering the ailing Pope John Paul II in the Vatican. As we approached the Notre Dame, we saw posted on the massive doors a notice stating: 'The Pope had died on April 2, 2005 at 09:27 p.m.' All night prayers were being held. The death of the first non-Italian Pope in 450 years, led to all flags to be drawn at half-mast.

The other ailing personality in Europe was Prince Rainier of the Principality of Monaco. With his marriage to American actress Grace Kelly, the tiny fairytale kingdom of Monaco came into international spotlight. It so happened that, in London - our next port of call - while coming out from Harrods department store, the *Evening Standard* posters declared 'Playboy Prince of Monaco Dead'.

In our frequent bus journeys on no. 80, we crossed the Place de I' Alma, above the tunnel where Princess Diana and her friend Dodi al-Fayed died in August 1997. It seemed to me that some people were hanging over the railing looking into the tunnel. I also spotted flowers lying at the base of the golden flame sculpture. Funnily enough, we were travelling on to London where Prince Charles and Mistress Camilla Parker Bowles were to finally tie the marital knot following a 'marathon three decades plus long love affair.

A bout of indulgence took place at the 'new' Sephora emporium near the Galeries Lafayette. The other 'new' for us - since our last visit to Galeries Lafayette - was the Maison Lafayette across the road, catering to all household functional and decorative needs. This could qualify as a museum of contemporary arts. The spacious layout, stunning interior and fabulous displays are striking and earmark it as a cutting - edge store. The ground floor bookshop caters to all architectural, decorative and garden needs. Gastronomic indulgence can be had at a delicatessen that offers apple strudel, baklava, couscous...a wide array of culinary fusion delights. The aroma of freshly brewed coffee floated across from the café. Maison Lafayette is an 'Icon of Flair' - another success story in both concept and implementation.

Another regular haunt is the American bookstore Brentano's near the Opera. Brentano's opened its doors for business in 1895. Many reference books on Paris have been bought here over the years. Two gems emerged this time. A researcher's dream come true on the city is the *Traveller's Literary Companion: France* by John Edmondson. My cup of luck overflowing, I also found the same on India - an indispensable literary aid for my book on travel in India.

A stroll down Champs Elysées is a leisurely exercise in the uplifting of the spirit. Who can fail to be awed by the magnificence of this grand tree-lined venue? Ask any first-time visitor to Paris and repeat the question to frequent visitors; not to speak of the locals; Les Champs Elysées enthrals all. In Edmondson's literary marvel I came to know that Charles Dickens stayed at No. 49 Champs Elysées in 1855. Dickens wrote affair "Each room has but one window in it, but we have no fewer than six rooms (besides the back ones looking on the Champs Elysées) with the wonderful life perpetually flowing up and down." Robert and Elizabeth Barrett Browning lived in an apartment at No. 138 in 1851.

I wanted to take in the special exhibition at Louvre of 'La France Romane' that covered the history of France in the tenth to twelfth centuries. Here were highlights of the increasing presence of the Church, the nascence of Gothic art, the First Crusade and names and events that rekindled childhood history classes - Hugh Capet, Eleanor of Acquitaine, William the Conqueror, the Battle of Hastings... Due to time constraints, I had to console myself with turning the pages of books available on the exhibit at the

Louvre Carousel - a marvellous two floor collection of books, cards, prints, models, paintings, jewellery.

I reached the Musee d'Orsay late. I am fascinated by the conversion of this nineteenth century train station into a twentieth century museum that houses an immense range of the fine arts between 1848 and 1914. I was not aware of a similar conversion - a tropical garden existing under the glass roof of the Atocha train station in Madrid. This is the imaginative contemporary use of old spaces. The huge Impressionist collection is the crowd-puller at the Musee d'Orsay. This is the place to see one's fill of Manet, Monet and Matisse. Only the bookshop was open for business. A brief visit followed. I turned the pages of a number of art books and books on Paris. I was sorely tempted to buy a new book on Orientalism. Both price and weight deterred me.

In London, a point of pilgrimage is the Victoria and Albert Museum in South Kensington. I must confess that an hour I allocate to the V & A boutique alone. It is a most satisfying museum boutique. I always manage to succumb to temptation and emerge with a V & A carrier-bag.

I recall my last viewing of 'The Lady of the Louvre' Mona Lisa in 1998. I thought it was high time to reacquaint myself. Part of the desire to revisit the world's most famous painting, was to see her again in her old location, before her transfer to the refurbished and redesigned Salle des Etats, a massive rectangular gallery within the Denon Gallery overlooking the Seine. I saw Mona Lisa in her old setting on 2nd April, she relocated on the 3rd April and was ready to receive visitors on April 5, 2005. It is a fact that some 80 per cent of Louvre's visitors, come to pay homage to the 'Lady with the Smile'. Some 6.6 million visitors annually target the Louvre. Amongst the incredible numbers, half are foreigners. And among the foreigners, some 2.2 million Japanese walk the *salons* of the Louvre. This probably explains the reason for Japan's Nippon Television Network paying $6.2 million for the renovation of the nineteenth century Salle des Etats. Apparently, they also paid for the cleaning of the Sistine Chapel at the Vatican in the 1980s. With reserve funds to spare, the television company will contribute $2.2 million to upgrade the Louvre gallery that displays the other 'Beauty at the Louvre' - the celebrated Venus de Milo-the prototype of Greek feminine beauty.

The iconic status that is 'Mona Lisa' now holds court amongst other Italian monumental works by Titian, Caravaggio, Bassano and Veronese. I had forgotten how small was the most famous painting in the world. A tiny lady of only 75 by 50 centimetres/30 by 21 inches dominates the global art world. In her new home, Mona Lisa stares enigmatically across Veronese's 'Marriage at Cana'. This painting measures only 9 by 6 metres/30 by 20 feet!

I bought *The Da Vinci Code* by Dan Brown for my in-flight reading on this trip. That did not happen. I, however, read the first fifty pages at one reading the first night in Paris. It seemed right to honour the book in its proper setting. Not only has Dan Brown written a thriller that cannot be put down but *The Da Vinci Code* reads like a travel book on the Louvre and Paris. With an extraordinary eye for detail, he takes the reader hand-in-hand through the museum and the city. I actually looked for the steel grates that locked in the Louvre's curator Jacques Sauniere in the Grand Gallery that is in fact the Salle des Etats. The steel grates exist. The description and controversy surrounding I.M. Pei's glass pyramid masterpiece entrance had me nodding my head in agreement. Dan Brown's mega-selling book is to be filmed by Ron Howard. Tom Hanks is to play the Harvard symbologist, Robert Langdon; the enigmatic French actor Jean Reno, Captain Bezu Fache and the immensely talented French actress Sophie Marceau, the cryptologist Sophie Neveu. The director Ron Howard was been given permission to shoot the film within the Louvre and more specifically, the Salle des Etats itself. This is an extraordinary book in an extraordinary setting.

On Sunday, we strolled through the weekly open-air market next door. We were sorely tempted to buy fresh bread, chunks of cheese, pickles, scores of vegetables that would make a succulent salad - mushroom, endive, water-cress, button-tomatoes, an array of lettuce; and to finish off-seductive strawberry tarts. This was a feast for the eyes and a lament for the taste-buds. We were leaving Paris shortly. In an act of compromise, I bought some *brie*, *roquefort* and *chevre* goat cheese and *baguette* bread to nibble on, as we continued our walk through a vista of endless charm.

Echoing Ernest Hemingway's heartfelt devotion to the City of Light in his ode to Paris, *A Moveable Feast*, I have to concur with him. "Three is never any ending to Paris and the memory of each person who has lived in it differs from that of any other. We always returned to it no matter who we were or how it was changed or with what difficulties, or ease, it could be reached."

The Parisian thread of memory lingers on...

Love Affair

A stay fuelled by curiosity and fascination ends with an unrequited love affair with the city of lights. I had not meant from the onset to develop a lengthy line of fascination on Paris. It simply emerged as I delved into the rich literature on Paris. Evidently, exuberance on the subject far outweighs the criticism. Yet here for the record – is an observation with a super-sting. William Gaddis, named as 'America's unknown great writer' by *The Economist*, had lived in Paris for a time and dismissed it. He declared, "Age cannot wither, nor custom stale, her infinite vulgarity."

Others have expressed somewhat different sentiments.

Add three letters to Paris and you shall be in paradise.
Jules Renard, French writer

To be in Paris is to be...
Enthusiastic correspondent, 1323

Whoever you may be, here is your master.
Victor Hugo

France is a man, Paris is the heart.
Henri IV

If I were God and had two sons, the eldest would have to be God after me, but I'd make the second King of France.
Maximilian I, Holy Roman Emperor

Paris, home of kings, whose wide brow has seen nothing of the like under the rolling clouds ...
Pierre Ronsard, sixteenth century French poet

Paris is an ocean in itself. There is always some spot

never seen before, some unknown cavern ... flowers, pearls, monuments, delights, hitherto unknown ...
Honore de Balzac

I only know that I found in Paris all and even more than I was expecting. I only know that I was charmed and elevated more than I can say.
A Paris-lover of more than a century ago

I cannot tell you what an immense impression Paris made upon me. It is the most extraordinary place in the world ... I cannot conceive any place so perfectly and wonderfully expressive of its own character.
Charles Dickens

Paris is a moveable feast.
Ernest Hemingway

To be a Parisian is not to be born there but to be reborn there.
Sacha Guitry, French actor and director, born in St. Petersburg, Russia

Every man has two countries, his own and France.
Benjamin Franklin

I have two loves; my country and Paris.
Josephine Baker, American dancer

Paris should be declared an international shrine. The World Bank should finance its economy. The people of Paris should work at no other job than simply that of being Parisians.
Joe Murray, 'International Herald Tribune'

I would admit that I idealise France.
Julian Barnes, British author of 'Cross Channel'

French sickness.
Yushin Fukuhara, Japanese founder of Shiseido Cosmetics

I had become a Parisian instantaneously. Paris was where I felt most at home.
Virgil Thomson, American composer

Whoever seems a little more distinguished than another has been to France.
George Moore, 1888

Bibliography

'Architecture in the 19th Century'; Beaux Arts, Publications Nuit et Jour, Paris, 1992.

Arnold, Wendy: *The Historic Hotels of Paris: A Secret Guide*, Thames and Hudson, London, 1990.

Buchwald, Art: *I'll Always Have Paris: A Memoir*, Ballantine Books, Random House, New York, 1997.

Chazelles, Amelie: *Montmartre: Vu par les Peintres*, Edition, S.A., Lausanne, 1987.

Chevalier, Maurice: *My Paris*, Macmillan Company, New York, 1972.

De Andia, Beatrice: *Le 16e: Chaillot, Passy, Auteuil – Metamorphose des trios villages*, Paris, 1991.

De Maupassant, Guy: *The Complete Short Stories of de Maupassant*, Rupa and Co., New Delhi, 1984.

Egyptian Art at the Louvre: Societie Francaise de Promotion Artistique, Paris, 1998.

Egypt: Yesterday and Today: Lithographs and Diaries by David Roberts, The American University of Cairo Press, Cairo, 1996.

Genevoix, Sylvie; *Paris: The Seine*, Pro Libris, Paris, 1993.

George, Adrian: *Paris in August*, Peter Owen Publishers, London 1994.

Grand Louvre: *The Palace, The Collections, The New Areas*; Beaux Arts, avenue de Maine, Paris, 1996.

Guadalupi, Gianni: *The Discovery of the Nile*, The American University of Cairo Press, Cairo, 1997.

Hankinson, Jim: *Bluff Your Way in Paris*, Ravette Books Limited, London 1993.

Hemingway, Ernest: *A Moveable Feast*, Arrow Books Limited, London, 1994.

Hugo, Victor: *The Hunchback of Notre-Dame*, Wordsworth Editions Limited, Hertfordshire, 1993.

Jacquemart-Andre Museum, Beaux Arts, avenue de Maine, Paris, 1996.

James T.G.H.: *Ancient Egypt: The Land and its Legacy*, University of Texas Press, Austin, 1998.

Johnson, Diane: *Le Divorce*, Vintage, Random House, London, 1998.

Karnow, Stanley: *Paris in the Fifties*, Random House, New York, 1999.

Lewis, Edward: *The French on Life and Love*, R.H.S. Publications, London, 1969.

Makine, Andrei: *Le Testament Francais*, Hodder and Stoughton, London, 1997.

Mayle, Peter: *A Year in Provence*, Pan Books, London, 1990.

Mayle, Peter: *Toujours Provence*, Pan Books, London, 1992.

Mayle, Peter: *Acquired Tastes*, Bantam Books, New York, 1993.

Mayle Peter: *Anything Considered*, Penguin Books, London, 1997.

Michelin Guide to France, Michelin et Cie, Clermont-Ferrand, France, 1996.

Mikes, George: *Little Cabbages*, Allan Wingate, London, 1955.

Museum International, UNESCO, Paris No. 4, October-December 1997.

Ogden, Christopher: *Pamela Harriman – Life of the Party*, Little, Brown and Company, London, 1994.

Paris, Casa Editrice Bonechi, Florence, 1995.

Paris: User's Guide: l'Office du Tourisme de Paris, les Champs-Elysees, Paris, 1996.

Places and History: Paris; Librarie Grund, Paris, 1997.

Rice, Jr. Howard C.: *Thomas Jefferson in Paris*, Princeton University Press, Princeton, New Jersey, 1991.

Robitaille, Louis-Bernard: *And God Created the French*, Robert Davies Multimedia Publishing, Quebec, 1997.

Rosenblum, Mort: *The Secret Life of the Seine*, Addison-Wesley Publishing Company, Paris, 1994.

Rutkowska, Wanda: *Famous People in Anecdotes*, Wydawnictwa Szkolna I Pedagogiczne, Warsaw, 1977.

Sagan, Francoise: *Those Without Shadows*, John Murray, London, 1957.

Sagan, Francoise: *Lost Profile*, Andre Deutsch, London, 1976.

Simenon, Georges: *L'Amie de Madame Maigret*, U.G.E. Poche, Presses de la Cite, l'Imprimerie Bussiere, Saint-Armand, 1996.

Taylor, Jennifer (ed.): *The Francophile's Quotation Book: A Literary Affair*, Robert Hale Limited, London, 1995.

Van der Kamp, Gerald: *Monet: A Visit to Giverny*, Editions ART-LYS, Versailles, 1997.

Vuitton, Louis: *L'Art de Traverser le Temps*; Louis Vuitton Malletier, Paris, 1996.

Welty-Rochefort, Harriet: *French Toast: A Humorous Tour of What Living in France is Really Like*, Anglophone SA, Montreuil, 1997.

White, Edmund and Sorin, Hubert: *Our Paris: Sketches from Memory*, Alfred A. Knopf, New York, 1995.

Wiser, William: *The Crazy Years: Paris in the Twenties*, Thames and Hudson, London, 1990.

Yapp, Nick and Syrett, Michel: *The Xenophobe's Guide to the French*, Ravette Publishing Limited, West Sussex, 1997.

Magazines

Chateaux et Demeures, Paris.

Economist, London.

Esquire, New York.

Geo, Paris.

L'Express, Paris.

Paris Capitale, Paris.

Time, New York.

Vanity Fair, New York.

Newspapers

International Herald Tribune, Paris.

Le Figaro, Paris.

Liberation, Paris.

Acknowledgements

The first words of appreciation are owed to Paris, a city that has inspired countless writers. Brentano's Galiganani, Shakespeare and Company, Tea and Tattered Pages and W. H. Smith bookshops in Paris have provided me with a wide range of literature on Paris. The number of newly published books on the City of Light that continue to adorn bookshops never fails to amaze me.

I renew my thanks and deep appreciation to Mohiuddin Ahmed of University Press, Dhaka for first publishing *Parisian Portraits* in 2000. Kudos and my personal gratitude to Anuj Bahri of Tara Press, New Delhi who found time to read my humble tribute to Paris and thus was born *Paris, A Homage*. Debbie Smith, editor at Tara Press, has been delightful to work with. Jehanara Wasi has painstakingly ploughed through the text for which I am most grateful. My husband Tufail K. Haider has indulged me and in the process succumbed to the charm that is Paris. Finally, *je remercie* readers over the years who have expressed their delight in finding themselves once again in Paris.

Raana Haider

Index